Literary Live

This classic and longstanding series has established itself making a major contribution to literary biography. The books in the series are thoroughly researched and comprehensive, covering the writer's complete oeuvre. The latest volumes trace the literary, professional, publishing, and social contexts that shaped influential authors—exploring the "why" behind writers' greatest works. In its thirtieth year, the series aims to publish on a diverse set of writers—both canonical and rediscovered—in an accessible and engaging way.

More information about this series at
https://link.springer.com/bookseries/14010

Jane McVeigh

Richmal Crompton, Author of *Just William*

A Literary Life

Jane McVeigh
University of Roehampton
London, UK

Literary Lives
ISBN 978-3-030-96510-5   ISBN 978-3-030-96511-2   (eBook)
https://doi.org/10.1007/978-3-030-96511-2

Cover illustration: Portrait of Richmal Crompton 1920s, Richmal Crompton Collection, Foyle Special Collections and Archives, University of Roehampton

This Palgrave Macmillan imprint is published by the registered company Springer Nature Switzerland AG
The registered company address is: Gewerbestrasse 11, 6330 Cham, Switzerland

"It was one of the world's great tragedies when philosophy parted company from theology and metaphysics."

"The proper study of mankind is man?"

"Exactly."

—Richmal Crompton *The Inheritor* (1960)

To
Kate Massey and Edward Ashbee
Richmal Crompton Lamburn's great-niece and great-nephew

Preface

This Life celebrates the centenary of the first two William books, *Just William* (1922) and *More William* (1922). It is an introduction to Richmal Crompton's less well-known fiction, as well as a study of her famous character William Brown and a story about her writing life. I hope it will both entertain Richmal Crompton's fans and other general readers and instigate further studies on her work and influence.

It features two main characters, the author Richmal Crompton, re-created here by me as her biographer, and her famous character William Brown, created by Richmal Crompton. In a form of show-not-tell, the sections on William, his family and friends are drawn from the William stories and are based on Crompton's storytelling. Crompton's and William's own voices and the views of their fans interweave alongside chapters that tell a story about Crompton's life and focus on themes in her fiction, especially her novels and the William stories.

The woman behind the author and her character, Richmal Crompton Lamburn, remains in the shadows, as she may have wished. There is limited autobiographical or other evidence available about her personal life. Family myth suggests that she may have destroyed many of her private papers. Nevertheless, this biography introduces new information about her. It suggests that we look at Richmal anew as a vibrant, imaginative, clever, humorous and strong woman who was the head of her immediate family living in Kent for most of her adult life. She was both extrovert and an expert performer on the page and in her professional life, as well as careful to protect her private life from external scrutiny.

The thematic sections aim to illustrate what Crompton cared about as an author. These chapters introduce aspects of her writing that warrant further detailed study in future, such as her interest in the role of mothers within families and what it means to behave in a grown-up way whatever age her characters might be. They address the extent to which she is a writer read by both young and older readers. This Life suggests that her fiction warrants a re-evaluation in the context of fiction by other women writers from the early to mid-twentieth century and the wider social and professional changes in women's lives in the interwar years. Crompton's concerns as a writer were influenced by her relationship with her father, her experience as a teacher, and her knowledge of classical literature, as well as her extensive reading of philosophy, theology, poetry and fiction.

Richmal contracted polio in her early thirties. Whether other people's view of her as a disabled person and her restricted mobility influenced her reputation and the opportunities that may or may not have come her way is hard to prove, but one can hypothesise that it did. The experience of disabled people is a significant theme in her fiction.

Richmal's niece Margaret remembers that her aunt enjoyed living alone when she was 'free to think her own thoughts without interruption.' Margaret describes her as a loner.[1] Yet there is a difference between someone who is content to be alone and those who avoid human company or feel lonely. Richmal relished a room and home of her own in which to write about people, her enduring passion. It is true that she often seems set apart, an observer, a chronicler, an amused bystander; Richmal was amidst yet often not one of the crowd.

There may be more evidence that comes to light about Richmal's life that might influence her story in future. I hope there is. In the meantime, this book is an attempt to fill in some, but not all, of the gaps based on what we know so far and to consider the perspective of some of her readers on her writing. Crompton inspired a new generation of writers and created one of the most influential literary cultural icons of the last hundred years and a classic of twentieth century literature.

London, UK   Jane McVeigh

Note

1. Disher, M., *Growing Up with Just William* (1990), 204–205.

Acknowledgements

This book could never have been written without the support of Kate Massey and Edward Ashbee, Richmal Crompton's great-niece and great-nephew and her literary executors. I am delighted to dedicate it to them.

Members of The Just William Society have been unfailing in their interest and help. I am grateful to the authors of articles in *The Just William Society Magazine* that have informed my research. David Schutte, as well as Nicholas Bennett, Simon Procter, Terry Taylor and Paula Wild, dealt generously with many queries; Margaret Sherriff, known professionally as the translator Margaret Jull Costa, supported my work on Crompton's impact in Spain; Tony Coles, Tim Havenith, Lez McLair, Miranda Pender, Jim Riddell, Alan Ring and Sandra Shastid kindly agreed to talk to me about their love of William.

I am hugely grateful to Anne Fine and Brian Jarman. Talking to them and their comments on an early draft enabled me to think through my perspective both on Crompton and on aspects of my own writing. David Schutte and Michael Wace also read versions of my manuscript and offered advice that improved the final book.

My Honorary Research Fellowship at the University of Roehampton has been invaluable, and I am especially grateful to Professor Laura Peters. Staff at Royal Holloway, University of London, have also been very helpful, and I am grateful to Professor Paul Layzell.

Crompton and William have been significant in many other people's lives. I have been helped by several who know the stories well. I am especially grateful to Professor Michael Gold, Martin Jarvis, Jonathan Massey and Deborah Moggach.

My Palgrave Editor, Allie Troyanos, has dealt with endless enquiries and anxieties and has been a kind and generous advisor throughout the two and half years when I was writing in earnest. The Society of Authors information was always useful. Harriet Sanders at Macmillan was also helpful.

Kornelia Cepok, Archivist for the Foyle Special Collections and Archives at the University of Roehampton, has guided me through the Richmal Crompton Collection for over ten years. I am hugely grateful for her support. Other archivists, librarians and staff have helped me throughout my research. I am grateful to Wendy Gradwell from Bury Libraries and Archive; Christopher Cipkin at Royal Holloway, University of London; Esther Seifert-Iseli, International Lyceum Club Archives, Switzerland; and staff at the BBC Written Archive, King's College London Archive, King's College Cambridge Archive, the Centre for Research Collections at Edinburgh University, the National Archives in Kew, the Wellcome Collection Library and the British Library.

When I visited St Elphin's old school building in Darley Dale, near Matlock, members of the Old Elphinians were on hand to give me essential background about the school. Mark Hone at Bury Grammar School Boys told me about Edward Lamburn's time there and Julie Hone translated a postcard from Edward to Richmal that is written in Latin. This book is built on these tiny, but significant details. Joanna Friel of the Chislehurst Society was a very helpful local guide. I am also grateful to Kripen Dhrona of the British Polio Fellowship for useful information and advice.

During my research many others have also given their support, including John & Evelyn Barclay; Professor David Buckingham; Philip W. Errington; Peter Elliott; Paul Gardner; Simon Higman; Julie Mills; Ann Montgomery; Guy Neely; Marleen Rensen and Christopher Wiley; Professor David Rudd; Alysoun Sanders; and Carola Scupham.

I am grateful to my mother, other family members and dear friends for their support too. Brian has spent years living with the haunting ghost of Richmal Crompton. I wonder if he will miss her as much as I will.

Praise for *"Richmal Crompton, Author of Just William"*

"Richmal Crompton was justly celebrated for her comic and satirical Just William books, but she was also a vastly prolific author of novels for adults. Jane McVeigh gives a comprehensive account of both aspects of her work, setting them in their contemporary context, and raises broader questions about the status and social significance of popular fiction aimed at both child and adult readers. Engagingly written, with a light touch, this literary biography casts new light on a somewhat neglected and enigmatic author, whose work deserves to be much more widely understood."

—Professor David Buckingham, *Emeritus Professor of Media and Communications, Loughborough University, UK*

"Jane McVeigh's literary biography of Richmal Crompton successfully reappraises Crompton's writing in the context of not only children's literature and crossover fiction but also mid-twentieth-century women's writing more specifically. McVeigh's reappraisal of this undervalued, and somewhat neglected, writer is an act of remembrance that is fluid in its approach and enriched by both the archival work that underpins it and the connections it foregrounds. By rejecting a more traditional single-life portrayal of its subject, McVeigh's literary life ensures that Crompton and her writing are potentially opened up to a range of new readers."

—Dr Keith O'Sullivan, *Associate Professor and Head of School of English, Dublin City University, Ireland*

Contents

List of Figures

1

Introduction

In one sense [William Brown] is Everyman – a part of us all. We recognise
our humanity in him and in his adventures. But, although he shows us the
foibles, fancies and achievements of our own society and our own century, he
also rides above us all. He's a kind of time-lord; what we'd hope to be. And his
glorious imagination cannot be confined.[1]

Martin Jarvis, well-known for his recordings of William stories enjoyed by
fans of all ages.

This literary life celebrates the hundredth anniversary of the first two William
books published in 1922, *Just William* and *More William*. It aims to give
some insight into the life and writing of the clever, outgoing, humorous and
courageous woman who published hundreds of stories about her infamous
hero William Brown aged eleven years old. During her lifetime, Crompton
published books over five decades, including: thirty-seven William books;
forty novels; *Just William: The Book of the Film* (1939); two books of *Jimmy*
stories about a boy aged seven years old; and ten books of other short stories.[2]
The final William book, *William the Lawless* (1970), was published after
her death. William's centenary is a timely moment for a re-evaluation of
Crompton's contribution to British literature in the early to mid-twentieth
century, based on a close look at the William stories, as well as her novels and
other short stories, and for a rethink about the kind of person, writer and
aunt she was. In any family there are secrets and in the case of Richmal some,
but not all, will remain hidden.

© The Author(s), under exclusive license to Springer Nature
Switzerland AG 2022
J. McVeigh, *Richmal Crompton, Author of Just William*, Literary Lives,
https://doi.org/10.1007/978-3-030-96511-2_1

This book considers what we know about Richmal Crompton Lamburn (1890–1969) and her alter ego Richmal Crompton, the author of the William stories. Her mother's maiden name was Crompton, and she published her work under this pseudonym. She was close to her family, including her mother Clara, with whom she lived for many years, and to her sister Gwen and niece Richmal. She did not marry. Some readers might expect her to be described as a sister and aunt who was rather stiff and remote, yet often kindly, and as a spinster who wrote funny stories for children and was always smiling and polite in public. In 1958, a newspaper article describes her as William's 'neat, soft-voiced exceedingly civilised creator ... the self-effacing ... spinster with cornflower-blue eyes.'[3] This staid, patronising version of Richmal Crompton Lamburn is not the view of her that the reader will find in this biography.

Richmal was a loving daughter; an aunt, a great-aunt and a niece with four aunts of her own. She was also a hugely successful though misremembered author, an experienced teacher and a knowledgeable classicist. The breadth of her imagination and creativity in fiction that ranges across novels, short stories and plays encompassing comedy, satire and tragedy has rarely been recognised. In her personal life, she was a loyal and caring friend and someone who was widely read. Richmal loved performing on the page, on the stage and at social events, and took on many roles in life. After the death of her father, she became the head of her immediate family, supporting her mother, sister and her children, and at times her brother and his family too, financially and emotionally, from her twenties and for the rest of her life. Most of all, she was a dedicated, driven and ambitious writer.

Richmal contracted polio as an adult. As a result, her right leg was impaired. Her disability did not define her sense of identity and she was not disempowered by it. Whether other people's view of her as a disabled person and her restricted mobility influenced her reputation and the opportunities that may or may not have come her way is hard to prove, but one can hypothesise that it did.

* * *

Crompton's writing as a whole is hard to pigeonhole: is she a children's author or a writer for adults; is she a novelist whose work has something in common with other writers of the interwar period; is she a writer of light-hearted comedy or more serious literature? This literary biography is an introduction to her novels, plays and short stories that do not feature William Brown, as well as a story about her life and her famous character. It aims to suggest that: she has been undervalued as a writer for both children and adults; her writing is set within the middle-class world she knew and has much in common with other contemporary twentieth century women writers; her fiction is sophisticated and satirical and covers a huge range of content, styles and forms, including plays, short stories and novels. Whether she is a good author and created serious literature it leaves to others to finally decide, but rest assured that, about writing, she was very serious indeed.

Crompton had wide-ranging intellectual inspirations, including a love of poetry and an extensive knowledge and love of classical literature, both of which are threads woven throughout her work and reflect her values and beliefs. Reading was a passion for Richmal and other literature influences much of her writing too. She was always reading at least four books, according to her family. In her library are both nineteenth and twentieth century poetry collections, as well as books on Christianity and spiritualism, alongside philosophy, contemporary plays and novels by canonical authors and her peers, such as Ivy Compton-Burnett and Rosamund Lehmann.[4]

The notes she kept on the art and craft of writing include her version of a quote from the French nineteenth century novelist Honoré de Balzac about the creative process:

> To plan, to dream, to imagine and work is a delightful occupation…. If the artist does not throw himself into the work like a soldier into the breach, like a miner buried under a fall of rock, the work will never be completed, [and] the artist will look on at the suicide of his own talent.[5]

Balzac's contemporary and compatriot Gustave Flaubert echoes this commitment to rigour and relentless graft: 'Inspiration consists of sitting down at one's desk at the same time each day.'[6] This was a dedication that Crompton brought to her own work. Neither her prolific output, her popularity as the author of the William stories, her stiff outward appearance in formal suits, nor her rigorous day-to-day routine of writing in conventional surroundings at home, mostly in the mornings, should allow us to misinterpret or dismiss the breadth, fluidity, creativity and depth of her imagination and intellect. Balzac and Flaubert are authors who committed their lives to writing. It is the vocation to which Crompton also dedicated her life.

* * *

Initially, Crompton wrote the William stories for adults, and they subsequently became popular with children. She felt like a wolf in sheep's clothing when she was described as a children's writer. When she first began to publish the William stories they were 'stories for adults about children.'[7] She commented in 1952 that:

> I think that it was not till the last war [- the Second World War -] that they found their way from the general shelves to the children's department in the bookshops. And even now I receive letters from adult – even elderly – readers.

In her view, it is important not to talk down to her readers who are children:

> Children enjoy assimilating new facts and ideas, but only if the writer is willing to rediscover these facts and ideas with the children, not if he hands out information from the heights of adult superiority.... There are some very long words in the stories ... The plots are not specially devised for children, but I think that if there's anything in the story that children don't understand they just don't worry about it.[8]

This Life will discuss the extent to which Crompton's fiction, including the William stories, can be understood as a bridge between children's and adult literature and as a form of crossover writing read by both children and adults.

In 1999, Canadian academic Sandra Beckett argues that crossover fiction transcends the boundaries of genre. She suggests that the 'largest group of crosswriters are, of course, the authors who address children and adults in separate works, and many of them continue ... to maintain a clear distinction between their two audiences.'[9] On the other hand, other contemporary writers 'now aspire to and engage in the form of cross writing that consists of addressing the same texts to young and old alike.'[10] These authors 'transcend or transgress the so-called borders between adult and children's fiction in order to address readers of all ages.'[11] Beckett argues that more and more books 'illustrate the limitations of audience age as a defining category and refuse to be confined by any such arbitrary boundary constraints.'[12] Crompton's work falls into both of these categories identified by Beckett.

Some of her novels, as well as the William stories, are examples of fiction suitable for both older children and adults. William attracts a dual audience of children and adults and several novels by Crompton had the potential to attract similar audiences when they were first published. However, they are unlikely to attract young adult readers in the twenty-first century, who would find them out of touch with their contemporary lives. The novels are interesting examples of a type of coming-of-age story, also known as bildungsroman, written from a young person's point of view. They follow young people from their childhood into early adulthood and we watch them as they, unlike William, grow up. In other novels, Crompton writes about what it means to behave in a grown-up way, a theme important in many of the William stories too, whatever a character's age. It is interesting to consider whether more proactive marketing of these novels when they were first published would have attracted both young and older adult readers.

Given that Crompton is an author who wrote a range of fiction for children or adults and other fiction for both children and adults, this may be one of the reasons why her novels have been undervalued. One senses that she was ambitious to write for different audiences and in doing so confused the gatekeepers who published, promoted, distributed and reviewed her work. Many of them pigeon-holed all of her novels as family sagas or quiet stories about village life and the William stories as children's literature, especially after the Second World War. Arguably, crossover writing remains a contested area in the marketing and study of literature, but that is a subject for another book about Crompton's work.

This Life will also consider Crompton's fascination with childhood and what happens in traditional families with two parents, as well as others in which children are brought up by an aunt or a sister. Crompton wrote about aspects of growing up all her life. She was not restricted by the constraints of age in her understanding of experience and many of her child characters are mature in the way they behave, whilst adults in her William stories and novels can be childlike in their approach to life and never grow up emotionally or intellectually. What it means to behave in a grown-up way and whether this is a state of mind that some can never achieve whatever their age interests her throughout her career.

* * *

Crompton wrote about the comfortable society she knew. From the nineteen twenties to the sixties, there was a massive increase in the size of the middle-class in Britain and their income rose throughout this period. The years from 1923 until the Second World War 'appeared a kind of golden age.'[13] The majority of the middle-class never experienced long-term unemployment and, despite changes to domestic service after the First World War, many were still able to afford residential or daily staff.[14] The thirties brought further prosperity to the South and Midlands in England. 'In 1931, nearly one in every five households still had at least one full-time domestic living in, while many more employed a "daily" to do most of the cleaning and cooking.'[15] Domestic service subsequently collapsed after 1940. The Brown's domestic arrangements in the William stories reflect these changes and their live-in servant finally disappears from the stories of the nineteen fifties and sixties.[16] She is replaced by Mrs Peters, a daily help.[17] Her novels and William stories provide a prism through which we see Crompton's perspective on this milieu in the early to mid-twentieth century. In this context, Crompton's fiction is in step with other contemporary children's literature of the period, which British children's literature specialist Dennis Butts notes 'tends to reflect the values of the prosperous and untroubled part of the population.'[18] The reader should note that this Life does not focus on Crompton's fiction in the context of children's literature from the early to mid-twentieth century. This too could form the basis of another book.

When she sets her novels amidst the mills of her childhood, the scars and hardship experienced in the North of England barely feature and they are ambivalent about the mills' influence on her characters' lives.[19] Occasionally Crompton uses language that is no longer acceptable in the twenty-first century and her fiction is representative of some of the prevailing attitudes of the early twentieth century that are no longer appropriate.

Crompton's novels are often concerned with the lives of women and the social changes brought by the interwar years and the two wars that framed them, including the impact of women's right to vote from 1918. She writes about the influence of modernity in relation to social mobility and how it affects women's lives who choose to stay within their family, and possibly marry, or leave to pursue a career or new adventures. For many of her characters, happiness is hard to find, especially if their childhood has been a battlefield, but there is hope for many of them and some find a place to belong and call home when they grow up. Life is complicated and Crompton offers no easy answers. Pathos can rest alongside humour and can be integral to comedy, but this is not pessimism.

British scholar Alison Light suggests that Crompton's writing be considered in the context of the conservative modernism reflected in the fiction by women novelists in the early twentieth century, such as novels by Winifred Holtby, Stella Gibbon, Ivy Compton-Burnett, Sylvia Townsend Warner and Rachel Ferguson.[20] She argues that novels by women writers in this period offer a more radical response to social, cultural and political changes in the interwar years of the twenties and thirties than has previously been acknowledged. These novels 'not only speak from their cultural moment but take issue with it,' writes Light. They offer a form of conservative modernity which, she argues, can 'simultaneously look backwards and forwards; it [can] accommodate the past in the new forms of the present.'[21] For Light this approach to modernity is based on the middle-class of the interwar years which represented Englishness 'in both its most modern and reactionary forms.'[22] As British academic Maroula Joannou suggests, in common with Light, many women writers in the interwar years were 'distinctly modern in such respects as style, outlook, and social attitudes,' yet 'they sought to deal with the contradictions of modern life by writing outside the framework of Modernism,' found in the work of authors such as Virginia Woolf, James Joyce and D.H. Lawrence.[23] The novels of these women writers not only speak within their cultural moment and take issue with it, exposing its confusions and imagining its problems in new ways, they also encompass a range of voices, languages and positions, and do not sustain a single 'argument' with the reader.[24]

Light suggests that the act of writing has a special place in women's lives, symbolised by a room of their own, 'which could be both domestic and public, private and professional.'[25] The image of women writers who needed a room of their own in which to write, famously advocated by Virginia Woolf in 1929, resonates with some of Crompton's women characters who are writers, or find solace in a study of their own for reading and private reflection.[26] This literary life will set Crompton's writing in the context of Light's approach, whilst not constraining our view of her within it, and look at some of the places where she studied and wrote herself.

As we shall see, Crompton cares about the home, a place or room of one's own for women, and social values that both underpin and challenge the influence of family relationships. She writes within the context of a middle-class world and this milieu provides a platform on which to showcase and perform in scenes, comic sketches and one-off episodes, her values about the nature of personal and social freedom, the importance of private, family, professional and social relationships, and how to live a good life in a philosophical, spiritual and intellectual sense. It is Crompton's understanding of human experience that captures her readers' attention, an experience that is not based on an essentialist view of age and which can capture youthful maturity and ageing delinquency.

* * *

A friend of Robert's, William's older brother, remarks that his friend's younger brother is, as ever, 'the ubiquitous William':

> William hoped that the look he received in return made him feel small. Ubiquitous indeed. When he'd washed his face, and brushed his hair, and put on his best suit, and looked as smart as any of them.[27]

This is one of many examples where Crompton's vocabulary sparkles. One reader will understand that William has misunderstood the meaning of ubiquitous and enjoy Crompton's comedy, whilst another, perhaps younger, reader will marvel at her language, albeit that William's response will not help them to learn the meaning of ubiquitous, a quality that he embodies.

A few words and a tightly structured phrase can encapsulate William's character. Crompton's fans often say that much of their enjoyment lies in the sharp satire inherent in individual sentences or short passages in which Crompton's narrator wryly observes William's world. For example:

> It is a great gift to be able to lie so as to convince other people. It is a still greater gift to be able to lie so as to convince oneself. William was possessed of the latter gift.[28]

> William had learnt that in dealing with ordinary limited human beings one's imagination should not be given too free a rein. He put the true artistic touch of restraint into his picture.[29]

> William realised that it is impossible to waylay a person who refuses to be waylaid. He lacked the optical power of the Ancient Mariner.[30]

Some of the distinctive characteristics in the William stories are vocabulary unfamiliar to many of Crompton's younger readers and sharp, piercing observations that still feel relevant to contemporary readers today.

Crompton wanted to be known as a serious author, as well as the comic author of the William stories. Of course, comedy can have serious intent, particularly when it is satirical. The William stories feature one of the familiar stereotypes of classic comedy, the trickster, who 'appears in the folk tales and religious myths of many cultures,' and is 'a witty and irreverent being who violates the most sacred of prohibitions. The trickster is not confined by boundaries, conceptual, social, or physical, and can cross lines that are impermeable to normal individuals.'[31] In doing so, she or he exposes many of the flaws in the world around them, as indeed William does, although his intentions are invariably good, rarely of a criminal nature and never malicious. As American academic Andrew Stott suggests, stories featuring a trickster 'usually conclude with the meddle-some actions of the protagonist coming to serve some useful or illustrative purpose.'[32] Not everyone would agree that the outcome of William's antics are useful, but the stories often illustrate a moral that exposes pomposity, greed and other adult flaws. In the case of a recurrent fool or trickster, there is a philosophical or mythic dimension 'that asserts the existence of a universe outside the individual and a higher power that controls it.'[33] This Life looks at the extent to which this is a significant quality inherent in Crompton's William stories that was informed by her father Edward's values and beliefs, her own extensive reading and her study and teaching of classical philosophy and literature. William's life is often plagued by the higher power of Fate, as we shall see.

American novelist and academic Alison Lurie argues that subversive children's literature makes 'fun of adult institutions, including school and family' and it appeals 'to the imaginative, questioning, rebellious child within all of us … and act[s] as a force for change.'[34] The William stories are subtly subversive in this way, although not in the sense that they seek to undermine the middle-class world in which William lives. They certainly 'make fun of honored figures and piously held beliefs; and they view social pretenses with clear-eyed directness,' whilst focusing on the world of home and family.[35] Crompton is an educator, a guide and a commentator, not a social reformer. The change she seeks is within individuals who may, or may not, face up to their mistakes or have enough self-awareness to see the flaws in themselves and others and to learn from them. By often taking a child's eye view of the world in her William stories, she understands that all of us were once children, who are part of what Lurie describes as 'an unusual, partly savage tribe, ancient and widely distributed.'[36]

In her comic novels that bear some similarity to the structure of the William stories and encourage the reader to smile, although not to laugh out loud as they do when reading William stories, a wry eye observing the world is a feature of domestic *flaneuse*-like characters, such as Euphemia, Beatrice and Matty. These characters appear in *The Odyssey of Euphemia Tracy* (1932), *The Old Man's Birthday* (1934) and *Matty and the Dearingroydes* (1956), respectively. In *Caroline* (1936), *Journeying Wave* (1938) and *The Gypsy's Baby* (1954), there is also a central comic character around which the plot revolves. In these novels, in a range of carefully structured scenes and anecdotes, each of the other characters are involved in some way in the central character's experience, as they invariably are in the William stories.

Crompton's satirical eye roves throughout many of her novels, which, like the William stories, expose complacency and pomposity and lift the roof off petty conventional behaviour. For example, the village life portrayed in *Leadon Hill* (1927) is claustrophobic, bitchy and uncomfortable for many of the village's inhabitants, several of whom would like to escape if they could. Anyone who rocks the boat or does not conform can be severely punished. The Faversham's young son Timmy has surgical boots and 'irons' on one leg, which suggests that he contracted polio as a child. In Leadon Hill, 'Acacia Road was very refined and very critical.' The people who live on the road disapprove of the Faversham family's children who are allowed to 'run wild.'[37] 'Acacia Road liked children to walk decorously in the village with nurse or governess, not tear up the road to the woods.'[38] They also fail to understand why Timmy is allowed to join his brother and sister in these activities.

In the novel, Miss Mitcham 'made it her business from childhood to know everything about everyone' and she was 'a power in the village'[39]:

> People were afraid of her and tried to placate her. They wished to get off as lightly as possible when Miss Mitcham sat in her little over-crowded drawing room in Acacia Road with her friends and set to work on the time-honoured task of ravelling reputations.[40]

Several reputations do indeed become tangled, confused, broken and discarded during the novel. Helen is a visitor to the village and fails to fit in. She plans an act of kindness that might avert someone's unnecessary death but her intentions are maliciously twisted and misrepresented by Miss Mitcham when she shares them amongst the other inhabitants of the village, who stand 'about in little groups gloating.'[41] The novel leaves the reader feeling uncomfortable and disappointed by pettiness and meanness.

We do not see Crompton's characters' subtlety evolve in her fiction but rather catch them at particular moments, in much the same way that her biographer will catch Richmal herself in this tale about her life of writing. In her novels, Crompton reimagines classical myths and allegories, and writes family sagas, tales of village communities, stories that focus on one woman's life, bildungsroman, anecdotal stories about a range of people who find themselves in a similar place and ghost stories, amongst others. Her novels include several comedies and a tragedy, *Narcissa* (1941). Crompton often takes a satirical and askance view of the day-to-day world and asks her readers to question conventions and notice inconsistencies and power imbalances, especially in the lives of women, as well as in the William stories. She asks her readers to think differently.

Unknown to many of her readers, Crompton also wrote adventure stories, which do not feature William as the hero and instead focus on crime. A collection of adventure stories initially published in the *Strand* magazine were brought together by the Folio Society in 1995 and includes "An Eventful Day in the Life of Miss Faversham" (1926) by Crompton.[42] As William knows, adventure can be found by Crompton's characters in the most conventional domestic surroundings as they go about their everyday activities.

Some of her darker characters suggest that she can fear the worst in others, but others are a counter to their narcissism and malevolence.[43] Much of her writing is full of hope and optimism, as any fan of William will know. To fully appreciate her approach, it is important to read the William stories, her novels and other short stories together to understand both what they have in common and how they differ.

* * *

This book is based on facts about Richmal's life, although many are missing. It does include moments of speculation. Gaps are filled by the voices of William, Richmal Crompton's other characters, her fans, especially members of The Just William Society, as well as Richmal herself, or at least a version of herself as the author Richmal Crompton that she portrayed in interviews and in her letters to her fans and other professional contacts. They all intervene at times to give their own perspective on her fiction and her life of writing.[44]

My copy of *William and the Pop Singers* (1965) was owned by Richard, who signs himself off on the inside cover as 'The King of the Earth.' No doubt, this is how William made him feel, and this description might also be Richard's perspective on William. The William books are entangled in their fans' lives. They are a touchstone that fans reread over many years and share with those they love. Fans' voices are integral to this story of Crompton's life. Novelist Deborah Moggach believes that the William books are the funniest books of all time. She has read them since she was eleven:

> There's a snobbishness in our literary world that equates laughter with shallow-ness.... [Crompton] understood that the basis for comedy is the disconnect between how we see ourselves and how others see us.... When we laugh at its protagonists, we also laugh at ourselves.... There's still a part of me who's an 11-year-old crashing around the countryside, unwittingly causing mayhem from often the best intentions.[45]

Wherever they come from, other fans share Moggach's sense that Crompton writes about a world made up of flawed people and relationships, and they too appreciate the serious intent of her comedy.

Many of Crompton's fans collect the William books and share the stories with their own children and grandchildren. The familiar characters and plots are an important part of the stories' appeal. British academic Victor Watson describes reading series fiction as 'going into a room full of friends.' Readers young and older enjoy the certainty of meeting familiar characters again and again in series fiction like the William stories, in which William remains eleven years old throughout. Watson suggests that in series fiction, the 'char-acters who remain the same age for ever inhabit an essentially magical and romantic world, however authentic the surface realism might be.' It is such a world to which William belongs. Watson also argues that series fiction can be underestimated, and that the literary quality of its writing and storytelling can be missed.[46] This is certainly true of Crompton's reputation to date and her association with series fiction might be one factor to explain why the quality of her novels has been overlooked. American academic Betty Greenway shares this view about the William stories and argues that William is distinct from other series fiction:

> Complex characterization, where the child is understood and the adult often pilloried, and an intricate, humorous, and satirical style go hand in hand in the William books, a combination not seen in other series books of their kind. The books are also an excellent example of cross-writing, and of cross-audiencing … The very literary style appeals to the adult, while the characterization appeals to the child, and of course also to the adult who was a child.… And it is William's great imagination, finally, that sets these books apart from other series about real children having adventures in the real world.[47]

Crompton's and William's imaginations are on display throughout this Life.

Few of Richmal Crompton's fans will realise that her William stories were censored in Franco's Spain where they were considered subversive. They are certainly funny, satirical and ironic, particularly those written in the nineteen twenties and thirties, and have been read across Europe and in many other countries by young and older readers.

Both Crompton and William look outwards onto the world. They are both thoughtful and strategic, but glimpses into Richmal's personal inner world where we can 'hear' her thinking are rare. There are no personal diaries or an autobiography in her archive, only a few personal letters, and a limited number sent to her by family, friends, fans and media and literary professionals. William acts on what he has been thinking about, Richmal's alter ego Richmal Crompton writes about it in her fiction and her perspective is reflected in a few published interviews and articles. How Richmal Lamburn really felt about her own life, her characters and her alter ego as a writer is largely absent in this Life, perhaps as she intended.

Crompton believed that as his success grew, she became William's puppet, and she commented that he pulled the strings:

> For he is resolute, indomitable, and inclined to be tyrannical. Like all characters who have been overindulged by their authors, he insists on having his own way. He refuses to cooperate in some plots. He makes fantastic demands on others. He pushes his way unceremoniously into situations in which he has really very little concern.[48]

The two main characters depicted in this biography are the domineering William Brown and Richmal Crompton. As Crompton knew, we cannot have one without the other. Occasionally they almost seem to meet in the stories. This Life hopes to illustrate that in fact William was expertly controlled by Crompton as he peers out from behind her shoulder.

One has a sense of her self-control in interviews with journalists in the nineteen fifties and sixties in which we have a rare opportunity to hear her speak in her own words. William was hugely successful, and Crompton had celebrity status by the mid-fifties, but her novels and other short stories were not well read. It would not be surprising if she were disappointed that the breadth and depth of her writing, including the genius of William, had been undervalued in her lifetime. In 1968, a few months before she died, there is an edginess in her comments about her writing in one interview. Crompton tells the journalist:

> I feel that 100 years hence it won't make any difference whether I have written stories, but it might matter if I have helped someone—that's more important than working on something that isn't going to be a masterpiece. More tea?
>
> She knows, she says, that she has not contributed to literature with a capital "L" and that her writing is on a very low scale. Most of it is escapist.[49]

There is a sharp edge to her tone here which implies 'I know I am not any good at this, or so everyone keeps telling me.' I do not believe that she accepted this for a minute. One fears the journalist has missed the bitterness in, 'More tea?', which gives her interviewer little opportunity to say something in reply, such as: 'Goodness me, no. Your character William is certainly a masterpiece and a number of your novels and other short stories are far more than mere escapism.' Perhaps Richmal knew that the journalist would not reply, as indeed she did not. One senses that Richmal had been told something similar by others before. Those who knew her suggest that she was always polite and calm, and she was certainly a consummate professional and rarely rude, but her reaction in this interview sounds like disappointment, even anger. This literary biography is a reply to her retort, 'More tea?', and one that, sadly, she did not receive in her lifetime.

* * *

The chapters in this literary life are organised within six sections, which include chronological biographical sections and others that are primarily thematic and take a close look at William and other characters in Crompton's writing from several different perspectives. A few illustrate some of the connections between William and aspects of Crompton's novels and other short stories.

Part I (1890–1911) covers her childhood and youth in Bury and at St Elphin's School in Darley Dale, a boarding school for the daughters of clergymen. It introduces her parents Edward and Clara and discusses the portrayal of Mr and Mrs Brown in the William stories, as well as Crompton's writing about mother figures in her novels.

Part II (1911–1923) is based on her life at university and her early years in Bromley, Kent, where she moved following the death of her father in 1915. Richmal Crompton and William are born in these years. The first two William books were published in 1922 and then in 1923 she contracted polio, in the same year as her first novel, *The Innermost Room*, was published. This novel is a bildungsroman about growing up and the choice a young woman makes between writing or marriage. Crompton's own life as a young woman was framed by the First World War, the three years she spent at St Elphin's as a teacher after leaving Royal Holloway College where she studied Classics, the death of her father and her move to Kent to join her mother and sister, and by illness. In this period she became a property owner, a hugely successful professional woman, the head of her family living in Kent and an example of what women could achieve after 1918, when women over thirty could vote for the first time.

Part III (1924–1938) covers a prolific period in Crompton's writing life, both on and off the stage, and the birth of Violet Elizabeth Bott, who proclaimed so proudly, 'I can.' There is little evidence available about her personal life in the years after she contracted polio. In the twenties, her drive to write remains undimmed and she introduces new comic characters who bear some William and Violet Elizabeth-like characteristics. Her interest in what it means to grow up is clear and darker themes appear in other fiction. Crompton emerges in the nineteen thirties on the stage and the fringes of literary London. This section also considers characters in her novels who share William's ability to live on the boundaries of the everyday and serve as a central character around which satirical plots revolve. They act like a *flaneuse* or a *flaneur* and sometimes as a guide on how to live a better life.

Part IV (1939–1945) covers her life and writing during the Second World War and reflects on William's heroic qualities. It is hoped that readers will enjoy the 'tongue in cheek' suggestion that he is comparable to Homer's Odysseus. There were many ordinary people who were heroes on the home front during the war and we read about some of them in her novels from this period, two of which address the experience of Jews in England and that of ordinary Germans in the late thirties.

Part V (1946–1969) takes us through the forties and fifties, when William became successful on radio and television, and to the end of Crompton's life in January 1969. We hear something of her 'voice' in media interviews late in life. The breadth of her writing remained overlooked. There is a poignancy in her last novel, *The Inheritor*, published in 1960 when she was seventy. She decided not to publish any further novels, yet she was writing and publishing William stories until the day she died.

The last section, Part VI, is dedicated to some of Crompton's fans, in particular: writers influenced by her fiction, including those who pay homage to William in their own fiction; Spanish fans living through the Franco era; and contemporary William fans in the UK. Crompton was not averse to poking fun at herself and she writes wryly about characters who are authors.

* * *

The image of a studious, demure and pensive young woman, a vibrant actor performing on and off the page and at events, a loving and caring friend, a funny, extrovert guest with a sparkling imagination and an astute observer of other people whatever their age, reflect the same person who was also a dedicated teacher, a devoted aunt and the head of her close family in Kent, as well as the frumpy, frail and formally dressed old lady who we see in photographs towards the end of her life. It is hard to know how her disability and a life of recurring pain and fatigue, both of which may be long-term consequences of polio, had an impact on Richmal. She performed many roles in life and her character is complex. Some of the roles she played are hard to reconcile with the wild, bumptious, mischievous character Crompton's fans love, but at heart Richmal and William have much in common.

I have spent many years in Richmal Lamburn's company and realise that there is still much about her that I do not know. I offer here my reading of her life of writing as Richmal Crompton and of her character William Brown, which have helped me to understand some of the things she cared about as a writer. I hope that it will inspire others to join me in reading more of her work. If it does nothing else, this Life will confirm what many of his fans already know, that William is a masterpiece of early twentieth century literature and that Crompton's novels, and other short stories are far more than mere escapism. It also hopes to reconcile what Richmal Crompton cared about in her novels and other short stories with her infamous character William Brown and the William stories. This Life considers Crompton's oeuvre across fifty years of writing, looking at William and all her other characters in novels, plays and short stories through the same lens and wonders what they have in common. Her writing takes centre stage in the eyes of her fans and in this biography.

Critic Alvara Santana-Acuna believes that one of the most familiar characteristics of a literary classic is 'its unstoppable power to be part of our lives.'[50] He describes a classic as a social institution that 'shapes the taste and actions of artists, art industry gatekeepers, influencers, and consumers across generations, nations, and cultures' and that supports a community of readers.[51] This literary life suggests that, on the basis of Santana-Acuna's definition, the William stories are a classic of twentieth century literature.

William and his friends Ginger, Douglas and Henry, known as the Outlaws, discuss the mysteries associated with grown-ups who, William tells them, have to say things in a way that is harder to understand than the 'ornery way.' They have a special 'langwidge' that helps them to become headmasters [and biographers].[52] As William says in another story:

> We've only got to listen to grown up people talkin'. They always talk about each other. I guess there isn't a single grown-up you couldn't find out all about by jus' listening to other grown-ups talkin'.[53]

Whether we should believe everything other people, biographers, writers and their characters say is one of the challenges facing any reader. In *The Inheritor* (1960), Mr Pelham writes popular biography, which he describes as 'a cross between unpopular biography and the historical novel, you know. I've got a sort of flair for it. But even so it means a certain amount of research and you've got to get your facts right.'[54] Mr Pelham is quite an innocuous character. It is a relief to note that his creator seems to bear him no ill will. Whether this biography is popular will be up to readers to decide. I certainly hope that it can be enjoyed as an entertaining and occasionally light-hearted story that is based on facts about the life of the writer Richmal Crompton, on her stories about her most famous character, and as an informative introduction to her other writing.

Notes

1. Jarvis, Martin. *The Just William Society Magazine 1*, 18. The magazine will be identified as *JWSM* in forthcoming notes.
2. Jimmy features in *Jimmy* (1949) and *Jimmy again* (1951). Armada later published three Jimmy books based on the stories in the first two books: *Jimmy* (1965), *Jimmy Again* (1965) and *Jimmy the Third* (1965). Please see the Appendix for a bibliography of many of Crompton books. *Enter*

Patricia (1927) is included as a short story collection. In a dedication To
The Reader the narrator suggests: 'With a respectful recommendation
not to read all the following sketches in one sitting.'
3. Kitchener, 4.
4. Richmal Crompton's library, taken from her last home, is located in the
Richmal Crompton Collection held in the Foyle Special Collections and
Archives at the University of Roehampton.
5. UoR RC/1/11. Notes on other authors.
6. Ibid.
7. *The Writer*, 4.
8. Ibid.
9. Beckett, xiv.
10. Ibid.
11. Ibid., 31.
12. Ibid., xviii.
13. McKibbin, 59.
14. McKibbin, 59–62.
15. Stevenson, 131.
16. Taylor, 38.
17. Ibid.
18. Butts, 120.
19. Dennis Butts notes that unemployment was 'most devastating in those
areas dependent on the older stable industries of textiles, iron and steel,
and mining, such as Lancashire, Scotland, the North-East and South
Wales' (120). Bury, where Richmal was born, is in Lancashire.
20. Light, 239.
21. Ibid., 2 and 10.
22. Ibid., 11.
23. Joannou 2013, 2.
24. Light, 2.
25. Ibid., 5.
26. Virginia Woolf wrote an influential essay, *A Room of One's Own* (1929),
based on lectures she gave at Cambridge University—see Chapter 9.
27. "William Starts the Holidays," 227.
28. "William's New Year's Day," 196. Christopher Ringrose celebrates
William's imagination when he lies: 'His capacity for carnivalesque imag-
inings, his disregard for the rules of evidence, his reckless lies, endorsed
by an indulgent narrator who devises a series of elaborate plot resolutions to extricate him from the consequences of his untruths, place the
William series at the aesthetic level of the treatment of truth and lies

in children's fiction.... it constantly reminds the reader of the limits of truth-telling and of the human need to experiment with veracity' (235).

29. "William and the Musician," 14. In this story, William is 'chagrined' at the misconception of one of these ordinary beings, who has misunderstood his loftier purpose, because in his imagination he had become 'the owner of all the land and houses as far as he could see' (13). Reality and veracity have their own meaning for William.

30. "William and Cleopatra," 77. In "The Rime of the Ancient Mariner" (1798) by Samuel Coleridge a stranger is spellbound by the eye of the Ancient Mariner and feels compelled to listen to his story.

31. Stott, 51.

32. Ibid., 54.

33. Ibid., 60.

34. Lurie, x–xi.

35. Ibid., 20 and 25.

36. Ibid., ix. Butts comments that the subversive nature of Crompton's William books, amongst others, continued the tradition of comparable children's literature by previous authors such as Lewis Carroll in *Alice's Adventure in Wonderland* (1865), Rudyard Kipling in *Stalky & Co* (1899) and Thomas Hughes's *Tom Brown's Schooldays* (1857) (137).

37. *Leadon Hill*, 13–14.

38. Ibid., 14.

39. Ibid., 32.

40. Ibid.

41. Ibid., 299.

42. See *Adventure Stories from the 'Strand.'* (1995) selected by Geraldine Beare. In this collection, Crompton is in the company of stories by Conan Doyle, H.G. Wells, Somerset Maugham, Sinclair Lewis and Graham Greene, among others. Also see "Miss Burford's Crowded Hour" *Annie Swann's Annual* 1928, 59–64, which is another crime story. Like William, Miss Burford longs for adventure (60). She finds it and to her surprise starts brandishing a revolver: 'Considering that she had only seen the action performed before in one or two melodramas acted by the Sunday school dramatic society, she did it remarkably well' (63). Further research will no doubt identify other similar stories.

43. British academic William Whyte argues that Crompton had a 'highly pessimistic view of human nature' (154) and there are certainly some dark themes in a few of her novels, such as *Narcissa* and *The House*, and in some of her short stories. However, in other work she is optimistic

and positive. This Life offers a more balanced view on the basis that Crompton was interested in people, for good and ill.

44. Kristin Barton suggests that there are varied reasons why people become fans and explains that 'being a fan allows us to express ourselves, it helps us connect to like-minded people, and it allows us to escape into a world devoid of the pressures of life, even if only for 30 min at a time. But more than anything, being a fan means being in love' (6). Most of the fans mentioned in this biography love the William stories and several have described their reading as a moment of escape. At the very least, fans of the William stories are more than readers because they return to the stories again and again as children and adults, and some have been influenced by Crompton in their own writing.

45. Moggach, 2017.

46. Watson, 6, 8.

47. Greenway, 108.

48. "Puppet Pulls the Strings," 41.

49. UoR RC/1/9/5. John London "The woman who is more than just William" *Evening News* 25 November 1968.

50. Santana-Acuna, 3.

51. Ibid., 4.

52. "The Outlaws Deliver the Goods," 142.

53. "The Outlaws and the Hidden Treasure," 127.

54. *The Inheritor*, 131.

References

Barton, Kristin M. and Jonathan Malcolm Lampley Eds. 2014. *FanCULTure: Essays on Participatory Fandom in the 21st Century.* London: McFarland and Company.

Beckett, Sandra. 1999. "Crosswriting Child and Adult in France: Children's Fiction for Adults? Adult Fiction for Children? Fiction for All Ages?" In *Transcending Boundaries: Writing for a Dual Audience of Children and Adults*, by Sandra Beckett Ed., 31–61. New York: Garland.

———. 1999. "Introduction." In *Transcending Boundaries: Writing for a Dual Audience of Children and Adults*, by Sandra Beckett Ed., xi–xx. New York: Garland.

Butts, Dennis. 2010. *Children's Literature and Social Change.* Cambridge: Lutterworth Press.

Crompton, Richmal. 1995. First pubished 1926. "An Eventful Day in the Life of Miss Faversham." In *Adventure Stories from the 'Strand'*, by Geraldine Beare Ed., 209–222. London : The Folio Society.

———. 1927. *Leadon Hill.* London: Hodder & Stoughton.

———. October 1952. "On Writing for Children." *The Writer Vol 10.4* 4–5.

———. December 1957. "Puppet Pulls the Strings." *Books and Bookmen* 41.

———. 1960. *The Inheritor.* London: Hutchinson.

———. 1999. First published 1930. "The Outlaws and the Hidden Treasure." In *William's Happy Days*, by Richmal Crompton, 106–132. London: Macmillan Children's Books.

———. 1951. First published 1929. "The Outlaws Deliver the Goods." In *William*, by Richmal Crompton, 138–163. London: George Newnes Ltd.

———. 1985. First published 1933. "William and Cleopatra." In *William - The Rebel*, by Richmal Crompton, 71–87. Basingstoke, Hampshire: Macmillan Children's Books.

———. 1949. First published 1932. "William and the Musician." In *William - The Pirate*, by Richmal Crompton, 13–35. London: George Newnes Ltd.

———. 1991. First published 1922. "William's New Year's Day." In *Just - William*, by Richmal Crompton, 186–204. Basingstoke, Hampshire: Macmillan Children's Books.

———. 1930. First published 1926. "William Starts the Holidays." In *William - The Conqueror*, by Richmal Crompton, 214–234. London: George Newnes Ltd.

Greenway, Betty. 2002. "William Forever: Richmal Crompton's Unusual Achievement." *The Lion and the Unicorn 26.1* 98–111.

Jarvis, Martin. December 1995. "An Interview with Martin Jarvis." *The Just William Society Magazine 1* 17–19.

Joannou, Maroula. 2013. "Modernism, Modernity, and the Middlebrow in Context." In *The History of British Women's Writing, 1920–1945*, by Maroula Joannou Ed., 1–20. London: Palgrave Macmillan.

Kitchener, Pamela. 1958. "William's Misdeeds." *Western Mail*, 14 February: 4.

Light, Alison. 1991. *Forever England: Feminity, Literature and Conservatism Between the Wars.* London: Routledge.

Lurie, Alison. 1990. *Not in Front of the Grown-Ups.* London: Cardinal.

McKibbin, Ross. 2000. First published 1998. *Classes and Cultures England 1918-1951.* Oxford: Oxford University Press.

Moggach, Deborah. 2017. "'I Fell Out of Bed Laughing': Writers on Their Favourite Funny Book." *The Guardian*, 7 January: https://www.theguardian.com/books/2017/jan/07/my-favourite-funny-book-jonathan-coe-nina-stibbe-david-nicholls-bridget-christie.

Ringrose, Christopher. 2006. "Lying in Children's Fiction: Morality and the Imagination." *Children's Literature in Education 37* 229–236.

Santana-Acuna, Alvaro. 2020. *Ascent to Glory: How One Hundred Years of Solitude Was Written and Became a Global Classic.* New York: Columbia University Press.

Stevenson, John. 1984. *British Society 1914–45.* London: Lane.

Stott, Andrew. 2005. *Comedy.* Abingdon, Oxon: Routledge.

Taylor, Terry. Summer 2013. "Where Did All the Servants Go." *The Just William Society Magazine 32* 30–38.

Watson, Victor. 2000. *Reading Series Fiction: From Arthur Ransome to Gene Kemp.* London: RoutledgeFalmer.

Whyte, William. 2011. "Just William? Richmal Crompton and Conservative Fiction." In *Classes, Cultures, and Politics: Essays on British History for Ross McKibbin*, by Clare Griffiths James Nott and William Whyte Eds., 139–154. Oxford: Oxford University Press.

Part I

(1890–1911)

2

Edward Lamburn and a Classical Education

In *Anne Morrison* (1925), the midday siren sounds loudly in Framhurst, Crompton's fictional mill town set in the nineteenth century, and 'crowds of mill girls' flood the streets:

> in shawls and clogs, with little bits of white fluff clinging to their clothes and hair. They besieged the trams or walked off in little groups. All of them seemed to be shouting to each other at the tops of their voices and uttering shrill screams of laughter.'[1]

Richmal Crompton Lamburn was born amidst such 'satanic mills' in Bury, Lancashire on 15 November 1890. Comparable mills haunt a few of the novels written by her alter ego, Richmal Crompton. In *Family Roundabout* (1948), the Willoughby family, headed by the matriarchal Mrs Willoughby, own the local monstrous, massive, barrack-like mill and are as dominating in the local area as the mill they own.[2] Mrs Willoughby herself is equally massive; solid, ugly and expensive, like the furniture in the grand family home.[3] Local mill-owning families and their properties embody the pervasive power they have in the town.

The mills define the lives of the people who live near them. Whether rich or poor, everyone is subsumed within their influence, with relish or reluctance depending on their nature. In *Millicent Dorrington* (1927), Millicent is born in a house next to the family's mill before her father builds a grander home in a more salubrious area favoured by other big mill-owners on the edge of the

© The Author(s), under exclusive license to Springer Nature
Switzerland AG 2022
J. McVeigh, *Richmal Crompton, Author of Just William*, Literary Lives,
https://doi.org/10.1007/978-3-030-96511-2_2

town. The owners and their families try to move away from the smoke, dirt and noise of the mills below them, but it is impossible for them to escape:

> The smoke from the crowded mill chimneys made housekeeping, as Mrs. Merton, who was cultured, put it, a "Sisyphean labour." Windows and curtains wouldn't keep clean for even one day, and however much you paid your gardener, everything in your garden was wizened and stunted and stained with smoke.[4]

Millicent's father is the successful owner of their family's mill, although his 'tastes and interests have more in common with the artistic than with the business world.'[5] In her fiction, Crompton consistently values characters who follow intellectual and artistic pursuits, such as Archie in the William stories who is a painter, as well as William's sister Ethel's hapless suitor. We shall meet him in a later chapter. In Crompton's novel, Mr Dorrington had always planned to leave his work at the mill, but when his own father died, he went to the mill 'just to tide things over.' He tells Millicent:

> I don't know why I stayed. I've never understood that. I suppose it was a sort of moral supineness. I got into a rut before I realised it and then found I couldn't get out. I began to like the work. A mill is ugly looked at from one point of view. Looked at from another it's a beautiful living organism.[6]

In *Anne Morrison*, Anne understands the positive influence of the mills too. Aged ten, she has three siblings: Lorna aged thirteen whom Anne joins at boarding school, Cathy who is seven and Paul who is eleven.[7] They live in Framhurst with their mother and father, who is a clergyman, where the hills, valleys and moorland 'were fouled by the myriad ever-smoking factory chimneys which stretched like an army as far as the eye could see. You could never get out of sight of those chimneys, for Framhurst was linked up with countless other little manufacturing towns.'[8] As a child, Anne hates the chimneys, their ugliness and the dirt they create as the surrounding woods and fields become smoke-grimed and soiled. However, when she returns as an adult, later in life, and 'looked down curiously at the forest of chimneys,' she too sees 'in their ugliness a beauty and romance.'[9] Anne's family is representative of the growing middle-class who relied on the success of the textile industry in northern towns and cities from the nineteenth century through to the nineteen twenties, when it began to decline.

Anne's father, Timothy, is a local minister who moved to the town after a troubled childhood. Timothy was disappointed in his own father, who was a drunk:

His childhood had been an unhappy one ... his memories of it were memories of misery and poverty, of a faded shadowy mother and a drunken father.... His mother had been warned against him. But he was a handsome man with a tall figure and flowing side-whiskers, and between his drinking bouts, charming.... To Timothy childhood had meant a ceaseless fear of his father's blind drunk rages, and an almost greater fear of the fits of maudlin sentiment into which his old charm had degenerated, a heart-rending pity for his mother and ineffectual attempts to protect her. He left home when she died and obtained a post as student teacher in a boys' school.... He was happy there.[10]

Timothy is fearful of his own father's faults which 'were branded deeply and with a sickening horror into his mind.' He marries and watches anxiously for signs of his father's failings in his own children, 'signs of the slackness, the shiftiness, the self-indulgence, that had been his father's ruin. Even traces of his father's easy charm in them frightened him.'[11] He dedicates himself to living a better life than his father and to giving his children the opportunities he never had.

His work as a teacher and a curate fills Timothy's days and Anne rarely sees him when she is growing up. However, on precious walks together he tells her stories of Ancient Greece and peoples her world with a wonderful assemblage of Greek heroes: 'He lived in her mind almost as a hero of fable himself.... He was Odysseus, Jason, Perseus.... Then he took more definite form. He became teacher now as well as storyteller.'[12] He is a romantic with Spartan ideals, at times entertainer or companion, whilst often teacher or guide.[13] As she grows up, Anne supplants her brother as the focus of her father's ambitions. They discuss her reading of Scott, Dickens, Trollope and Thackeray on long walks together:

She owed much of her development to those walks with Timothy. It was during those walks that he told her of his own childhood, his unhappiness and fear of his father.... She became aware that, unconsciously, he had singled her out and bestowed upon her a different kind of love from that which he gave his other children, and in return her love for him grew deeper and stronger.[14]

Richmal's father, Edward Lamburn, would have understood the beauty and romance of the mills that Anne Morrison values when she grows up. Richmal shared with him a love of classical literature and languages, teaching and study.

Edward was a lasting influence in Richmal's life. She grew up to achieve more than her father could ever have imagined. The reading they shared became a lifelong passion. Throughout her writing, as we shall see in a later chapter, Crompton is interested in her characters' reading and familiar canonical stories feature in some of her most enjoyable stories. She is also fascinated by what it means to behave in a mature grown-up way, whatever age her characters are, and she writes often about childhood and the impact it has, for good or ill, on her characters.

* * *

Edward came to Bury as a young man to face the challenges of a densely populated, noisy, thriving town, which was a far cry from the rural, pastoral community in which he grew up. In 1854, he was born into a family of farmers from Charndon, a small hamlet in Buckinghamshire. Steve Lawson, a William fan, discovered that the Lamburns 'had farmed in the county of Buckinghamshire for generations.'[15] In 1876, Edward was appointed Assistant Master at Bury Grammar school where he stayed for thirty-nine years until his death at the age of sixty-one in March 1915, whilst in hospital for an operation. He was curate of Radcliffe Parish Church and, in 1897, became the stipendiary curate for the parish of Thornham-with-Gravel-Hole. He walked the twenty-mile round trip from his home in Bury to take church services there each Sunday. During the week, he got up at five every morning and went swimming in a reservoir, taking a candle and a hammer with him in winter. The candle was to guide his way and he needed the hammer to break the ice.[16] His rigorous, spartan daily routine' consisted of this early morning swim in Clarence Park Reservoir, attendance at St John's in Bury for the morning service, followed by a full day's teaching at Bury Grammar School, as well as private tuition of two pupils at his home.[17]

Over his first ten years in Bury, Edward established himself in the town and fell in love with his future wife, and Richmal's mother, Clara Crompton. In their early letters, we hear two nervous young people becoming friends and then lovers. Edward's tone was terse and constrained at times, as Clara pointed out to him. We do not know if she was a little taken aback to receive his marriage proposal by letter in January 1886. He told her that 'the special circumstances of my own case' had led him to write, even though he believed that what he called verbal declarations are best. He asked her to marry him with some reservation:

> I have hesitated somewhat in taking this step from a natural reluctance to bring forward family matters of an unpleasant character. My father, some years ago, fell into drinking habits which of course brought great trouble upon us. He has however recently gone to a fresh school near Newmarket, and I have every reason to think he is quite reformed.[18]

Edward's father, Edward Lamburn senior, had a history of drinking. He was a schoolmaster too, but he had to keep moving across England from school to school because of his drinking.[19] When Edward's mother Mary died, he moved to the North of England and a new life away from his father's influence. In his proposal to Clara, he was clearly worried that his family's circumstances would influence her decision. He ended his letter with a formal note that his present income was £200 per year.

She replied the following day with equal restraint. Her parents believed she was old enough to know her own mind and advised her to follow the dictates of her heart. She accepted him and was prepared to wait for him, as he had asked, whilst he built his career.[20] During their engagement, Edward told her that he had plans for further studies, which he hoped would help him 'secure a good position in the scholastic world.' He had already gained a university degree in 1882.

The experience of his childhood made Edward a tentative lover and drove him to achieve the highest moral, intellectual and professional standards. His Christian values, sense of duty, dedication to hard work and high expectations of others, including his own children, were important to him in every aspect of his life.

From February 1886, in their letters we can hear the couple getting to know each other better. Clara worried that she was not 'a grand and noble woman, as I am afraid you think me, but just a weak, foolish girl, with very undisciplined feelings. I think I am younger than my years for I have always been so free from care and responsibility, but you will help me, I know, to become better.' She was jealous of his work commitments and wanted to spend more time with him. Edward hoped and believed that 'as we go through life together, our attachment to each other will become deeper.' Nevertheless, he shared and understood Clara's concern that they still had so much to learn about each other:

> You say you feel as if you did not half know me; no doubt both of us have much to learn about the disposition of the other; but the main outlines of our character are, I feel sure, well known to each. And I venture to think that during the month which has elapsed since our engagement this mutual insight has vastly increased.

Clara asked if he could sign his letters as Eddie, rather than Ned. Edward suggested she chose whatever name she liked. 'Eddie, of course, sounds more familiar and homely, but I do not know that anything else can be said in support of it,' he commented dryly. Eddie, he became.[21]

By April 1886, the tone in their letters was already lighter and more familiar. He was ordained in the summer, although he remained in teaching. Her letters are full of spring cleaning, obligations to look after her parents, the local church and going out to tea or entertaining. Clara feared that their engagement did not mean as much to him, 'for love and marriage is always more in a woman's life than in a man's,' she wrote. Whilst she was cloistered at home, he was full of his studies, teaching, church duties and his travels to different parts of the country. It is no wonder that she felt disappointed and was frustrated by his absence at times. He worried that his letters sounded too formal. On New Year's Eve 1887, he sent her one of these more stilted missives:

> We must not expect to go through the world without some cares – such a life would not be the best life for us, but, if we are really true to each other and endeavour to help each other, troubles will be a blessing in many ways.[22]

This stoicism would certainly be needed in later years when troubles did indeed come their way.

On 1 August 1888, Richmal's parents were married at St John's Church in Bury. His brother, Thomas Lamburn, was Edward's best man, and two of Clara's sisters, Ada and Richmal, were bridesmaids. Edward's other brother George, and Alfred Crompton, Clara's uncle, were amongst the guests.[23] In a letter written shortly after their marriage, Edward told her of his happiness:

> A fortnight of our married life has now nearly passed by, and I do not think I ever spent two weeks so pleasantly…. one cannot know any person truly until they have lived with them. I thought we should be happy … [and I] look forward without or almost without any fear to a happy and useful life together.[24]

Another sermon, but this one is full of love and hope for the future. For Edward, being useful was central to his character.

The couple went on to have four children. Gwen, christened Mary Gwendolen, was born in 1889, Richmal in November 1890, known in the family as Ray, Jack, christened John Battersby Crompton, in 1893, and Richmal's younger sister, Phyllis, who died in 1895, after contracting whooping cough at the age of fourteen months. By Edward's death in 1915, his remaining children had grown up and left Bury. In 1914, Gwen married Thomas Disher and moved to London and then Kent. Jack had emigrated to work in Rhodesia (Zimbabwe today) and China. Richmal followed in her father's footsteps and went on to become a classics teacher, first at St Elphin's School in Darley Dale, where she had been a pupil, and later in Bromley, Kent, where she moved after her father's death. Teaching and classical literature were central to both their lives. Her father's example of a life inspired by duty, dedication to both his professional life and family, his Christian beliefs and his support for her intellectual and spiritual development, despite her gender, were positive and influential guides in the years ahead, although Crompton is not afraid to parody the church or the teaching profession in her William stories. Edward and Richmal were both inspiring teachers, and not adverse to performing on and off the stage. Edward could be as eloquent as William Brown when given the opportunity.

Edward was nicknamed Lammie by his pupils and was hardworking, enthusiastic, cheery and impassioned, 'a man with a heart of gold but many quaint ways.'[26] One pupil remembers sitting on a bench in his classroom one day:

> when the door opened and in rushed Lammie, his face covered with blood. He had slipped in his own room when teaching his form and caught his forehead on a corner of a desk and cut it badly. He really was an appalling sight. Arthur … just in front of me, fainted outright and other boys almost followed suit. Half a dozen of them … had to be taken out into the yard to receive restorative treatment.[27]

A postcard to Richmal from her mother, whilst she was away at boarding school, suggests that this incident happened in 1903. She confirms that about six boys fainted, frightened by the sight of blood when Edward knocked his head and bled profusely. Edward adds a reassuring note to tell his daughter that he feels 'quite well' after the incident.[28] When there was a fire at the school: 'The buckets were passed along the line and the last boy in the line threw as much water as he could on the masters – chiefly "Lammie".'[29] We are told that Edward was:

> the most bullied of all masters, surely. He could be led on a false scent at the beginning of a lesson and the time would be half gone before he realised that he hadn't really begun the lesson. He was a man of many gifts and no-one was remembered with more affection by old boys, but his weaknesses were obvious, and boys are cruel animals. He had a rough time with us. He was excitable and when roused used to say the queerest things: 'Brown, boy, what is your name?' 'Is anybody here absent?'[30]

Sadly, we know nothing about this Brown family and their son. In the classroom, Edward sounds like someone with passion and wit, plus a hint of

Fig. 2.1 Edward Lamburn[25]

misadventure, which contradicts the image of the rigorous spartan we see in his daily routine.

Edward was not promoted during his long career and remained in charge of the third form of younger boys for his thirty-eight-year tenure.[31] He was remembered with respect and fondness by staff and pupils alike. On 27 March 1915, Edward's obituary in the local *Bury Guardian* states that 'he was not a man of whom it could be said that he loomed very largely upon the horizon.' Nevertheless, it portrays him as 'a man of sterling worth, who conscientiously discharged his duties, and his unostentatiousness endeared him not only to his pupils and fellow masters, but to the community generally.'[32] An old boy reflects in the school magazine that Edward was 'a conscientious and capable master,' and a 'true personal friend.'[33] A poem written by another pupil hints at his reputation for eloquence:

Mute is the voice that once we knew so well,
Empty the customed place he so long filled —
Silence and emptiness unchangeable –
The presence gone! The well-known accents stilled![34]

The headmaster, Mr Howlett, reflected that Lammie was known 'in the highest terms' for his sermons, his fame on speech days and his delight in Shakespearean speeches: 'He never courted popularity, and yet none of us can ever forget the spontaneous outburst of enthusiasm when he rose up at our Old Boys' Dinner to respond to the toast.'[35] One ex-pupil reflected that, 'Many will remember the twelve months' hard gruelling work they did in [his] form' and, 'To every old Boy there will come the recollection of incidents innumerable in which "Lammy" was the central figure.'[36] He was a master feared, hardworking and respected as a teacher, who could also turn even the most everyday event into a dramatic performance and memorable incident.

Edward spent his life trying to be everything his father was not. He was a man with high moral standards, as well as compassion and an understanding of human nature. In February 1902, Edward wrote to his eldest daughter Gwen, in response to her last letter from boarding school. He asked her not to judge others too harshly, whilst also offering her some practical down-to-earth advice:

You must remember that we all have failings and remembering our own failings, we ought to bear with those of others. The habit of evil speaking grows upon one unless it be effectually checked and leads to much misery & unhappiness in the world. We all should try to make people happy, for sorrow will come soon enough and if we are censorious it makes others dislike us and they try to pay back with interest. Good words are worth much and cost little.... A kind word is a great help in the battle of life.[37]

This is more like a sermon, or a lesson, than a loving letter from a worried parent, and it is unlikely that Gwen would have been charmed by it. On the other hand, it is full of humility and suggestive of some bitter experience. It is a letter that Gwen kept all her life. It was inspired both by his love for his children and by his attempt to guide them as they grow up. He is encouraging Gwen to behave in a less childlike way, to think of others first, rather than herself. As we shall see in later chapters, Richmal in her writing is also concerned about the implications of 'the habit of evil speaking' and she was guided by his advice to put others before herself. The letter is an indication of the qualities Edward believed his children needed as they grew older and became adults.

Two of his surviving children found themselves in later life immersed in study, literature and writing. Richmal and Jack went on to become published writers. Gwen's daughter, another Richmal, worked alongside her husband Paul Ashbee throughout his career as a distinguished archaeologist and undertook her role as her aunt's literary executor for many years after her death. All of this was to come when they left Bury and had grown up, leaving their childhood behind them. Both Gwen and Richmal spent their teenage years away from home at a boarding school for daughters of clergymen.

* * *

Richmal's father, Edward, came to Bury from humble beginnings and never joined the highest ranks of Bury society. Whether his background inhibited his ability to rise, or whether he did not care about status and increased wealth, we do not know. He offered Richmal his Christian values, his knowledge of the classics and a lifelong commitment to education and a love of learning, all of which fed into her writing and the themes that she critiques within it. At times we can see a version of his childlike self, as his misadventures and eloquent speeches at school are enjoyed by his pupils. However, far more significant is the way he dedicated himself to becoming a hardworking teacher and curate, with a strong sense of duty and purpose, who could rise above the circumstances of his childhood. Edward was respected as a teacher, and he was committed to helping others.

Notes

1. *Anne Morrison*, 92.
2. *Family Roundabout*, 7.
3. Ibid., 36.
4. *Millicent Dorrington*, 3.
5. Ibid., 4.
6. Ibid., 39.
7. *Anne Morrison*, 8, 9, 14, 15.
8. Ibid., 26.
9. Ibid., 57.
10. Ibid., 22.
11. Ibid., 25.
12. Ibid., 29.
13. Ibid., 30.
14. Ibid., 138.
15. Lawson, 23–24.
16. UoR RC/1/9/5. "The Woman Who is More Than Just William." John London. *Evening News*, 25 November 1968.
17. Disher, M., 64 and Denny, 9.
18. From letters that are part of family records.
19. Disher M., 61.
20. From letters that are part of family records.
21. Ibid.
22. Ibid.
23. Denny, 7.
24. From letters that are part of family records.
25. UoR RC/3/6/048.
26. *I Remember*, memories of Frank Louis Buxton, born 17 November 1890, 7. Also, obituary notice by W.H. Howlett, the Headmaster, who knew 'Lammie' throughout his years at the school. Both Bury Libraries and Archive.
27. Ibid., 8.
28. UoR RC/2/1/1/5. Postcard from Clara 3 October 1903 (date approx).
29. Buxton, 7.
30. Ibid., 8.
31. Fallows, 341.
32. Denny, 19.
33. *The Clavian* April 1915, 192. *The Clavian* was Bury Grammar School's magazine.

34. Ibid., 175.
35. Ibid., 174.
36. Ibid., 193–194.
37. UoR RC/2/1/1/1. Letter to Gwen from Edward, 16 February 1902.

References

Crompton, Richmal. 1925. *Anne Morrison.* London: Jarrolds.
———. 1949. *Family Roundabout.* London: Hutchinson Universal Book Club.
———. 2017. First published 1927. *Millicent Dorrington.* London: Bello.
Denny, Mavis. 1990. *Richmal Crompton 1890–1969.* Bury: Bury Metropolitan Borough Council.
Disher, Margaret. 1990. *Growing Up with Just William By His Sister.* London: The Outlaws Publishing Company.
Fallows, I.B. 2001. *Bury Grammar School: A History c.1570 to 1976.* Bury: The Estate Governors of the Bury Grammar Schools.
Lawson, Steve. Winter 2006/2007. "Who Do You Think You Are … William Brown?" *The Just William Society Magazine 19*: 21–25.

3

William and Mr Brown

Family legend suggests that Edward was a good, kind, but strict father. Mr Brown can also be a daunting figure in the life of his son William. He works in the city, although his job is not made clear in the stories. In January 1969, a journalist reported in an obituary that Crompton had said: 'I think he probably runs a small family business in the City—leather handbags, perhaps.'[1] This does seem the sort of unadventurous career in retail that Mr Brown might have pursued. There are no indications that his older son, Robert, had any plans to join him in the business. Mr Brown rarely sympathises with his younger son's plight. Nevertheless, occasionally he rewards William for the unforeseen benefits of his adventures and is delighted when, thanks to his son, an unwelcome visitor departs in haste.

This chapter introduces some of William's main characteristics and the essential features of Crompton's writing. It is one of the few chapters that focus exclusively on William's character and the William stories and is intended to set the scene for the rest of this Life in relation to her writing. Some of the values and moral purpose that feature in these stories, as well as the character types and scene setting that she deploys, are typical of her oeuvre, as we shall see in later chapters. Crompton's approach to language and vocabulary is central to the stories' success as William mishears and misinterprets much of what the adult world, including his parents and other figures of authority, are trying to teach him. His distorted logic is quite rational from

© The Author(s), under exclusive license to Springer Nature Switzerland AG 2022
J. McVeigh, *Richmal Crompton, Author of Just William*, Literary Lives,
https://doi.org/10.1007/978-3-030-96511-2_3

his point of view and encourages his readers to look at life from his perspective, which his father persistently misconstrues, as other grown-ups often do too when they try to communicate with other people whatever their age.

* * *

From the opening story in *Just William* (1922), his father has no doubt that a series of misadventures instigated by his son prove that William is mad (repetition is one of Crompton's comic techniques and it is replicated for effect here). William is 'brutally assaulted by a violent and unreasonable parent' as a result. William, we are told, 'began to wonder if his father drank.'[2] He does not, although he might have been driven to it by his son: "'He's mad," said Mr Brown, with conviction. "Mad. It's the only explanation."' [3] He says that he finds it 'difficult to describe the atmosphere of peace and relief that pervades the house when [William] is out of it.'[4] William's father prefers 'people who haven't met him. They can't judge me by him.'[5] William knows that he goes to Sunday school because his father said, 'that he might as well go into an asylum straight off if he couldn't get a little peace from that boy on Sunday afternoons.'[6] Mr Brown even contemplates drowning his son, except it is against the law:

> "Poor William," murmured his wife, "he *means* well— and such a lot of people say he's like you."

> "He *isn't*," said his father indignantly, "I'm more or less sane, and he's a raving lunatic. He can't possibly be like me."[7]

In one of his longest speeches, Mr Brown draws a deep breath and continues to berate his son:

> Haven't you any sense at all? Are you a complete and utter imbecile? Haven't you any ideas in your head but tomfoolery and wanton destruction? You aren't fit to be a member of a civilised community and you seem to grow less fit with every day that passes.[8]

On yet another occasion, his father asks him again if he is insane. William says he isn't.[9] His father continues throughout the William series to think that his son is raving mad. He reflects that lunatic asylums across the country must be full of men who have had sons like William.[10]

Mr Brown wails to his wife, as he reclines in an armchair after a trying day, with one hand pressed to his aching brow: 'You ought to take him to the doctor and get his brain examined.'[11] Mrs Brown lays aside the sock she has been mending: 'It certainly sounds very silly, dear ... But there might be some explanation of it all, if only we knew. Boys are such funny things.'[12] William is equally concerned about the sanity of adults: 'He'd have come to the conclusion that grown-ups were mad, if he hadn't already come to it years ago.'[13] As William knows, it is, of course, the world of adults that is mad, and Crompton's readers know that even though William is funny, adults are certainly peculiar.

Not only is Mr Brown insistent that his son is mad, but he is also dismayed by William's constant chatter:

"William," he said, "the effect upon the nerves of the continued sound of your voice is something that beggars description. I would take it as a personal favour if it could kindly cease for a short time."[14]

Even Ginger, William's loyal sidekick and a member of the Outlaws—William's gang made up of Ginger, Henry and Douglas—agrees that William talks too much, although his logic 'was of course unassailable.'[15] At the end of another exciting day, William wants to tell his father about his adventures. Mr Brown looks around wildly for escape but sees none: 'Nemesis had over-taken him. With a groan he gave himself up for lost, and William, already thrilled to his very soul by his story, the memories of his exciting day already dim, pursued his ruthless recital.'[16] William is Mr Brown's Nemesis, and we shall meet William's, Violet Elizabeth Bott, in a later chapter.

Mr and Mrs Brown search for an explanation for their youngest son's behaviour, but they fail to find a satisfactory one. In the last William book published during Crompton's lifetime, *William the Superman* (1968), Mrs Brown is struck with horror for the umpteenth time when she looks aghast at her youngest son's dishevelled and dirty clothes on his return home: 'Jus' – jus' normal wear an' tear, I'spect," he said, remembering a phrase he had heard used in connection with an insurance claim.'[17] He is covered in cement. His parents are sitting together in the sitting room and William's bedtime approaches. Mrs Brown sighs, looking forward to her own bedtime, for she has had a long and tiring day. William considers her comment—he often considers his position on many things—and agrees, 'that's the sort of one I've had, too.'[18] Certainly his parents must be exhausted after so many years of tiring days trying, and failing, to get to grips with their son.

* * *

William is a past master at listening to grown-ups and repeating whatever phrase might be useful. As Crompton's narrator comments, when he does so 'he considerably overworked it,' and of course he misses its irony.[19] 'Talk about bad luck,' he cries at the end of one story, 'I'm simply statin' a fact. Talk about bad luck!'[20] William heaves a deep sigh and passes his hand over his brow having found that, 'Life was very wearing.'[21] Margaret and Ben Sherriff, both William fans, have identified other adult cliches misinterpreted by William, such as 'there ought to be a law about it, Parliamentary inquiries (or inquests as William would have it), [and] brain fever (a term perhaps gleaned from the romantic novels Ethel or his mother reads).'[22] Crompton was fascinated by the expressions she overheard. In 1953, she told her niece Richmal that she had made a note of 'She reared up alarming,' a phrase William might well have used himself.[23]

As well as repeating adult colloquialisms, without fully appreciating their meaning, William misrepresents some of the subjects he is taught at school. As a result, the logic of the lessons his teachers struggle to explain are viewed through Crompton's humorous eye. In one example, William asks his father about something he has learnt that day:

> "Father," said William suddenly, "s'pose I came to you an' said you was to give me a hundred pounds an' I'd give you five pounds next year an' so on, would you give it to me?"
>
> "I should not, my son," said his father firmly.
>
> William sighed.
>
> "I knew there was something wrong with it," he said.[24]

Whilst his intentions are good, his literal understanding of life is often less than helpful, albeit funny. When Mrs Brown discovers that William is responsible for some local disaster and asks her husband whether the culprit is always William, Mr Brown rises wearily, '"Of course," he said. "Isn't everything *always* William all the time?"'[25] There are times when William is weary of this lack of appreciation, and he develops a misanthropic view of life. He decides 'not to waste another moment of his life in uncongenial surroundings.'[26] He sometimes goes off in search of a new life, but usually returns in time for lunch.

* * *

Most of William and the Outlaws' pocket money goes towards repairing the damage they cause to windows, greenhouses, paintwork and ornaments, which seemed to the boys to self-destruct on their approach.[27] William is 'constantly being amazed and horrified by his parents' lack of credulity in his versions of affairs,' when these incidents, and many others like them, occur.[28] The other members of the Outlaws all experience 'similar examples of almost incredible ingratitude from the grown-up world' and they feel misunderstood by their parents.[29]

Their parents are equally incredulous, and they form a sort of Parents' Union in order to work in concert to address the consequences of their sons' misadventures.[30] Mr Brown and the other long-suffering fathers of the Outlaws are accustomed to receiving letters of complaint from Hubert Lane's father. Quite often they do nothing at all about them beyond dropping them into the wastepaper basket.[31] Hubert is the leader of a rival gang constantly battling with the Outlaws:

> It was an ancient enmity, and no one knew in what it had originated. Hubert Lane was fat and pale, easily moved to tears, slow to endanger his personal safety, given to complaining to his parents and masters when annoyed…. And Mr Lane was in every way worthy of his son, and that is all that need be said about *him*.[32]

It is rumoured that Mr Lane is a cad who dabbles in the black-market during wartime. He is certainly not an upstanding member of the local community like Mr Brown and the Outlaws' fathers.

William stories feature other older men who, unlike Mr Brown, rekindle some of their love of life and look at their circumstances differently when they meet William. William's antics have a positive effect on a psychiatrist who is lifted out of his boredom and general malaise. This does not happen after he has talked to William about his 'mental troubles,' but when he sees rivulets of yellow paint trickling down the face of another of William's patient victims. His laughter takes on Homeric proportions.[33] The story is vague about the meaning of 'mental troubles' reflecting William's complete lack of understanding on the subject. In another story featuring 'A Great Man from the Cabinet,' instead of addressing his father's political meeting, the illustrious guest mistakenly ends up in the audience for one of William's plays. He is a wistful-looking old man, absorbed in the performance, cheering with his top hat raised.[34] Even august politicians can enjoy the antics of make believe and the qualities of farce. 'A Great Actor' is absorbed in another performance, a chaotic play by the local Literary Society in which William fails miserably to create the required wind and storm sound effects. As the actor's spirits are lifted by the chaos caused during the performance, he is cured of his 'nervous breakdown' and heads back to London. The revelry takes him out of himself. He invites William to see William Shakespeare's *Macbeth*. William 'didn't think much of it, and he could have made a better storm himself.'[35] The irony being, of course, that he is like a devastating storm wherever he goes, and he clearly goes down like one.

Grandfathers can be far more understanding than fathers and William helps one of his to rediscover his childlike self. Mike Hepworth argues that William's contact with older people, not adults like his parents or those of the Outlaws, but rather grandfathers and their peers, are often treated sympathetically in the stories. In their encounters with William they experience what he calls infantalisation, which can be 'a rejuvenating and sometimes death-defying force.' Hepworth describes this as 'a process of mutual liberation through resistance.' He suggests that in one story:

> The old man wishes to capture his boyhood … for William and the old man [their] encounter is mutually rewarding because it dispenses with the mask of age the old man is in effect expected to wear. Because he has an old body he is expected to behave as if he has an old self.

In these stories, he writes, it 'is only the staid, the pretentious and the self-important who lose face.'[36]

William's grandfather is staying with them and reacts with glee when William plans to go to the circus. They slip out of the house together: 'William felt that he had found a kindred spirit.'[37] When they meet William, these men come to see not only the fun in his misadventures, but another more light-hearted side of themselves. In taking their circumstances and themselves less seriously and looking at them in a different way, they gain some perspective on life.

* * *

In the William stories, anecdotes conjure up farcical scenes and comic moments that remain with us long after we have finished reading them. For many readers, both men and women, these moments are evocative of their own childhood experiences, or those they wish they had had. The tone, narrator's voice and sharpness of Crompton's writing brings each scene to life. They capture in an ordinary everyday setting Mr Brown's assertion that his son is mad, when we know that he is not. William's arguments are, in his mind at least, logical and reasoned; whether his parents agree with him is another matter. His arguments are often flawed, as he misinterprets most situations and lacks adequate or accurate information on which to base his decisions. He is, nevertheless, a serious, well-meaning boy, although not quite as innocent as he seems. William does not grow older and remains eleven years old. He is not attracted by the prospect of becoming an adult. They make so many mistakes, and they are often pretentious, vainglorious and pompous and fail to understand anyone else's point of view, as we shall see.

Notes

1. UoR RC/1/9/13. Pottersman, Arthur. *The Sun* 13 January 1969, 8.
2. "William Goes to the Pictures," 30.
3. Ibid., 28.
4. "William Below Stairs," 73.
5. Ibid., 73.
6. "The Sunday School Treat," 142.
7. "The Terrible Magician," 51.
8. "William the Tree Dweller," 60.
9. "The Ghost," 124.
10. "William Finds a Job," 182.
11. "William Goes to the Pictures," 31.
12. Ibid.
13. "William and the Vanishing Luck," 142.
14. "The Circus," 182.
15. "The Outlaws Deliver the Goods," 141.
16. "A Dress Rehearsal," 252.
17. "William's Long and Tiring Day," 118.
18. Ibid., 135.
19. "The Outlaws," 158.
20. Ibid., 166.
21. "William and the Chinese God," 67.
22. Sherriff, *JWSM* 17, 10.
23. UoR RC/2/1/2/3. Letter from Richmal Crompton to Richmal Ashbee, 25 October 1953. Other examples of colloquial expressions that caught Crompton's attention are written on scraps of paper held in the Richmal Crompton Collection at the University of Roehampton.
24. "The Fall of the Idol," 81.

25. "William All the Time," 74. Mr & Mrs Brown's first names, John and Mary, are hardly mentioned in the stories. They have a rare conversation in which they speak to each other using their first names in "William and the Paying Guest," *William the Explorer* (1960).
26. "William Below Stairs," 60.
27. "William the Money-Maker," 97.
28. "William Plays Santa Claus," 80.
29. "William and the Fairy Daffodil," 40.
30. "William the Money-Maker," 97.
31. "Revenge is Sweet," 247.
32. "The Magic Monkey," 138.
33. "William the Psychiatrist," 28.
34. "What Delayed the Great Man," 27–29.
35. "William the Great Actor," 62.
36. Hepworth, *JWSM* 3 14.
37. "The Circus," 194.

References

Crompton, Richmal. 1953. First published 1924. "A Dress Rehearsal." In *William - The Fourth*, by Richmal Crompton, 227–252. London: George Newnes Ltd.

Crompton, Richmal. 1930. First published 1926. "Revenge is Sweet." In *William - The Conqueror*, by Richmal Crompton, 235–249. London: George Newnes Ltd.

Crompton, Richmal. 1961. First published 1923. "The Circus." In *William Again*, by Richmal Crompton, 180–195. London: George Newnes Ltd.

Crompton, Richmal. 1990. First published 1922. "The Fall of the Idol." In *Just - William*, by Richmal Crompton, 75–93. Basingstoke, Hampshire: Macmillan Children's Books.

Crompton, Richmal. 1959. First published 1922. "The Ghost." In *More William*, by Richmal Crompton, 112–125. London: George Newnes Ltd.

Crompton, Richmal. 1927. "The Magic Monkey." In *William - In Trouble*, by Richmal Crompton, 135–156. London: George Newnes Ltd.

Crompton, Richmal. 1990. First published 1922. "The Outlaws." In *Just - William*, by Richmal Crompton, 150–167. Basingstoke, Hampshire: Macmillan Children's Books.

Crompton, Richmal. 1951. First published 1929. "The Outlaws Deliver the Goods." In *William*, by Richmal Crompton, 138–163. London: George Newnes Ltd.

Crompton, Richmal. 1930. First published 1926. "The Sunday School Treat." In *William - The Conqueror*, by Richmal Crompton, 142–156. London: George Newnes Ltd.

Crompton, Richmal. 1984. First published 1927. "The Terrible Magician." In *William - The Outlaw*, by Richmal Crompton, 18–51. Basingstoke, Hampshire: Macmillan Children's Books.

Crompton, Richmal. 1961. First published 1923. "What Delayed the Great Man." In *William Again*, by Richmal Crompton, 13–29. London: George Newnes Ltd.

Crompton, Richmal. 1953. First published 1924. "William All the Time." In *William - The Fourth*, by Richmal Crompton, 59–74. London: George Newnes Ltd.

Crompton, Richmal. 1927. "William and the Chinese God." In *William - In Trouble*, by Richmal Crompton, 61–79. London: George Newnes Ltd.

Crompton, Richmal. 1927. "William and the Fairy Daffodil." In *William - In Trouble*, by Richmal Crompton, 39–60. London: George Newnes Ltd.

Crompton, Richmal. 1987. First pubished 1939. "William and the Vanishing Luck." In *William and the Air Raid Precautions*, by Richmal Crompton, 139–165. Basingstoke, Hampshire: Pan Macmillan Children's Books.

Crompton, Richmal. 1990. First published 1922. "William Below Stairs." In *Just - William*, by Richmal Crompton, 57–74. London: Macmillan Children's Books.

Crompton, Richmal. 1984. First published 1927. "William Finds a Job." In *William - The Outlaw*, by Richmal Crompton, 176–204. Basingstoke, Hampshire: Macmillan Children's Books.

Crompton, Richmal. 1990. First published 1922. "William Goes to the Pictures." In *Just - William*, by Richmal Crompton, 13-32. Basingstoke, Hampshire: Macmillan Children's Books.

Crompton, Richmal. 1984. First published 1927. "William Plays Santa Claus." In *William - The Outlaw*, by Richmal Crompton, 78–99. Basingstoke, Hampshire: Macmillan Children's Books.

Crompton, Richmal. 1948. First published 1928. "William the Great Actor." In *William - The Good*, by Richmal Crompton, 31–62. London: George Newnes Ltd.

Crompton, Richmal. 1948. First Published 1928. "William the Money-Maker." In *William - The Good*, by Richmal Crompton, 97–119. London: George Newnes Ltd.

Crompton, Richmal. 1992. First Published 1964. "William the Psychiatrist." In *William and the Witch*, by Richmal Crompton, 1–29. Basingstoke, Hampshire: Macmillan Children's Books.

Crompton, Richmal. 1991. First Published 1956. "William the Tree Dweller." In *William and the Space Animal*, by Richmal Crompton, 53–83. Basingstoke, Hampshire: Macmillan Children's Books.

Crompton, Richmal. 1993. First published 1968. "William's Long and Tiring Day." In *William the Superman*, by Richmal Crompton, 113–135. Basingstoke, Hampshire: Pan Macmillan Children's Books.

Hepworth, Mike. 1996. "William and the Old Folks." *The Just William Society Magazine 3*, December: 10–14.

Sherriff, Margaret and Ben Sherriff. Winter 2006. "Richmal Crompton and Langwidge." *The Just William Society Magazine 17*: 9–12.

4

Clara Crompton and Her Family in Bury

In the thirty years before the death of her husband in 1915, the life of Crompton's mother Clara had been comfortable and conventional, although touched by tragedy. At the end of the nineteenth century, she was from one of the most successful local families in Bury. The homes her family lived in embodied this world.

Clara's own mother, born Richmal Openshaw, was a member of a local mill-owning family and became the first Richmal Crompton when she married John Crompton. Richmal Crompton Lamburn, the woman hidden behind the writer, was the first Richmal Crompton's granddaughter. The name Richmal had been in the family since the early 1700s.[1] As Steve Lawson has identified, the name Richmal is part of Bury's local history; most of the children given the name between 1837 and 1890 are from the Bury area.[2]

It was strange to see the name Richmal Crompton on a letter written by Clara's mother. In August 1887, Edward receives a gentle reminder about his responsibilities as a fiancé in a letter from his future mother-in-law thanking him for her birthday present. She encourages him, no doubt at Clara's behest, to take a break during the summer:

> It will scarcely seem like holiday time to you having to work so hard. I am sure if you could manage it a little rest would do you good. With kind love from all at home.
>
> I remain your affectionate mother
>
> Richmal Crompton.[3]

© The Author(s), under exclusive license to Springer Nature Switzerland AG 2022
J. McVeigh, *Richmal Crompton, Author of Just William*, Literary Lives, https://doi.org/10.1007/978-3-030-96511-2_4

A simple message, and one that Edward failed to heed then and in the future. His passion to rise above his father's inheritance never left him.

One of Clara's sisters was another Richmal, Richmal Ellen Crompton, known to many as Re. She is the second Richmal Crompton. Clara's own daughter Richmal was known in the family as Ray, which no doubt helped to avoid confusion at family gatherings when all three Richmals were present. Re, our Richmal's aunt, lived all her life in Bury, where she was well-known for her work with the church and local charities. She was an active member of the local Temperance Society and qualified as a Sunday School Teacher in July 1890.[4] Whether she enjoyed crotchet, as William believes all aunts do, we do not know. Clara's niece, Rene, her brother Henry Crompton's daughter, who was also christened Richmal, often visited her aunt and cousin when they lived in Kent.[5]

Clara's father, John Crompton, was 'a well-to-do Lancashire retail chemist, whose business had included the manufacture of paint and other requirements for many mill-owners.'[6] John and his brother Alfred followed their father Henry Crompton into the family business as chemists. In 1892, when Mary, his youngest child, was eighteen, and four years after Clara's marriage and the birth of two of her children, John took his own life by drinking prussic acid, more commonly known as cyanide. The local newspaper records that he 'had not been in good health for the last two or three weeks and had been rather despondent,' because his wife was ill and away from home. During the inquest, his local doctor confirmed that John Crompton had been undergoing treatment over the last nine to ten days. The doctor reported that John had 'seemed to be suffering from nervous exhaustion due to anxiety, arising from his wife's illness.'[7] His death certificate records the cause of death as 'suicide by poisoning whilst temporarily insane.'[8] His wife did not die until January 1904. Whatever the cause for his severe anxiety and depression, as a chemist the poison was readily available to him: 'the bottle ... was one that was kept on a shelf in the shop.'[9] John would have known that his act was illegal. Despite the social stigma associated with suicide and the potential consequences for his family, including the impact on their position in the town, his despair nevertheless drove him to his death. This was a huge tragedy for him, his wife and his family.

John and Richmal had eleven children over twenty years, seven of whom survived into adulthood. Clara had four sisters, Hannah, Elisabeth, Re and Ada, and two surviving brothers, Henry and John, known as Harry and Jack.[10] John also went into teaching and was Headmaster of Hereford Grammar School 1919–1926.[11] Hannah married into the Wrigley family, another influential mill-owning dynasty in the Bury area. Her son, Sir John

Wrigley, was a senior civil servant and was closely involved in planning the evacuation of children from cities to the countryside in the Second World War.[12] In later life, our Richmal took his three children, Christopher, Martin and Elizabeth, to theatres in London and *William's Happy Days* (1930) is dedicated to them.[13] Once married, Clara had regular visits from her sisters, Aunts Lizzie, Re and Ada, both at her home in Bury and later when she moved to Kent.[14] Ada, Richmal's favourite, and Clara were close. Margaret Disher, Crompton's eldest niece, suggests that she 'was perhaps the prototype of the more attractive aunt that William liked.'[15] Ada had two sons, Arthur and Harry, both of whom went to Bury Grammar School with their cousin Jack. Both died during the First World War.[16]

In January 1916, Harry died whilst training with the Royal Fusiliers at Aldershot. Arthur served amidst the horror of the trenches in France until he was killed in battle in June 1918. He was just twenty-one years old. Other families in Bury shared similar tragedies. Arthur and his brother Harry are one of seven pairs of brothers commemorated on the Bury Grammar School Great War Memorial.[17] By 1916, Richmal was away teaching at St Elphin's, her father had died, and her sister Gwen was married and living in London where Clara had joined her. Nevertheless, the tragic loss of Ada's children would have brought the war close to home.

* * *

In 1896, Edward and Clara moved from their first house in the heart of the town to an attractive Victorian terrace on the edge of Bury, in an area known as Chesham. Ada and her family lived on the same road. Moving to the Chesham area was a step up for Edward and Clara. It was originally a farming community, then in the late eighteenth and early nineteenth centuries it was developed to house wealthy mill-owners, who were joined by middle-class families as the suburb grew away from the noise and pollution of the mills.[19] Clara's mother came from the Openshaw family. Openshaw cotton mills were based in the Bury area. The family had wealth and influence. They supported the building of the local St Paul's Church and donated land for Openshaw Park.[20] In 1889, the John Openshaw Scholarship, in memory of Clara's grandfather, was established by the family at Bury Grammar School where Edward taught.[21] As well as owning local chemists, the Crompton's owned large mills. James R. Crompton and his brothers manufactured paper at Elton Mill from 1856.[22] The Crompton and Openshaw families owned

Fig. 4.1 Clara Crompton Lamburn[18]

large properties in the Chesham suburb when Edward and Clara moved there. Edward had married into two of the most influential families in the town.

Clara and Edward's new home was a pleasant three-storey brick-built house with four bedrooms and space for servants' quarters in the attic. It was comfortable with high ceilings and well-proportioned rooms. This home was resoundingly middle-class, but the houses owned by some of Clara's nearest relatives were larger and more prestigious. Material success meant wealth and influence in business or notable civic positions amongst the higher echelons of Bury society. The pressure to succeed for Clara's father must have been tremendous. Her husband's success lay in his responsibilities as an ordained member of the church and in teaching rebellious, rough-and-tumble young boys.

* * *

After eleven years in Bury attending local schools, Richmal left the family home in Chesham and joined Gwen as a boarder at St Elphin's School in Warrington for the daughters of the clergy, where she was known as Ray Lamburn. In *Anne Morrison*, the vicar for the church where Anne's father is a curate 'had been able to secure a bursary for Lorna [Anne's older sister] in a good boarding-school where he paid only half-fees, and even that was drain enough on his finances. He had offered to do the same for Anne.'[23] The fees for Gwen and Richmal would have been supported in this way, which explains why they did not attend school in Bury, like their brother. In 1904, the decision was made for the school to move following worrying bouts of scarlet fever in the heart of Warrington. It was established in an old hotel in a rural setting in Darley Dale, not far from Matlock in Derbyshire.[24]

In the school magazine for 1918, Richmal wrote about her memories of Warrington, before the move. She remembers 'dark corners and narrow, mysterious passages,' and the old school peopled 'freely with ghosts' in every corner. A bathroom 'was haunted by a very inoffensive nun who was generally considered rather uninteresting.'[25] One can almost hear the voice of Moaning Myrtle and other echoes of Hogwarts. Richmal described the big schoolroom at the school. Four classes were held in this large room, one in each corner, with the dreaded headmistress sitting on a small platform behind a desk at one end. She missed nothing and would pounce on teachers and pupils alike, striking terror into their hearts.[26] Richmal was not averse to a spot of adventure, as she explained:

> For the adventurous ... there was always the chance of trying to climb the trees.... Moreover, there was a point in the Moat at which it was possible (not easy) to jump across and stand perilously and uncomfortably on the opposite bank between a fence and the Moat itself. This was a great attraction, and the performers of the feat were held in great respect and admiration.[27]

On visiting the new school in Darley Dale for the first time, Richmal's adventures continued. The new dining room was not quite finished, so the girls 'made a point of going in and out of the window frame for no apparent reason except that it was more difficult and dangerous than using the front door.'[28]

These are tame adventures, but they offer a tiny window into Richmal's schoolgirl world.

Richmal was writing from an early age. Before she went to school, she wrote a magazine called *The Rainbow* which she read to a small circle of dolls and her younger brother. It contained poems, stories and other items, such as 'Advice to Parents.'[29] Her niece Margaret recalls, 'Under her father's guidance she read a great deal of poetry so it was not surprising that her first efforts were rhyming verses'[30]:

> She started to develop her talent for writing in her early teens with contributions to the school magazine. Later she kept a Private Eye type of journal containing satirical descriptions of school personalities and events, which she allowed selected friends to read.[31]

In 1906, Richmal's essay in the school magazine was a ghost story, 'The Planting of Trees.' The story is set in 1905 and is based on a true event when pupils planted trees on a patch of waste ground outside the playing field. Richmal planted a maple tree. In her story, on the event's centenary ex-pupils return to the school in ghostly forms to haunt what had now become a forest that 'stood tall and gloomy, overshadowing the field.'[32] Richmal's thin spectre is amongst them. As an author, she returned to writing ghost stories many years later.[33] As a pupil, Richmal ran a secret literary society to which members contributed their own writing. Each week the members' contributions were read aloud, and members voted for the best.[34]

During the school holidays when Gwen and Richmal were still pupils at St Elphin's, they would return to Bury, or join their family on holiday elsewhere. In Crompton's novel *The Holiday* (1933), a vicar's family join him for a holiday, whilst he takes up a locum role to earn some extra income. The novel is written from the point of view of both children and adults. One can hear the children's voices as they grow up over the summer and their mother realises that they will never be quite the same again. She worries about her husband, Timothy—a vicar like his namesake in *Anne Morrison*—and the pressures that continually assail him: 'People, people, people, clinging to him, exhausting him, surrounding him on all sides, keeping him from her.'[35] The novel portrays him as a monk-like, intellectual figure seeking solace in the wilderness:

> Timothy followed the path that wound up the hillside among the bracken and the silver birches. When he reached the tumbled down wall that bounded the moor and from which one could see the whole valley outspread like a picture

before one, he sat down and took out a book from his pocket. It was his custom to sit here for a few minutes reading before he started on his walk.[36]

Timothy is not necessarily a portrayal of Edward, yet he shares some of his activities. To supplement the family's income, Edward took temporary roles as a curate in the summer holidays.[37] In *Anne Morrison*, Crompton is a young author writing about the world she knew.

When she was away at boarding school, Edward wrote a postcard to Richmal telling her about his plans to go to Thurnscoe, a coal-mining village in South Yorkshire, with her brother John, for the month in August.[38] He told her that she will join them there with her sister Gwen and their mother. The postcard is written in Latin. In 2019, the postcard was translated by Julie Hone, formerly Head of Classics at Bury Grammar School Boys, and her husband, Mark Hone, who was Head of History and Politics at the school. In 2022, Mark is in his thirty-second year of teaching at the school, similar to Edward almost a century before him.

From 1908, Richmal stayed on at St Elphin's for three years as a teacher. Becoming a pupil-teacher was one of the few options open to educated young women who needed to earn their own living and becoming a teacher was the most acceptable career for female graduates.[39] Ex-pupils without another source of income could be exploited when they took on teaching responsibilities, working long hours at the whim of senior staff, and isolated from family and friends.[40]

In 1911, Richmal won a University of London scholarship to study classics at Royal Holloway College. According to a contemporary local journalist: 'Mr Lamburn was successful in classics.'[41] Clearly, he thought the scholarship must have been given to a man called Richmal and, as many of Crompton's readers will attest today, this is a common misunderstanding based on the assumption that Richmal is a derivative of Richard. Richmal is in fact based on the names Richard and Mary. He had also failed to appreciate that St Elphin's was a school for girls. Richmal received the scholarship on the proviso that she would return for three years to teach at the school, which she duly did from the autumn term of 1914 after she had completed her studies at Royal Holloway.[42] In 1917, she moved to a new teaching role and a new life in Kent.

Richmal kept in touch with staff and pupils from St Elphin's for many years and attended reunion meetings in London.[43] Margaret Flood was headmistress at St Elphin's when Richmal was at the school as both pupil and teacher. Margaret Disher, Richmal's niece, was born in 1917 and became Miss Flood's goddaughter and was named after her.[44] Miss Flood subsequently banned Anne Morrison (1925) in St Elphin's, fearing that she was depicted in the character of Miss Rose, the fictional headmistress featured in the novel.[45] However, Richmal and her old headmistress met again in the nineteen fifties. These two successful women, who perhaps tussled for authority and influence during their years at the school, decided to forget the past.[46]

In 1952, Richmal wrote a review of a book by Miss Flood, *The Message of Love*, on the epistles of St John. Richmal reflects that 'St John was writing in the period that ushered in the downfall of ancient civilization, and the times in which we live have a disquieting resemblance to that period.'[47] As discussed in a later chapter, allusions to the contemporary relevance of ancient Greek society and culture are significant throughout Crompton's own work. She looks at the contemporary world and its people through the myths and epics of classical literature, which she first learnt about from her father, studied as a pupil and student at Royal Holloway College, and taught for many years.

* * *

Looking back on Edward and Clara's life we can see Richmal's childhood touching on the fringes of the wealthy community in the town. The Crompton family were part of the comfortable business community whose wealth grew in Bury at the end of the nineteenth century. Crompton was a keen observer of family life and as a novelist she is primarily known to date as an author of family sagas that chart the world she knew. The few sagas that she did write echo the milieu familiar to the Crompton and Openshaw families.

Richmal and her mother lived together for over twenty years in Kent. The houses Clara lived in with Edward, and later with Richmal, are representative of her life and those of other middle-class women like her whose lives revolved around family and home in England in the first half of the twentieth century. The relationship between mothers and their children, and whether all mothers are as understanding and tolerant as Mrs Brown, are key themes in Crompton's writing.

Notes

1. Bury Libraries and Archive, Richmal Crompton Exhibition May 2017.
2. Lawson, 25.

3. Letters that are part of family records.
4. *Bury Times*, 23 May 1908, 10 and *The Manchester Courier and Lancashire General Advertiser*, 5 July 1890, 8.
5. Disher M., 60.
6. Disher, T., 48.
7. Denny, 12. *Bury Guardian* 4 June 1892.
8. UoR RC/2/1/6. Death certificate for John Crompton.
9. Denny, 12.
10. Disher, T., 48, Disher M., 60, and Bury Libraries and Archive.
11. Disher, T and UoR RC/3/6/136.
12. Disher M., 59.
13. Ibid.
14. UoR RC/2/1/1/5. Postcards from Clara to Richmal 1903–1904.
15. Disher, M., 60.
16. Ibid., 59.
17. I am grateful to Mark Hone, Bury Grammar School Boys for this additional information about Richmal's cousins. See:
    http://bgsarchive.co.uk/Filename.ashx?tableName=ta_boys_rollofhonour&columnName=filename&recordId=16
    http://bgsarchive.co.uk/Filename.ashx?tableName=ta_boys_rollofhonour&columnName=filename&recordId=86
18. UoR RC/3/12/032.
19. file:///C:/Users/janem/Downloads/cheshamwoodleaflet_350111088.pdf.
20. https://prestwich.org.uk/history/places/chesham.html#danesmoorr
21. Denny, 6.
22. https://www.gracesguide.co.uk/James_R._Crompton_and_Brothers
    https://www.gracesguide.co.uk/1891_Cotton_Mills_in_Bury
23. *Anne Morrison*, 25.
24. UoR RC/1/1/2/3. Manuscript for Magazine of Harris Public Library, Preston, November 1964 and *The Elphinian* 1990, 71.
25. *The Elphinian* 1990, 59.
26. UoR RC/1/1/2/3.
27. *The Elphinian* 1990, 60.
28. Ibid., 73.
29. Harmsworth, 16–17.
30. Disher, M., 52.
31. Ibid., 53.
32. *The Elphinian* 1990, 77.
33. See a selection published in *Mist and other Stories* (1928).
34. Disher M., 55.

35. *The Holiday*, 158.
36. Ibid., 166.
37. Disher M., 61.
38. UoR RC/2/1/1/5. Postcard from Edward to Richmal in Latin.
39. Robinson, 202.
40. Ibid., 28.
41. *Sheffield Daily Telegraph*, 9 August 1912, 8.
42. Jane Robinson notes that in the nineteenth century students financed by King's scholarships from the Board of Education were required to teach in the classroom for at least three years (203).
43. Issues of the school magazine, *The Elphinian*, record Richmal attending reunions in 1948, hosted by Margaret Flood (*St Elphin's Magazine*, September 1948), and 1950 (*St Elphin's Magazine*, July 1951). A list of members of the Old Girls' Guild lists Richmal as one of their members in 1964 (UoR RC/2/7/1).
44. *The Elphinian* 1990, 80.
45. Tribute by Sybil Osmond, *Elphinian* 1990, 82.
46. Ibid., 82.
47. *St Elphin's Magazine* 70, July 1952, 24.

References

Crompton, Richmal. 1925. *Anne Morrison*. London: Jarrolds.
Crompton, Richmal. 1933. *The Holiday*. London: Macmillan.
Denny, Mavis. 1990. *Richmal Crompton 1890–1969*. Bury: Bury Metropolitan Borough Council.
Disher, Margaret. 1990. *Growing Up with Just William By His Sister*. London: The Outlaws Publishing Company.
Disher, Thomas Frederick Rhodes. 1954. *Sixty Odd Years*. London: Clerke & Cockeran.
Harmsworth, Madeleine. 1968. "William and the Old Lady of Beechworth." *Daily Mirror*, 20 November: 16–17.
Lawson, Steve. Winter 2006/7. "Who Do You Think You Are ... William Brown?" *The Just William Society Magazine 19*: 21–25.
Robinson, Jane. 2009. *Bluestockings: The Remarkable Story of the First Women to Fight for an Education*. London: Penguin.

5

William, Mrs Brown and Mothers in Crompton's Fiction

In the Brown family, Mrs Brown is certainly not the dominant mother figure feared in some of Crompton's novels and she is more tolerant towards her son than her husband. Mothers who are overbearing and controlling within the home and who interfere in every corner of their families' lives are a feature of Crompton's other fiction. The power in the Brown household, whether they admit it or not, lies with William. The battles in Mrs Brown's home are invariably instigated by William and, unlike Mrs Willoughby or Mrs Wilding, the matriarchs in *Family Roundabout* (1948) and the Wildings trilogy—*The Wildings* (1925), *David Wilding* (1926) and *The Thorn Bush* (1928)—she very rarely wins them. She is more like Mrs Fowler in *Family Roundabout* and is William's ally through thick and thin. Her dedication can be trying at times. In the William stories, other older women can be as pompous as their male counterparts.

* * *

Mrs Brown is a bridge between William and other members of her family. Robert is aghast because William always messes everything up: "'Nonsense, dear,'" said Mrs Brown. "'He sometimes makes mistakes, of course, but he always means well.'"[1] When something goes missing from the kitchen Mrs Brown is sanguine. She had not been William's mother for many years without knowing what to do: 'She went wearily up to William's bedroom.'[2] Mrs Brown, 'in whose breast hope sprang eternal,' is always optimistic about

J. McVeigh, *Richmal Crompton, Author of Just William*, Literary Lives, https://doi.org/10.1007/978-3-030-96511-2_5

her son and she is 'the one being in the world who never lost faith' in him.[3] From her, William has inherited a glorious optimism and, like him, she is always hoping for the best:

"Yes," said Mrs Brown, "I'm *sure* that he'll do his best. I know that he sometimes makes mistakes, but he's really a very good boy."

Mrs Brown frequently made this statement, in the vague hope apparently that if she said it often enough it might become true.[4]

However, 'Mrs Brown's rather pathetic faith in William's latent powers of goodness was unshared by any other of his family.'[5] She tells him that he must learn to behave like a civilised human being, but he is quite adamant that he does not want to: 'I'd rather be a savage any day,' he tells her.[6] William's mother is normally calm but there are a few cracks in her armour. She would have made it a law that no school holidays could be longer than a week and that free treatment for nervous breakdowns should be available for all mothers.[7]

There are rare occasions when William's parents almost get the better of him. Mrs Brown asks him to help on a white elephant stall at the local fete. His father warns him to be careful because they are difficult beasts to handle, and William assures him that he is not afraid of any old elephant. Mrs Brown leaps to William's defence and asks her husband not to tease him. She tells William that white elephants are things you do not need:

"I know," said William, "I know I don't need 'em but I s'pose some people do or you wun't be sellin' 'em."

With that he left the room.[8]

In this scene, and many others, Mrs Brown is the calm, deadpan stooge who provides the supporting dialogue for William's comic turn. In November 1919, Richmal was teaching in Bromley, Kent and was familiar with the ups and downs of local fetes and comparable events: 'Miss Drake and Miss Lamburn presided over a stall for household utensils' at a Bromley High School Sale of Work, the first they had held since 1913 because of the First World War. It is not known if there were any white elephants on Miss Lamburn's table.[9]

* * *

Turning to Crompton novels and other mother figures in her fiction, traditional matriarchal figures rule resplendently in their own comfortable homes in Crompton's family sagas. The Wildings trilogy is a saga published in the nineteen twenties, followed by *The Ridleys* (1947) and *Family Roundabout* (1948) published twenty years later. These are well-crafted traditional tales, in keeping with another contemporary and more famous trilogy published from 1906 to 1921, and subsequently published as *The Forsyte Saga* (1922) by John Galsworthy. These novels conform to our expectations about a realistic, chronological portrayal of the day-to-day lives, loves and losses of wealthy middle-class dynasties. It is these family sagas and the matriarchal figures they celebrate with which Crompton's novels have most commonly been associated. They are different from her more allegorical novels that focus on key themes and the values she cared about, such as *Roofs Off* (1928), *The Odyssey of Euphemia Tracy* (1932), *The Old Man's Birthday* (1934) and *Narcissa* (1941), as we shall see in later chapters. Some of her other novels are more like village sagas, such as *Leadon Hill* (1927), *Abbots' End* (1929) and *Steffan Green* (1940), in which different figureheads in a small village community tussle for influence and social superiority.

Mrs Wilding is an imposing matriarch guiding her offspring with a stern hand through the different stages of their lives. She is a robust, stately and overbearing mother whose magnificence as a charismatic figure who manages to guide, or rather direct, her family through thick and thin is overshadowed by her bullying and emotional intransigence. One can respect her total commitment to her family, whilst fearing her ability to get what she wants on almost every occasion. After their marriage, her son David and his young wife Hero briefly escape the confines of Mrs Wilding's orbit. David tries to build a life as a poet and critic. He stoically realises that his talent is a mediocre one and the couple reluctantly return home to face his mother, the family business and conventional family life.[10]

Metaphorical allusions to literature can be found throughout Crompton's fiction. We know from her involvement in school amateur dramatics at Bromley High School that she knew Shakespeare's plays well. In *The Wildings* (1925), Hero and David go with his sister Clare to a local production of *Hamlet*. David declares that Hamlet would have had a tragic life whatever circumstances he had been born into:

> He'd have—beaten himself to death against the walls of any cage. Sooner or later, I suppose, we all discover that we're in cages, and—some take it harder than others. He'd always have taken it the hardest.[11]

Hero fears that they too can never be free from their particular cage.[12] As the novel ends another young man from the family has rushed off to London. His mother is distraught, but David advises her to wait. In the last line of the novel, David tells her, "Let him go," he said dreamily. 'He'll come back.'[13] As indeed he does.

In another intertextual reference, in the last book in the Wilding series, *The Thorn Bush* (1928), David's niece, Veevie, is reading the first novel in Galsworthy's trilogy, *A Man of Property* (1906), and she compares Irene in the novel to her aunt Hero, David's wife. Galsworthy's saga moves from the nineteenth into the twentieth century. The lives of the central couple, Soames and Irene, who 'might have existed anywhere and at any time almost,' straddle the centuries.[14] Here Crompton tempts us to consider whether she has written a parody in honour of Galsworthy. When Hero leaves David, as Irene leaves her husband Soames, to embark on a career as a professional singer and a possible love affair, Mrs Wilding decides that she is 'not going to have this sort of thing in the family' and makes it crystal clear that it is David's responsibility to make sure his wife returns. So, as instructed, he goes after her. Hero is constantly infuriated by David's acquiescence every time his mother asks him to do something. She feels controlled not so much by her husband, as Irene does, but by her mother-in-law. Both Soames, who is a solicitor, and David, who manages the family bookshops, are successful middle-class businessmen. Soames seeks to lay down the law, whilst David follows the law laid down by his mother.

The cultural capital inherent in music, literature and art are revered in Crompton's writing. Artists and musicians live parallel lives amidst their conventional, bourgeois peers, or they escape to London or abroad to fulfil their dreams or fail remorsefully in their attempt to do so. In *Millicent Dorrington* (1927), Millicent plans a career as a singer and Caroline, in *Caroline* (1936), tries to prevent her younger sister Fay pursuing a career as a pianist, hoping that she will become a teacher instead. Archie in the William stories is an artist and a positive, albeit hapless, role model. He is poor, disorganised and perhaps the least pompous, pretentious and self-serving man throughout the stories. He is respected by the Outlaws for his dedication to his life as an artist, although their attitude towards him may have more to do with his attractive bohemian lifestyle and disregard for convention. As Pierre Bourdieu argued influentially later in the twentieth century, in the interwar period 1918–1939, cultural capital was important to the bourgeois and 'nothing more clearly affirms one's "class", nothing more infallibly classifies, than tastes in music.'[15] Once again, Crompton reflects the values of the world she knew.

She often uses strong metaphors to reflect the themes in her novels. In *The Thorn Bush*, Veevie finds it hateful having a large family. Her friend Doreen disagrees:

> "I shouldn't hate it … A large family seems like a lovely big tree always covering and protecting you."

> "It's the sort of tree then that's nicer to look at from a distance than to be under like a—like a—"

> "Thorn bush," suggested Doreen.

> "Yes. A thorn bush. They look awfully pretty, but they're uncomfortable to be in and, of course, they'd protect anything….[16]

David and Hero do indeed feel both uncomfortable and safe. *Family Roundabout* (1948), published over twenty years after the Wildings trilogy, follows two families in the years before the Second World War. In another striking example, Mrs Fowler reflects that family life is 'like a sort of roundabout … You get one lot more or less settled and then, before you know where you are, it's all starting again with the next.'[17] The novel opens as she looks back on her thirty-year marriage and the growth of her family.

Since the death of her husband, Henry, she has continued to act out the role of a docile mother and wife. Mrs Fowler understands the two sides of her own character: 'Her name was Millicent, but Henry … had called her Milly. She always thought of the quick-witted, quick tempered girl who still existed somewhere within her as Millicent and Henry's wife as Milly.'[18] We follow Milly and Millicent as Mrs Fowler tries to live with both of them as she grows older. After her husband's death, will she follow Millicent's dreams of travelling, or stay home to look after her family, who still need her even when they are adults? Mrs Fowler is the 'good' mother contrasted with the monstrous Mrs Willoughby who, like Mrs Wilding, is controlling and domineering. Her son-in-law must weather her interference.[19] She is outraged when Mrs Fowler encourages young people in both their families to follow their dreams and do what they think is for the best. Her granddaughter speaks to Mrs Fowler who advises her that 'everyone must decide things for themselves and not just do what other people would do.'[20] When she tells Mrs Willoughby about this, her grandmother is shocked into silence. Mrs Fowler wonders herself if she is doing the right thing:

> She had this feeling of uncertainty and inadequacy with all her children. She shrank from bringing pressure to bear on them in any way or obtruding on

Fig. 5.1 Richmal, Clara and Gwen[22]

their privacy, and so, she suspected, she often failed them. They wanted help and advice and she had none to give…. Her thoughts went to Mrs Willoughby. She can always give people advice. I'd be better if I had more of her in me. A little smile twitched her lips. And perhaps she'd be better if she had more of me in her.[21]

We do not know if, like Mrs Fowler, Ray tussled with Aunt Richmal, Miss Lamburn or Richmal Crompton to find a similar balance in her own personal and professional lives and whether she questioned the advice and support she gave to members of her immediate family and her students. One senses that she did.

Crompton takes a look at the demands of grasping mothers in many other stories. In two novels from the late nineteen twenties, several mothers try to control their children. In *Roofs Off* (1928), a local doctor believes that a 'spontaneous friendship between a parent and an adult son or daughter based on similarity of tastes is one of the most beautiful things in the world, and the domination of the parent over an adult son or daughter is one of the ugliest. It's unnatural.'[23] And in *Abbots' End* (1929), Beatrice, after a month's holiday following an illness, resolves to settle 'back on her throne' from which she rules supreme in her empire as mistress of her household. She struggles to come to terms with her young adult daughter's passion for moving to London, failing to understand that it is natural for Mavis to want her independence and that she must let her go. A visiting vicar helps her to move on and build a new relationship with her daughter based on trust, not control. He tells her a 'sort of parable':

> You can hold together in your hand a lot of wires that are really trending in widely different directions. You open your hand and let them go. In a second, they spring far apart to their natural positions. It would take much longer than a second to get them all together in your hand again. It might even be impossible.... at one stage in a woman's life she must readjust her relations with both her husband and her children.... You'll only keep your hold over them by letting them go.[24]

Reviews of Crompton's novels and non-William short stories published in her lifetime rarely identify the nuances within them. However, one review of this novel, *Abbots' End*, is an exception:

> We have, with the exception of Mr Galsworthy, no better chronicler of family life than Miss Richmal Crompton. Nothing escapes her: she watches her characters playing upon each other.... torturing each other with forced intimacies. To her every drawing room is a stage and every conversation a drama. Her new book *Abbots' End* ... gives an excellent portrait of a possessive mother.... There are one or two tragedies and several small comedies. But in spite of all this by-play the author never for one instant loses sight of her main idea. Beatrice's jealousy runs like a yellow thread throughout the book.... It is a very notable study both of jealousy and of village life.[25]

In *Ordinary Families* (1933) by E. Arnot Robertson (1903–1961), a contemporary novelist concerned with similar themes to Crompton, the narrator comments:

> In very few of the thousands of good homes, from which the children struggle to escape, can the truth ever be told, I suppose, even in the heat of a family row – the unfortunate truth that devotion easily grows unbearable when it is given to the young by those whose own lives are no longer, for some reason, of self-absorbing interest.... Such people crave for companionship, and it is their need which makes willing companionship impossible.[26]

In a later novel by Crompton, *The Gypsy's Baby* (1954), another mother tries to hang on to her daughter, insisting that she belongs to her. A friend gives her a similar message, 'You'll have to let her go, you know, if you want her to belong to you. Nothing really belongs to anyone till they've let it go.'[27] Crompton takes a hard look at this lack in the lives of some mothers and interrogates why there is a struggle for power and control in many families, as well as between families in small communities.

The tussle between controlling mothers and the need for their offspring, especially daughters, to break free is a theme throughout Crompton's fiction outside the William stories. Mrs Fowler wonders if her life could have been other than it was, a question faced by David and Hero too. For other mothers, motherhood gives them the right to control and constrain the lives of their children. Their homes are both safe and uncomfortable, thorny places in which many of the same tensions and battles just keep revolving in a never-ending cycle over the years. If only all mothers could be like Mrs Brown or Mrs Fowler. Mrs Brown offers the nurturing that perhaps every mother should aspire to achieve, and yet she fails to control the behaviour of her son.

A sense of not being able to follow your dreams and do what you want, which William Brown usually seems able to do, is a haunting presence in the life of Hero, David, and other Crompton characters, including Millicent in *Millicent Dorrington* (1927), as we shall see. Throughout her writing life, Crompton questions why other people cannot be more like William and pursue their own adventures. William's sense of freedom, confidence and hope represents the life they might have had, although another of his qualities is being able to make the best of any situation whether he achieves his initial plans or not. This sense of being able to make the best of anything and everything is endearing and a valuable asset when things, as they often do, go wrong. A sense of freedom for Crompton is not only to be found in a place, whether in rural or urban settings, travel, education and study, or a career, but within one's self. Whether this is enough, or whether her characters other than William delude themselves into accepting second best or can accept their circumstances whether they achieve their dreams or not, is a theme Crompton returns to again and again. It features in her final novel *The Inheritor*, discussed in a later chapter, which was published in 1960 when she was seventy.

* * *

Crompton's writing reflects aspects of the domestic modernism described by Chiara Briganti and Kathy Mezei who argue that writers such as Virginia

Woolf, Katherine Mansfield, Ivy Compton-Burnett, E.M. Delafield, Elizabeth Bowen and EH Young 'subjected house and household to critical
scrutiny.'[28] They 'unveiled the extraordinary in the ordinary.'[29] In the work of
these and other women writers, such as Crompton: 'Inter war fiction is both
responsive to the imagined possibilities offered by the domestic and subtly
critical of it.'[30] In common with her contemporaries, Crompton gives us a
critique of middle-class society and family values in her fiction, and this is
particularly sharp in her comedies.

In *The Gypsy's Baby* (1954), Drusilla is a housemaid who works for the
local vicar. She is pregnant, although she says that she does not know who
the father is. Her lack of concern about this and the vicar's wife's dismay
about her attitude kicks off the social comedy in this novel to a good start:
Mrs Medway asks, '"who's the father?"

"I don't know, ma'am," said Drusilla, and added in a tone of wistful innocence,
"I don't know how you tell which it is."[31]

Much of the comedy lies in the extent to which the reader believes, as Mrs
Medway does, in Drusilla's apparent innocence. Some women in the village
decide that they would like to adopt Drusilla's baby as, in their minds at least,
they believe they can offer more as a kind of surrogate mother than she can
as the baby's mother. They lack the self-awareness to understand that their
concern about the baby's future meets a lack in their own lives.

Putting Mrs Brown to one side, older women in the William stories,
are sometimes silly and foolish and lack similar self-awareness. They are
figures who have much in common with Mrs Willoughby and Mrs Wilding
and share their snobbishness, pomposity and bossiness. William wages a
war against them that he usually wins. A new neighbour, Miss Montagu,
writes complaining letters to William's father, underlining key words, such
as 'completely' spoilt, 'early' morning, 'headache', 'most disastrous' effect and
'persecutions'.[32] She clearly feels harassed by William's early morning antics,
which have completely spoilt her day, amounted to persecution and was disastrous for her health. Miss Montagu lies, telling her neighbours about six
burglars who she alleges have ransacked her house. William was in fact the
lone intruder, and spotting the opportunity for revenge, over his 'inscrutable
countenance there flickered just for one moment a smile.'[33] William might
be well-meaning, but he is not always innocent or without guile.

Societies for ladies who think they are better than everyone else, and each
other, are especially pilloried in the William stories. A meeting of the Anti-
Vivisection Society has decided to challenge the local scientist, Mr Gabriel

Simpkins. On the whole, the members of the society have a distinct lack of interest in the subject: 'Up to now there had been little scope in the village for their activities, though they had all much enjoyed the monthly meetings at which they had had tea and cakes and discussed the various village scandals.'[34] In another story, the Society of Ancient Souls, who all appear to be ancient, are led by William's neighbour Miss Gregoria Mush. She is shown no mercy by William when she is pompous and attention-seeking. Her other neighbour, the aptly named Mr Gregorius Lambkin, is not confident that he can avoid Miss Mush's demands on him. He has the clouds of Fate gathering around him—'what can one do against Fate?' comments the narrator.[35] William looks on as the society's members attend a special meeting in fancy dress; a meeting that Mr Lambkin has been persuaded to attend: 'A gorgeous scene met [William's] eye. Noah conversed agreeably with Cleopatra in the window seat, and … Nero and Dante arrived, having shared a taxi from the station.'[36] Miss Mush has mercilessly insisted that Gregorius Lambkin comes to this meeting dressed as Julius Caesar and he looks as unhappy as it is possible to look.[37]

Next morning is April Fool's Day and William's family watch him fearfully. However, this year his target lives elsewhere. In her garden, Miss Mush sweeps up for an appointment with the figure of Julius Caesar, who has his toga drawn over his head, and declares that they are to be married. As she leans forward, no doubt expecting a passionate embrace, the toga falls and a turnip attached to the top of a broomstick bears the sign, April Fool. A deep sigh of satisfaction comes from the other side of the garden fence.[38]

Miss Euphemia Barney is the President of the Society for the Encouragement of Higher Thought, which shares some of the features of the equally pilloried New Era Society, the Society of New Thought and the League of Perfect Health. Terry Taylor, a William fan, argues that these societies:

> underline the fact that [the stories] were written primarily for an adult audience that would recognise the character types [Crompton] was sending up. At least half a dozen of these stories must rank among the funniest that she wrote and well illustrate why she is regarded as one of the leading humourists of the twentieth century.[39]

Fans Ben and Margaret Sherriff agree that Crompton:

> takes a particular delight in unmasking and delightfully punishing characters who are ignobly dishonest or are self-deluding. (William's occasional dishonesties are, of course, necessary to survival in a harsh world.) … in the best

of the William stories, laughter and a gift for irony cleanses away whatever is foolish, or dishonest, or ... self-deluding.[40]

Quite so.

Whether Richmal's own mother Clara was more like Mrs Fowler than Mrs Willoughby, or whether Richmal felt that she had anything in common with Millicent or Milly, are questions that her biographer has constantly asked herself. They are ones to which we do not have any conclusive answers. What we do know about Ray, who her friends and family knew at home, Miss Lamburn, known to her pupils at school, and the fiction of the author Richmal Crompton, familiar to her fans, suggests that she brought her vivid imagination and mischievous, satirical and vivacious humour to her work as both a teacher and an author.

Clara's life is divided by her childhood and marriage in Bury and her move, following the death of her husband, to her new life in Kent from 1915, where she lived first with Gwen and then Richmal. Clara took care of their home, whilst Richmal pursued her careers. But first, in 1911 Richmal embarked on a new life as a student at Royal Holloway College.

Notes

1. "A Night of Mysteries," 208.
2. "A Busy Day," 25.
3. "William's Birthday," 99 and "William and Photography," 30.
4. "William Helps the Cause," 69.
5. "William Spoils the Party," 186.
6. "William and the Masked Ranger," *3*.
7. "William Starts the Holidays," 215.
8. "William and the White Elephants," 101.
9. *Bromley High School Magazine* 1920, 5.
10. *The Wildings*, 171.
11. Ibid., 88.
12. Nicola Humble suggests that novels in this period by other women writers reflect family life as 'simultaneously a haven and a cage' for women (*Feminine Middlebrow* 149).
13. *The Wildings*, 320.
14. *The Thorn Bush*, 108.
15. Bourdieu, 18.
16. *The Thorn Bush*, 201.

17. *Family Roundabout*, 270.
18. Ibid., 6.
19. Ibid., 38.
20. Ibid., 155.
21. Ibid., 164.
22. UoR RC/3/9/022.
23. *Roofs Off*, 199.
24. *Abbots' End*, 310.
25. Anon, "Village Jealousy", *The Yorkshire Post* 14 August 1929, 6.
26. E. Arnot Robertson, 217.
27. *The Gypsy's Baby*, 139.
28. Briganti and Mezei, 1.
29. Ibid., 2.
30. Ibid., 11.
31. *The Gypsy's Baby*, 8.
32. "The Midnight Adventure of Miss Montague," 101.
33. Ibid., 113.
34. "The Terrible Magician," 40.
35. "William and the Ancient Souls," 218.
36. Ibid., 217.
37. Ibid.
38. Ibid., 225.
39. Taylor, 31.
40. Sherriff 2006, 12 and 15.

References

Bourdieu, Pierre. 1984. "The Aristocracy of Culture." In *Distinction: A Social Critique of the Judgement of Taste*, by Pierre Bourdieu, 11–96. Cambridge, Massachusetts: Harvard University Press.

Briganti, Chiara and Kathy Mezei. 2006. *Domestic Modernism, the Interwar Novel and E.H. Young*. Hampshire: Ashgate.

Crompton, Richmal. 1959. First published 1922. "A Busy Day." In *More William*, by Richmal Crompton, 13–32. London: George Newnes Ltd.

Crompton, Richmal. 1985. First published 1934. "A Night of Mysteries." In *William - The Gangster*, by Richmal Crompton, 207–230. Basingstoke, Hampshire: Pan Macmillan Children's Books.

———. 1929. *Abbots' End*. London: Hodder & Stoughton.

———. 1949. *Family Roundabout*. London: Hutchinson Universal Book Club.

————. 1928. *Roofs Off.* London: Hodder & Stoughton.

————. 1954. *The Gypsy's Baby.* London: Hutchinson.

Crompton, Richmal. 1930. First published 1926. "The Midnight Adventure of Miss Montagu." In *William - The Conqueror,* by Richmal Crompton, 97–117. London: George Newnes Ltd.

Crompton, Richmal. 1984. First published 1927. "The Terrible Magician." In *William - The Outlaw,* by Richmal Crompton, 18–51. Basingstoke, Hampshire: Macmillan Children's Books.

————. 1928. *The Thorn Bush.* London: Hodder & Stoughton.

————. 1925. *The Wildings.* London: Hodder & Stoughton.

Crompton, Richmal. 1953. First published 1924. "William and Photography." In *William - The Fourth,* by Richmal Crompton, 28–41. London: George Newnes Ltd.

Crompton, Richmal. 1959. First published 1922. "William and the Ancient Souls." In *More William,* by Richmal Crompton, 212–225. London: George Newnes Ltd.

Crompton, Richmal. 1993. First published 1966. "William and the Masked Ranger." In *William and the Masked Ranger,* by Richmal Crompton, 1–26. Basingstoke, Hampshire: Pan Macmillan Children's Books.

Crompton, Richmal. 1984. First published 1927. "William and the White Elephants." In *William - The Outlaw,* by Richmal Crompton, 100–127. Basingstoke, Hampshire: Macmillan Children's Books.

Crompton, Richmal. 1999. First published 1930. "William Helps the Cause." In *William's Happy Days,* by Richmal Crompton, 59–73. Basingstoke, Hampshire: Macmillan Children's Books.

Crompton, Richmal. 1984. First published 1925. "William Spoils the Party." In *Still - William,* by Richmal Crompton, 184–207. Basingstoke, Hampshire: Macmillan Children's Books.

Crompton, Richmal. 1930. First published 1926. "William Starts the Holidays." In *William - The Conqueror,* by Richmal Crompton, 214–234. London: George Newnes Ltd.

Crompton, Richmal. 1999. First published 1930. "William's Birthday." In *William's Happy Days,* by Richmal Crompton, 86–105. Basingstoke, Hampshire: Macmillan Children's Books.

Humble, Nicola. 2001. *The Feminine Middlebrow Novel 1920s to 1950s.* Oxford: Oxford University Press.

Robertson, E. Arnot. 1982. First published 1933. *Ordinary Families.* London: Virago.

Sherriff, Ben & Margaret. Winter 2006. "William Among the Writers." *The Just William Society Magazine 19*: 10–15.

Taylor, Terry. Summer 2006. "William and Those Eccentric Societies." *The Just William Society Magazine 18*: 22–31.

Part II

(1911–1923)

6

Royal Holloway College, the First World War and Women's Suffrage

From the autumn of 1911, following three years as a pupil-teacher at St Elphin's, Richmal was a university student in Classics, and she embraced wholeheartedly all that Royal Holloway College had to offer. In 1914, she returned to teaching at St Elphin's for another three years. We know relatively little about her life in these years, but we can glimpse her amidst her studies at university and the turmoil of the First World War.

1918 brought the end of the war and women's right to vote. Crompton reflects on the lives of women in her fiction and the extent to which the emancipation they anticipated failed to materialise. Yet, in her case, by the early nineteen twenties, she was a successful professional woman and the head of her family living in Kent. The foundations of her achievements were laid in her relationship with her father, her experience as a pupil and teacher at St Elphin's and as a student at Royal Holloway College.

* * *

Women keen to make their mark in the world beyond home and family relished the opportunities offered at university. Richmal joined their ranks at the age of twenty-one.[1] She was part of a privileged body of women who were breaking new ground in higher education. At the turn of the century, women comprised only sixteen per cent of the university student population in England.[2]

Thomas Holloway founded Royal Holloway College, 'to afford the best education suitable for women.'[3] Holloway believed that the College should

© The Author(s), under exclusive license to Springer Nature Switzerland AG 2022
J. McVeigh, *Richmal Crompton, Author of Just William*, Literary Lives, https://doi.org/10.1007/978-3-030-96511-2_6

not be considered as merely a training college for teachers and governesses and that the subjects studied 'should not be exclusively regulated by the tradition and methods of former ages.'[4] The College opened in June 1886 and the first twenty-eight students began their studies in October 1887. It promoted intellectual rigour and offered an inspiring environment for teaching, study and research.

In the early decades of the twentieth century, the College's rules are evocative of sepia-tinted days gone by:

> No hair to be thrown out of windows; permission to be sought for biking on Sundays; chapel doors to be shut on the fourth strike of the bell, and all students not inside by then to be punished; smoking only allowed in the afternoons in the remotest part of the grounds, and only after 4.00pm in public corridors; no tennis on Sundays; stockings to be worn at all times and in all weather, even on the river.[5]

Students were even forbidden from borrowing teaspoons from the kitchen, which sounds like one of the rules made to be broken, as no doubt many of them were.[6] College life brought new freedoms to young women who had been closely supervised as they grew up, although the period in which they lived nevertheless expected that their activities would be restricted. Royal Holloway's regulations required that:

> Students must consult the Principal or her assistant before giving or receiving invitations, before going on the river unless with a lecturer, or undertaking expeditions. They are requested not to walk or bicycle alone beyond the grounds, and to be within the grounds by sunset.[7]

Chaperones for women students keen to go out and about were part of university life in all comparable institutions until the nineteen twenties.[8]

The architecture of St Elphin's School is subsumed by the awe-inspiring grandeur of Royal Holloway's Founder's Building where students lived and studied. One ex-staff member, W.E. Delp, recalled that: 'What inevitably struck the newcomer most in 1908 [when she joined the College] was the building: its sheer size, its elaborate ornamentation and the still flaming red brick which fairly scorched the eye.'[9] Each student had her own bedroom and a separate study.[10] These two rooms were a luxury in comparison with other colleges.[11] They offered Richmal the privacy she had lacked during her many years at St Elphin's. The students' hours were regulated and focused on their studies; privacy 'was fundamentally privacy to work.'[12] High academic standards and hard work were demanded from all of them.

Staff and students changed for dinner and 'the catering at Royal Holloway was far superior to that of other women's colleges.'[13] One of the most distinctive features of college life was the system of dinner-partners, which encouraged staff and students to pair up with someone different each evening. Their conversation continued with coffee in staff members' studies where they 'chatted over the fire' with students.[14]

Richmal was one of a small number of students funded by a scholarship that contributed to the annual fee of one hundred pounds for board, lodging and teaching.[15] To compete for the award, she attended a week-long examination period at the College from June 26th to 1st July 1911. She needed to satisfy the examiners in several subjects, including four exam papers in Classics.[16] In the summer of 1911, sixty-one candidates sat these exams. Four Founder's Scholarships of sixty pounds a year and eight Entrance Scholarships worth fifty pounds per year were awarded to successful applicants. Richmal was awarded a Founder's Scholarship.[17] Subsequently, she was awarded two further scholarships which provided additional money to cover her fees and recognised her potential.[18] Her awards suggest that money was not forthcoming from other sources, including her family. However, supporting students without access to private sources of income was not their only purpose; scholarships were provided 'in order to secure students of ability whose work could set a high standard.'[19] They offered exceptional young women, irrespective of wealth, the freedom to study and develop their intellectual and academic potential.

There were approximately one hundred and sixty students each year during the period Richmal was at Royal Holloway.[20] She would have stood out as a high achiever. Her first year must have been even more challenging when, at a meeting of her peers, Richmal was elected the Senior Scholar for first year students. She made a speech on the need to preserve unity in the year, another tiny detail from her youth that is suggestive of her confidence, ambition, drive, leadership abilities and her ability to cope under pressure, as well as her outstanding intellectual prowess.[21] At Royal Holloway, we catch sight of Richmal as a vibrant, extrovert and exceptionally clever young woman, both immersed in her classical studies and enjoying the independence and new challenges that university life could bring. She was Secretary of the Classical Club, Treasurer of the Christian Union and a member of the tennis, boating and hockey clubs, and she took a leading part in college theatricals, as she had at St Elphin's.[22]

Young women cloistered at university lived in a climate of tight-knit relationships and fervent opportunity. In Crompton's early novels, *The Innermost Room* (1923) and *Anne Morrison* (1925), we join two young girls, Bridget and

Anne, on their journeys into adulthood. When they reach college, they touch on subjects that are out of bounds at home. In *The Innermost Room*, away from the ever-watchful eyes of her older sister and formidable aunts, Bridget feels she belongs at university, where she makes friends with her peers, Susan, Diana and Faith:

> There was so much to do and think about. They belonged to the usual innu-merable societies. They went joyfully from a Browning discussion to modern poetry readings, from that to a socialist society, from that to a debating society and from that to a dramatic society. They were keenly alive and inquisitive and ardent and young, with all the pathos of youth to which youth itself is mercifully blind. They wanted to reform the world. They were impatient of the years of waiting.[23]

Curled up by the fire in their dressing gowns late at night, Bridget and Susan drink cocoa and discuss everything under the sun: 'They worked together—reading … or writing essays and always comparing results.'[24] At college, Bridget only shares her poems and stories with Susan. In her better known *bildungsroman* from the same period, *Dusty Answer* (1927), Rosa-mond Lehmann evokes other similar nights at college for students Judith and her friend, Jennifer, who while away the hours sprawled across their rooms drinking cocoa and eating buns with friends, discussing 'earnestly, muddle-headedly – sex, philosophy, religion, sociology, people and politics; then people and sex again.'[25] On their own, they languish together in the early summer sun:

> Slowly they opened books … turned to smile at each other, to talk as if there could never be enough of talking; with excitement, with anxiety, as if tomorrow might part them and leave them for ever burdened with the weight of all they had had to tell each other.[26]

This is an exciting time for these young women as they throw themselves into impassioned conversations, driven by the optimism of youth, on subjects that are new to them, and experience freedom they have never had before and which they would no doubt struggle to find again in future.

Nicola Humble suggests that a surprising number of women's novels written in the nineteen twenties, thirties and forties concentrate on adoles-cence: 'Among them are novels which have been read by generations of teenage girls.'[27] This focus is reflected in Crompton's novels featuring young characters who we follow as they grow up into early adulthood, and they are discussed in a later chapter, including *The Innermost Room* (1923), *Anne*

Morrison (1925), *The Four Graces* (1929), *Blue Flames* (1930), *Quartet* (1935), *Frost at Morning* (1950) and *Four in Exile* (1954).[28] Sadly, these novels were not discovered by readers of the William stories or other women's novels in the nineteen twenties and thirties. These readers may have known other comparable and better-known novels from this period such as *The Constant Nymph* (1924) by Margaret Kennedy, and *Ordinary Families* (1933) by E. Arnot Robertson.

* * *

In 1914, the challenging and exciting days at Royal Holloway came to an end when Richmal returned to teach at St Elphin's. The school had supported her move to study for a degree on the proviso that she returned to teach at the school.[30] In common with many of her peers from similar backgrounds, Richmal went to university expecting to earn her own living if she did not marry. Teachers were the largest group of professional women, followed by nurses, and it was the most popular career for women after the First World War.[31] Richmal's return to life at the school would have meant the loss of the relative freedoms she had enjoyed at college and the luxury of full-time study.

Having completed her three years at St Elphin's and following her father's death, she decided not to stay on at the school and instead to join her family in the South of England, where she had secured a new teaching post at Bromley High School for girls. Margaret Flood, the headmistress at St Elphin's, wrote a reference for Richmal that is full of praise. The letter is, not surprisingly, formal and lacks warmth. She emphasises that Richmal has a considerable talent for organising the school's plays.[32] As a young teacher she was clearly outgoing, a leader, and someone who excelled in her classical knowledge and in the performing arts. She can direct both in the classroom and on stage and these dramatic, performative qualities would become a feature of her writing.

Another more emotional and personal letter gives us a greater insight into the impact Richmal had on pupils at the school. To the end of her life, Richmal kept a letter from one of the girls at St Elphin's, who wrote to her when she was leaving:

Dear Miss Lamburn,
   I just want to write a few words to thank you for what you have done for me. By far the largest share in any honour I have gained by winning the scholarship belongs to you. I could not have done it without you. During my time at St.Elphin's my work was mostly in your hands and you pulled me through.... your teaching won the scholarship for me and the opportunity of college work and life. I thank you for it sincerely.[33]

Fig. 6.1 Richmal Crompton Lamburn circa 1912[29]

A pupil with the same ambition to go to college kept in touch with Richmal until her death many years later. Joan Braunholtz was one of the girls Miss Lamburn supported at Bromley High School with her college application and she secured a place at Oxford University. Joan was unhappy at home, and she was profoundly influenced by Miss Lamburn's serene and happy temperament with its underlying simple faith in the rightness of things, her lively mind, her humour and her love of classical literature, particularly of Homer. She taught Joan to love Greek, and it was through her that she came to realise the beauty and nobility of Greek poetry and thought. Also, she offered Joan some sense of security in the present and hope for the future. Miss Lamburn became like a mother substitute, and later they became lifelong friends.[34]

The support of hard-working and ambitious teachers like Richmal was often the main reason why young women were able to access higher education in this period:

> The orthodox route to university admission was via school. Teachers identified likely candidates, coached them carefully, crammed them and drilled them if necessary, made inquiries about scholarships and grants and arranged the entrance exams and interviews.[35]

Richmal knew from her own experience how to support younger girls who dreamed of following the same path as herself.

Richmal, or Miss Lamburn as she was known in school, became a classics mistress in charge of the Lower Third Form at Bromley High School for Girls. Unlike her father's long career in teaching, she would only stay for six years. She lost none of her ability to inspire her pupils when she changed schools. Richmal had a 'deep faith in the essential rightness of things' and her pupils at Bromley High School came to know her for her 'love of literature—English, Latin, but most of all Greek.'[36] There is no doubt that she would have continued to empower the lives of many young women had she spent her working life in teaching. It was a career to which she was ideally suited, and she maintained the same commitment to knowledge and learning in her life as a writer.

The pedagogy she drew on for both her teaching and fiction was based on the art and craft of storytelling. A pupil at Bromley High School describes how she 'was always tolerant and patient and her keen sense of humour was a great help; amusing stories, atrocious puns, silly jokes, impressed rules and vocabulary on our minds where learning by rote would have failed.'[37] She brought this creativity and humour to her writing and continued to tell stories for the rest of her life. Creativity, a vibrant imagination and maturity, the ability to build strong relationships and offer intellectual guidance through stories and laughter are qualities and skills that embody Crompton's professional life.

* * *

In *The Wildings* (1925), in an early visit to her future husband's bookshop, Hero picks up a book and is 'lost to everything' as she reads aloud a narrative poem she loves, *Reynard the Fox* (1919) by John Masefield (1878–1967).[38] In the poem, the fox flees his hunter, and the poem evokes terrifying scenes of battle:

> Though his death seemed near he did not blench,
> He upped his brush and he ran the trench.
>
> He ran the trench while the wind moaned treble,
> Earth trickled down, there were falls of pebble.
> Down in the valley of that dark gash
> The wind-withered grasses looked like ash.
> Trickles of stones and earth fell down
> In that dark alley of dead men's town.[39]

Masefield wrote the poem in the wake of the First World War. He describes the hunted fox as the image of his subject, Britain at war:

> For more than four years before I wrote, something primitive, wild, beautiful and strange in the Spirit of Man had been pursued through most of Europe with the threat of death. It had survived the chase, but as a hunted fox may survive a long run, to lie panting somewhere till the heart stops beating. It was my hope that my fox's heart should not stop beating.[40]

Masefield's fox survives as does Britain, only to face another war twenty years later. Both wars had an impact on the lives of tens of thousands of families and Richmal's was one of them. Her writing life was just beginning in 1918 and the First World War is briefly featured in her early novels, although her more mature novels published during the Second World War when she was in her fifties are more powerful.

Richmal was teaching in both the north and south of England during the First World War, which was never far away from either school. Close to St Elphin's, bombs were dropped by Zeppelins.[41] Meanwhile, at Bromley High School they 'heard the thunder of the troop trains rushing through Bromley South Station' and the school gardens were turned into vegetable plots and were also used to keep chickens.[42] In 1916, the Headmistress, Miss Hodges, wrote to old girls asking them to volunteer for national service. She urged them to consider that so 'great an opportunity of rendering service to our country at a time of grave need and anxiety has never before arisen.'[43] As time went on, one ex-pupil remembered that 'more and more girls lost fathers, brothers, cousins, and each morning another girl would arrive with a tear-stained face.'[44] One girl arrived at the school in 1917:

> at the very worst period of the war. Food supplies were very bad. In the holidays we went to a Communal Kitchen, in the town, where meals were cooked. We must all have been suffering from some degree of malnutrition—coughs and colds, chilblains and fainting fits were the result of this and the Spanish influenza raged in 1918.... The long casualty lists sometimes included the brothers and fathers of girls, who stayed away from school and left classes in tears.[45]

A pupil remembers that the 'lack of young men gave us a different adolescence from the girls who grew up before and after World War I.' Facing everything they had to cope with, 'Life became sad.'[46] The loss of young men on a tragic scale meant that peace-time expectations about romance, marriage and becoming parents were shattered for tens of thousands of young people. One teacher at the school reminisced after the war that one colleague, 'like so many of our teachers, had lost a fiancé in the Great War and so never married.'[47] The war changed life for everyone. Women experienced new responsibilities in munitions factories, working on farms, as ambulance drivers, and in blue- and white-collar jobs for civilian and military services, whilst others continued to support families, often on their own, at home.

From March 1918, the Spanish Flu pandemic killed millions of people across the world over the next two years, surpassing losses during both the First and Second World Wars.[48] Laura Spinney suggests that in the continents most engaged in it, the First World War had a greater impact than the flu. In Britain, three times more deaths were associated with the war than the pandemic and there was a similar pattern across Europe and the US.[49] However, on every other continent, 'more died of flu than war.'[50] In 1918, despite the availability of vaccines, mostly 'they had no effect: those who were vaccinated continued to fall ill and die.'[51] As the pandemic a hundred years later proved, some vaccines have been more effective in the fight against subsequent viruses.

The Bromley and Chislehurst areas where Richmal, Gwen and Clara moved during the First World War experienced the fighting in the skies overhead at close hand. From August 1914, the army were based in Chislehurst. A local landowner, Agnes Tiarks, recorded her experience of the war in her diary, and watched the movement of artillery on the local common. By May 1915, Zeppelins were reported to be bombarding Southend and London. However, their threat was short-lived; Zeppelins proved easy to shoot down. Not so the newly emerging airplanes, deployed by Germany over England from June 1917: 'We heard the air raid over London - in our peaceful garden. Bombs dropped in the City, great damage, many killed and injured,' she wrote.[52] In late 1917, food rationing was introduced.[53] Agnes used much of her estate and farm for growing food, and many other local people did the same in their gardens and allotments.

Wounded soldiers were treated by local young women who became volunteers in VAD hospitals (voluntary aid detachment) in Bromley and Chislehurst. One of the hospitals was based at The Rookery, owned by the Norman family since the mid-eighteenth century, which was close to Bromley Common where Richmal and her mother moved in 1917.[54]

* * *

In 1918 women over thirty were given the right to vote, whilst younger women had to wait until 1928 to attain full voting rights with men from the age of twenty-one. In the years before 1918, suffrage societies were active in women's colleges, including Royal Holloway:

> Membership was divided between suffragists, who promoted votes for women and tried to win support through debate and ideological persuasion, and suffragettes, attacking the political status quo through physical protest and violence. Bluestocking suffragists affiliated themselves to national societies, held meetings, wrote letters, sewed banners, and joined marches; the militant suffragettes courted publicity by shocking the public into taking notice. Both these sisterhoods attracted ridicule, within their universities as well as the world outside, and from women as well as men.[55]

In 1913, during Richmal's time at the College, the suffragette and Royal Holloway alumna Emily Wilding Davison was killed when she 'threw herself in front of the King's horse' during the Epsom Derby. Royal Holloway was represented at her funeral.[56] As a student, Richmal may have supported women's suffrage and attended a few meetings without necessarily getting directly involved in campaign activities. It is unlikely that she would have supported direct action of any kind. As a Senior Scholar her focus would have been on her studies and her responsibility to act as a role model for other students. Also, it is hard to imagine her sewing anything, let alone a banner, or clutching one at a meeting. It is intriguing to wonder what she really felt about the suffrage campaigns. It feels safe to assume that she would have supported the campaign. In her fiction, she is certainly committed to advocating greater freedoms and career opportunities for women.

Women's suffrage and their experiences on the home front during the First World War in a range of jobs previously undertaken by men, heralded new opportunities and offered hope for vocational recognition after five years of conflict. Richmal was one woman who went on to achieve the professional success craved by many of her peers. However, whilst the right to vote raised women's expectations, for many their lives continued to focus on nurturing family and home life. Other additional or alternative opportunities, responsibilities and careers remained out of reach for many.

By the mid-nineteen thirties, Crompton reflects in her fiction on the disappointment experienced by countless women, and one has a sense of her empathy with other women's experience. In a short story, "Family Group," published in *The First Morning* (1936), Joanna is married with children and for her:

> the years following the granting of the vote to women had been a slow and bitter disillusionment. Women had won the vote, but the millennium did not come.... Women did not at once exceed men in every sphere of professional life. They did not even seriously rival them. A few famous women doctors seemed the sum total of it. The doors had been beaten down, but where was the triumphant procession that should have entered them? Where were the famous woman barristers, lawyers, politicians, diplomats?[57]

Joanna's parents were happy for her to have a conventional sheltered life of domestic duties, and 'when she joined the militant suffragettes they had felt as much disgraced as if she had committed a crime.'[58] In Crompton's novel *Steffan Green* (1940), the vicar's wife, Mrs Fanshaw, was also a militant suffragette in her youth. She wanted her freedom and a career: 'I was fighting for all the women who were to come after me. I put matches in pillar-boxes and chained myself to railings and went to prison.'[59] She felt that she was fighting for her daughter's future, but when her daughter grows up all she wants is the life of marriage and domesticity that her mother had hoped she would at least delay until she was older. Later in life, Mrs Fanshaw believes that the battles fought by the suffragettes were rather futile: 'We were fanatics. We thought that the vote would bring the millennium and it didn't. Except for a few women doctors and MPs, we're pretty much as we were.'[60] Even by 1945, despite more equal political, legal and economic rights and status, women's lives had not changed fundamentally. The number of women in the upper echelons of politics, other professions and the arts was still small.[61] A woman's place remained primarily in the home.[62] In common with the women characters portrayed in Crompton's fiction, veterans of the suffragette movement felt their high ideals had been sold cheaply for short-term benefits and relative improvements.[63]

* * *

From the age of eleven until she left Darley Dale to join her family in Kent and start a new teaching role at Bromley High School in 1917, when she was already twenty-seven, Richmal's day-to-day life was dominated by two residential institutions, Royal Holloway College and St Elphin's School, where she had been a pupil, student and teacher. Study, teaching, and Greek and Latin classical languages and literature lay at the heart of her life in this period. She would continue to teach until 1923, although from 1917 she was living at home with her mother, rather than within an educational institution day and night. Since she was eleven years old, for over fifteen years she lived and worked alongside other women and girls in sheltered environments. In common with her peers, there would have been few opportunities to meet a potential suitor or husband, to find out about a professional life outside teaching, or a different kind of social life. Nevertheless, despite her inexperience of other professional networks and social circles, by 1923 she was established as a successful popular writer. Richmal's ambition and drive to succeed in her professional life are palpable and her courage to take on the complexities of a career as a writer is significant given her relatively cloistered life as she approached her thirties.

Notes

1. Royal Holloway College opened for women in 1886. It remained an exclusive college for women until 1945.
2. Robinson, 55.
3. RHC Royal Holloway College Calendar 1911–1912, 1.
4. Ibid., 1–2.
5. Robinson, 115.
6. Ibid., 125.
7. Delp, 10. See "Royal Holloway College 1908–1914" by W.E. Delp based on a talk given at Royal Holloway on 21st January 1969, RHC 378.421.DEL.
8. Robinson, 49.
9. Delp, 1.
10. Ibid., 11.

11. Robinson, 111.
12. Bingham, 82.
13. Ibid., 62.
14. Delp, 10.
15. RHC Royal Holloway College Calendar 1911–1912.
16. RHC Royal Holloway College Calendar 1910–1911, 19–22.
17. RHC Royal Holloway College Calendar 1911–1912, xxxv.
18. RHC AR/230/28 and UoR RC/2/2/3. Reference by Ellen Higgins, Principal of Royal Holloway College, July 1914.
19. Bingham, 74.
20. Delp, 2. There were one hundred and sixty-three students in 1914.
21. RHC AS/140/1, First Year Minute Book 1907–1916.
22. UoR RC/2/2/3. Reference by the Principal Ellen Higgins.
23. *Innermost Room*, 106.
24. Ibid., 103.
25. Lehmann, 130.
26. Ibid., 137.
27. Humble, 77.
28. See Chapter 12 for further discussion on this theme.
29. UoR RC/3/6/061.
30. Jane Robinson notes that in the nineteenth century students financed by King's scholarships from the Board of Education were required to teach in the classroom for at least three years (203).
31. Beddoe, 76 and Robinson, 211.
32. UoR RC/2/2/3. Margaret Flood 31 March 1917.
33. UoR RC/2/1/1/1. Letter from Eileen Thomas 14 April 1917.
34. I am very grateful to Carola Scupham, Joan's daughter, for this information.
35. Robinson, 100.
36. *Schoolgirl Voices*, 42.
37. Ibid., 41.
38. *The Wildings*, 68.
39. Masefield, 57.
40. Ibid., 109. This quote is from Masefield's introduction to the poem published in 1962.
41. *The Elphinian* 1990, 79.
42. *Schoolgirl Voices*, 26.
43. Ibid.
44. Ibid., 27.
45. Ibid., 28.

46. Ibid., 27.
47. Ibid., 29.
48. Spinney, 4.
49. Ibid., 6.
50. Ibid., 7.
51. Ibid., 98.
52. Allen, 9–10.
53. Ibid., 8.
54. See: Kent 50 Voluntary Aid Detachment | People | Bromley First World War.
55. Robinson, 175.
56. Bingham, 126. No specific evidence that she attended women's suffrage meetings at university has been identified for this book.
57. "Family Group," 193.
58. Ibid., 193.
59. *Steffan Green*, 27.
60. Ibid., 29.
61. Stevenson, 174 and Beddoe, 7.
62. Beddoe, 7. Beddoe comments, as several of Crompton's women characters know, that 1918 was a partial success for women's suffrage: 'winning the vote had not changed the world or heralded in a brave new era of sex equality in which women's moral values prevailed. The optimism of 1918 was replaced by a more cautious and tentative approach by the late 1930s. The number of women MPs was small and women's advance in the profession was disappointing: women came to realise that nothing had changed fundamentally.'
63. Stevenson, 181.

References

Allen, Tony. 2015. *Agnes Tiarks War Diaries 1914 to 1918*. Chislehurst, Kent: The Chislehurst Society.

Beddoe, Deirdre. 1989. *Back to Home and Duty: Women Between the Wars 1918-1939*. London: Pandora.

Bingham, Caroline. 1987. *The History of Royal Holloway College 1886-1986*. London: Constable.

Bridge, Marie Ed. 1983. *Schoolgirl Voices, Bromley High School 1883–1983* . Dorchester: Henry Ling.

Crompton, Richmal. 1936. "Family Group." In *The First Morning*, by Richmal Crompton, 187–205. London: Hutchinson & Co.

———. 1940. *Steffan Green*. London: Macmillan.

———. 1923. *The Innermost Room*. London: Andrew Melrose.

———. 1925. *The Wildings*. London: Hodder and Stoughton.

Humble, Nicola. 1998. "Eccentric families in the Fiction of Adolesence from the 1920s to the 1940s ." In *Childhood Remembered*, by Kimberley Reynolds Ed., 77–89. London: National Centre for Research in Children's Literature.

Lehmann, Rosamond. 1996. First published 1927. *Dusty Answer*. London: Flamingo.

Masefield, John. 2008. First published 1919. *Reynard the Fox. Introduced by Philip W. Errington*. Manchester: Carcanet Press.

Robinson, Jane. 2009. *Bluestockings: The Remarkable Story of the First Women to Fight for an Education*. London: Penguin.

Spinney, Laura. 2018. *Pale Rider: The Spanish Flu of 1918 and How It Changed the World*. London: Vintage.

Stevenson, John. 1984. *British Society 1914-45*. London: Lane.

7

Birth of Auntie and the Story of a Marriage

In 1917, when she left St Elphin's for the last time, Richmal was enveloped once again in family life and became the main breadwinner and supporter, emotionally and financially, of her mother and sister Gwen and her children, who knew her as Auntie. Gwen's marriage was fraught and unstable, and the support of her sister was ever present. After Jack's return to England in 1931, Richmal occasionally supported her brother and his family too, although to a lesser extent. From an early age she became the head of her family living in Kent and the need to earn a living for herself and her close relatives was at the centre of her life, for the rest of her life. In the six years from 1917, Richmal was juggling two careers, as a teacher and an emerging author.

On her move to Kent, Richmal was not only a property owner, the head of her family and an experienced teacher in Classics, she was also on the cusp of a life of writing. William and the writer Richmal Crompton are 'born' in these early years, as we shall see in the next chapter, and fame and fortune beckon. She became the successful author of William, first published in 1919. Her first two William collections, *Just William* (1922) and *More William* (1922), were hugely successful following the initial publication of the individual stories in magazines. William's status as a classic of English literature was established quickly in this period.

In her private life, the lives of Richmal and her sister embody some of the tensions in the experiences of women in the interwar years. Some, like Gwen, gave up a future career to marry and have children whilst others, like Richmal, did not marry and, in her case, pursued a successful career. What emerges in

© The Author(s), under exclusive license to Springer Nature
Switzerland AG 2022
J. McVeigh, *Richmal Crompton, Author of Just William*, Literary Lives,
https://doi.org/10.1007/978-3-030-96511-2_7

telling their story is that both women continued to care for members of their family throughout their lives, irrespective of their marital status.

By 1910, Gwen had left St Elphin's and was studying at home in Bury and Richmal had become a pupil-teacher at the school.[1] The first jobs undertaken by Gwen before her marriage and by Richmal, in secretarial work and teaching respectively, reflect two of the most acceptable and common career options for women of their class in the early twentieth century. In 1913, Gwen completed her studies and became Mathematical Mistress at Grange School, Buxton.[2] The appointment was short-lived. In 1914, she was looking for administrative roles in London when she met and quickly married Thomas Disher in October. Gwen's marriage was unhappy and a battlefield on the home front during the First World War, and for the next twenty years. Although Gwen's life took a different direction from Richmal's, when Richmal joined her mother and sister in Kent, the two sisters once again became part of each other's day-to-day lives and saw each other frequently.

After the failure of Gwen's marriage, according to her eldest niece Margaret, Auntie Ray became what she calls 'a surrogate father for Gwen's family.'[3] As we shall see, she was already helping her sister by 1919, before she became successful as a writer. Richmal's rising income and her willingness to share it enabled her sister to live reasonably comfortably when her children were small and her husband was unable or unwilling to support his family.

* * *

Thomas Disher was a former priest who worked for the Colonial Missionary Society in Newfoundland from the age of twenty. He moved to a similar role in Western Canada, where he lost his faith whilst living in extremely cold and primitive living conditions.[4] In July 1914, having left his career in the church, he was working in wholesale confectionary when he advertised for a secretary.[5] Mary Gwendolen Lamburn, known as Gwen, 'interested' him most. It was a whirlwind romance. On the day she came to see him, he took her to tea at his parents and on to the theatre, escorting her to Euston for the night train home to Bury.[6] On 4th August 1914, Britain declared war on Germany. Early in August, Gwen began her duties as his secretary and Thomas spent the August Bank Holiday weekend with her family in Bury. Meanwhile, his daughter Margaret comments that, 'all over the country, Army reservists were travelling to their depots, preparing for the start of war.'[7] In Bury, Thomas met Richmal, who was home for the summer holidays after leaving Royal Holloway and on her way back to teach at St Elphin's for another three years. Margaret recalls family legend that 'With the exception of Richmal, Tom was well received by the Lamburn family.'[8] Richmal never accepted him. Shortly after the visit to Bury, Thomas tells us in his autobiography that he asked Edward for Gwen's hand in marriage, and they married in London in October 1914.[9]

According to his account of their courtship, the couple were engaged no more than six weeks after their first meeting, and they were married within three months. Six months later, Edward died following an operation and Clara joined Gwen and Thomas in London. As a widow, Clara had limited choices after the death of her husband. For many women, becoming a widow brought poverty, isolation, and displacement, so a move to live with one of her daughters might have been Clara's only option.[10] Richmal was away teaching at St Elphin's and spent her holidays with Gwen and Clara in Dulwich, London until her own move to teach at Bromley High School.[11]

Gwen and Thomas were married in the early months of the First World War. When the war was declared in August 1914, Disher's brother Archie 'at once successfully applied to be transferred [from the Territorials] to a Fusilier Battalion going to the front and was blown to pieces a few weeks later.'[12] Both his younger brother, Maurice Willson, and Thomas himself were exempted from military service on medical grounds. Maurice Willson Disher was disabled 'early in life by hip trouble, which necessitated years of hospital residence.'[13] Thomas was flat-footed and had an umbilical rupture.[14] He felt that he would have been in 'hot water' had he joined the army, because he would have 'raised hell' about 'many of the crazy orders given by incompetent generals.'[15] He was never someone who took kindly to being told what to do by anyone. His sister Ethel was a nurse during the war, and another, Muriel, was still at school. In 1917, Ethel married and had seven children before her early death at forty-two in 1931. In common with many women, her life was cut short after fourteen years of childbirth and hard physical work maintaining a home.

By July 1915, when their first child, Tommy, was born, Gwen and Thomas had moved to a large property in Denmark Hill in London where they lived for six years.[16] The house had nineteen rooms, a large garden and a tennis court, and was looked after by several staff, including a cook, maid and a gardener. Thomas claimed that the dining room could seat one hundred and fifty people.[17] In June 1917, the couple's daughter, Margaret, was born.

In preparation for her birth, and to give Gwen some respite, their two-year-old son was sent for a month to an institute that trained children's nurses. He became seriously ill and was rushed home 'at the point of death.'[18] Thomas claimed that the after-effects of Tommy's illness persisted for many years. His father believed that his son's illness was caused by physical neglect during his stay at the institute. However, further evidence in his sister Margaret's memoir suggests that Tommy found life difficult for reasons that might not have had an organic cause and related to his inability to cope effectively with other people and day-to-day challenges.

Throughout his life, Tommy struggled to maintain the boundaries of conventional behaviour and found it difficult to understand why some of the things he did might be considered wrong. He had a troubled history at work, leaving jobs after only a few months. He first joined the army early in the nineteen thirties. Richmal paid for his discharge when he lost his rifle, and Tommy was advised to try another career.[19] He joined a local bank, with his aunt's help, where he also struggled. He was completely unselfconscious and had few inhibitions, telling the truth to such an extent that at times he was rather tactless. He did not change his behaviour as he grew up, saying whatever was on his mind, which was often disconcerting. He bored easily and was a poor listener, absorbed in himself. He could be bad-tempered, impatient and rude if he did not get his own way. He was then surprised when his mother was shocked by his actions.[20] Fortunately, neighbours made allowances for his eccentricities, even when he asked them for help at 7.30 am.[21] He was well-known in the area.

Tommy carried childhood antics into his adult years and on into his sixties. His sister asks, 'How many men in their sixties have proposed to the same girl for weeks, taking an offering of a single flower, until the mother practically slams the door in his face?'[22] After he died in October 1983, when Margaret was clearing his home, she found that many parts of the house were sticky with honey and blackcurrant juice, and in some places dust and a tacky surface had formed a congealed layer. Cutlery was distorted and misshapen.[23] Her description of a man who has died at sixty-eight paints a dismaying picture of someone who is childlike and unworldly, and unable to look after himself. One might speculate whether the family received any support with his inability to connect with the adult world, concentrate, and form long-standing relationships, although this is doubtful, and they might not have wanted to draw attention to it anyway. Gwen looked after Tommy throughout their life together, except for the period when he was away in the army during the Second World War. She washed and repaired his clothes, made his bed, and cooked his meals. The roles of mother and son were reversed when Tommy took over the cooking and cared for Gwen for five years before her death. He continued to live in the house and died only two years later. One has a sense that he was lost without her.

From early in their marriage, her husband Thomas left Gwen to bring up Margaret and Tommy on her own for months at a time, whilst he travelled in Britain and abroad to pursue his business interests. At sixty-six years old Thomas Disher published his autobiography, in which he celebrates his successful career. He opens his book declaring that 'Life has been and still is for me a great adventure.'[24] After his early life in the Church, he moved into commerce. His wholesale confectionery business was based in Lewisham in London, which was not far from Bromley, where Gwen would move some years later. In 1917, he also bought into a sauce and pickle manufacturing business. The wholesale confectionery business distributed several hundred packs of milk chocolate each week during the First World War until what he calls a 'crazy rationing scheme' was introduced by his supplier. He explains that it did not take him long to devise a way out of the difficulty this had created.[25] By the end of the war, he had a weekly turnover across his businesses of five thousand pounds.[26] However, by 1919, Thomas's business ventures 'had taken a dive downwards,' and he looked for opportunities abroad. He went on to buy land in Tahiti in the winter of 1920. He was away from his young family for six months at a time, 'without providing adequate financial support.'[27] In 1921, the family moved out of their Denmark Hill home into 'rooms' in Bromley.[28] The 1921 census shows Gwen and Margaret living with Richmal and Clara, so the family must have moved in with them shortly afterwards. His career diversified and, whilst Thomas continued to maintain businesses in England, he moved into the tourist business, arranging touring holidays in Europe, and he also invested in property in other parts of the world.

By this point, Thomas's income was not sufficient to provide for his family, so additional funds were needed to support Gwen and her children. Margaret comments that her Aunt Richmal was a very strong character, 'despite the impression she gave of being gentle and accommodating. I have seen her very, very angry and frequently this was caused by her brother-in-law.'[29] Richmal arranged for Gwen to join her in a teaching post at Bromley High School and to live with her and Clara during Thomas's frequent absences.[30] She also found and paid the fees for a boarding school in rural Kent for Margaret and Tommy, aged six and four, where it was hoped their father would not be able to find them. Gwen had decided to separate from her husband and to hide her children in Kent.[31] Thomas, however, did manage to find them and he abducted both Margaret and Tommy. In early 1922, Thomas informs Gwen that he is taking the children to Germany. Gwen had little choice and, in the Spring, she joined him and their children on his package tours of Germany and Austria.

During a short return to England towards the end of 1922, Gwen left her job at Bromley High School.[32] At the end of the year, Thomas took Gwen and both children on a world tour, including Australia. The tour ended in Tahiti where Thomas already had a house:

> built of posts of coconut palms ... The floor was some eight feet above the beach, the roof was of niaou—plaited coconut leaves—and in place of walls [he] had made, of the same material, screens which could be raised to act as walls whenever it rained.[33]

He bought land in Tahiti to grow vanilla, oranges, bananas, and limes for export. Thomas returned on his own to spend the winter in Tahiti for the next eight years.

After living a very different life in Tahiti, in 1923 the family travelled home to England via the US.[34] After only half an hour's driving lesson, Thomas drove them from San Francisco to Montreal.[35] He had never driven a car before, so the car salesman gave him ten minutes driving instruction and sat alongside him for the first twenty-five miles of the family's journey.[36] The salesman then returned to San Francisco with his wife, who had been driving behind them. The Dishers made it to their destination, although they often ran out of money because of the cost of repairs to the car, which was frequently damaged during the trip.[37]

In the summer, Gwen and her children were back in England to find that Richmal had been diagnosed with polio whilst on holiday in Cromer. Gwen refused to return to Tahiti later in the year and Thomas went back alone.[38] He spent most of the rest of his life living abroad. He could only tolerate the English climate, he wrote in his autobiography, 'if there were compensations in the way of outlets for my energies—but confiscatory rates of taxation made business expansion financially dangerous' in Britain.[39] It is possible he was in dispute with the UK tax authorities, and he certainly felt that British taxation inhibited his business prospects. Looking ahead to 1927, the sauce business was in trouble. He bought all the shares 'except for a few hundred put up by "Richmal Crompton."' [40] Thomas makes no other comment about his sister-in-law's support for him or, more probably from her point of view, for his family. Despite this investment, the business continued to struggle, in common with most of his other ventures.[41]

Thomas continued to keep in touch with his family on his frequent stays abroad, visiting occasionally. He lived with Gwen for short periods after the birth of their third child, Richmal, in March 1929.[42] His older daughter, Margaret suggests that:

> he wanted power over people and tried to dominate everyone in the family and his businesses. But he was up against Aunt Richmal. Twice he upset Mother

Fig. 7.1 Richmal and Gwen as girls[48]

so much that I had to phone Auntie to come to the house, which she did immediately. She was strong enough to oppose his bullying.[43]

In 1931, Gwen's marriage drove her to a nervous breakdown and Richmal sent her to a nursing home.[44] Thomas went abroad once again, leaving the children in Aunt Richmal's charge. On Gwen's return, she finally decided to divorce him, but Thomas was not asked to go for the last time until 1934. Richmal bought Gwen a house near to her own, which remained Gwen and Tommy's home until his death in 1983.[45] Richmal did not arrange for the house to be made over to Gwen until twenty years later, well after her divorce was finalised, thereby ensuring that it was not available as a capital asset to her ex-husband.[46] Thomas Disher married for a second and then a third time. He remained in touch with Gwen and asked her for help on occasions. Gwen and Thomas's second wife Freda were in touch with each other too. At the end of his autobiography, he writes that the unfairness of tax laws and the costs and difficulties of divorce inflicted on married men seemed incredible to him.[47] To say that he was a difficult man might seem like an understatement.

* * *

Crompton's novels touch on a fear of sex. Sex becomes a weapon for those men who seek to control their wives.[49] In *The Hidden Light* (1924), Crompton's second novel, Monica is struggling in her marriage and is suffocated by her husband Kenneth's emotional abuse and infidelity: 'He delighted to put her in a position of intolerable impotence.'[50] He is weak, selfish and incapable of understanding her.[51] Her husband is reluctant to go into detail about his business dealings, merely explaining to Monica that they involve buying and selling, sometimes in large quantities. When she meets him, he is running a wholesale stationery business that had belonged to his uncle. He is vain and 'always exaggerated the importance of anything connected with himself and was very sensitive as to whether his descriptions were entirely believed.'[52] Despite his affairs, Monica initially persuaded herself that it was her duty to stay with him and to keep the family together. When she leaves him, he hurts her in the most effective way possible by abducting their children and threatening that he will never allow her to see them again. She returns but refuses to have sex with him: 'He was beside himself. His face was ugly with passion…. A sudden murderous hatred of her was at his heart…. He could have killed her at that moment.'[53] Instead, he flings himself out of the house. Monica feels soiled and ashamed and 'even the hidden light of her spirit seemed darkened.'[54] He continues to lust after her, but she refuses to become one of his 'chain of mistresses.' Then, finally, he resorts to violence: 'Blind with rage he lurched towards her and shot out his fist. It caught her on the shoulder, and she fell back, catching at the bed-post as she fell.'[55]

Monica reflects painfully on what has happened: 'Where had she failed?'[56] In common with other women who have experienced domestic abuse, Monica's confidence has been completely undermined and she blames herself for the failures in her marriage. The blame, of course, lies with her husband, yet her experience of emotional abuse means that she tells herself that she should have tried harder and that if she had loved him enough the abuse would not have happened. When she is with her children, Sheila and Jimmie, life is not futile, and she feels able to carry on. Monica finds a potential escape route when she meets Phillip, an artist who falls in love with her. She decides that she cannot leave her husband because of her children.

At the end of the novel, Kenneth conveniently dies in a car crash, and she can be together with Phillip at last. In this early novel, the ending is romanticised, clichéd and unconvincing, but Crompton's description of Monica's abusive relationship with her husband is not. These are scenes of physical and emotional domestic abuse, in which Monica's confidence is destroyed and she feels that she must protect her children by staying. It can take many similar incidents, and even years, before some women in similar circumstances can overcome their lack of confidence and fear for themselves and their children and feel they can leave an abusive relationship, whilst many others are trapped and even killed. As Monica discovers, leaving, or threatening to do so, can be dangerous for both a woman and her children.

Crompton's novel reflects the lives of many women in the nineteen twenties and beyond. Domestic abuse was hidden within the boundaries of family life for thousands of them. They were ignored or criticised if they spoke about their abuse outside the home and many had to endure years of suffering in silence. Into the nineteen fifties 'many women remained silent and were silenced by family and friends on the question of abuse in the home.'[57] It was the early nineteen seventies before women's refuges and other services developed. The oppressive power of coercion, feelings of failure, concern about their children and the threat of or actual physical abuse, as well as poverty and the lack of financial independence, stifled women's ability to leave. They were often isolated and had no-one around to help or talk to them.

* * *

In comparison to Gwen's life, the life of William's sister is comfortable and secure. Ethel finds William annoying, and he tends to create havoc at events that she is either attending or organising. She is convinced, like her father, that William is mad. Ethel enjoys helping her mother with lunches, parties and local events, playing tennis, and worrying about love and marriage. She is one of William's 'permanent grievances against Life'[58]: There is a continual state of warfare between William and Ethel[59]:

> What Ethel gained in the authority that accrued to her added years she lost by that respect for appearances that frequently laid her at William's mercy, and so they were about equally matched as adversaries.[60]

William 'always avoided walking with Ethel. She objected to any interesting mode of progression.'[61]

The female sex is a mystery to William: 'Except in the case of his mother, he could see no reason for their existence. Yet he grudgingly admitted to himself that Ethel's admirers had not been useless to him.'[62] Hector, Ginger's older brother, and George, Douglas's brother, admire Ethel, much to the Outlaws' horror. William feels as 'deeply outraged as any of them.'[63] William has various battles with Ethel's boyfriends, and he only endeavours to improve her love life if it is to his own advantage.

For her part, Ethel cannot understand why her parents cannot do something about him, such as sending him to an orphanage, despite the fact that he is not an orphan, as Mrs Brown reminds her daughter.[64] Ethel is emphatic that William is unspeakably awful. Mrs Brown placidly points out that there are times, when he has a new suit on, that he looks quite sweet. William would not have been pleased to hear it.

Notes

1. Disher M., 56. Gwen may have attended Owen College in Manchester, where her father studied. It became the University of Manchester in 1903. Her course would have been under the auspices of the University of London.
2. *The Elphinian* 1990, 78.
3. Disher M., viii.
4. Ibid., 26–28.
5. Ibid., 28.
6. *Sixty Odd Years*, 48.
7. Disher, M., 26.
8. Ibid.
9. *Sixty Odd Years*, 49.
10. Stevenson, 136.
11. *Sixty Odd Years*, 49.
12. Ibid.
13. Ibid., 52.
14. Ibid., 49.
15. Ibid.
16. Disher, M., 29.
17. Ibid.
18. *Sixty Odd Years*, 50.
19. Disher M., 147.
20. Ibid., 21.
21. Ibid., 11.
22. Ibid., 25.
23. Ibid., 7.
24. *Sixty Odd Years*, 1.
25. Ibid., 56.
26. Ibid., 44.
27. Disher M., 29–31.

28. 31 and 68.
29. Ibid., 31.
30. Ibid. Also, *Bromley High School Magazine* 1921, 2.
31. Ibid., 32.
32. *Bromley High School Magazine* 1923, 4.
33. *Sixty Odd Years*, 95.
34. Disher, M., 47.
35. Ibid.
36. *Sixty Odd Years*, 97.
37. Disher, M., 48.
38. *Sixty Odd Years*, 111.
39. Ibid., 311.
40. Ibid., 137.
41. Ibid., 226.
42. Her full name was Richmal Crompton Lamburn Ashbee. She is usually known as Richmal Ashbee.
43. Disher, M., 129.
44. Ibid., 129.
45. Ibid., 130.
46. Ibid.
47. *Sixty Odd Years*, 312.
48. UoR RC/3/12/024.
49. For example, *Naomi Godstone, The House*.
50. *The Hidden Light*, 251.
51. Her ghost story *The House* (1926) and *Naomi Godstone* (1930) also feature an unhappy marriage in which a husband has been unfaithful.
52. *Hidden Light*, 31.
53. Ibid., 246.
54. Ibid., 247.
55. Ibid., 304.
56. Ibid., 307.
57. Fitz-Gibbon and Walklate, 132.
58. "William the Match-Maker," 133.
59. "William and the Spy," 23.
60. Ibid.
61. "The Sunday School Treat," 143.
62. "William and the White Cat," 92.
63. "Parrots for Ethel," 145.
64. "William and the Match-Maker," 152.

References

Crompton, Richmal. 1948. First published 1928. "Parrots for Ethel." In *William - The Good*, by Richmal Crompton, 145–178. London: George Newnes Ltd.
———. 1924. *The Hidden Light.* London: Hodder & Stoughton.
———. 1930. First published 1926. "The Sunday School Treat." In *William - The Conqueror*, by Richmal Crompton, 142–156. London: George Newnes Ltd.
———. 1984. First published 1925. "William and the Match-Maker." In *Still - William*, by Richmal Crompton, 127–152. Basingstoke, Hampshire: Macmillan Children's Books.
———. 1951. First published 1931. "William and the Spy." In *William's Crowded Hours*, by Richmal Crompton, 13–29. London: George Newnes Ltd.
———. 1961. First published 1923. "William and the White Cat." In *William Again*, by Richmal Crompton, 92–107. London: George Newnes Ltd.
Disher, Margaret. 1990. *Growing Up with Just William By His Sister.* London: The Outlaws Publishing Company.
Disher, Thomas Frederick Rhodes. 1954. *Sixty Odd Years.* London: Clerke & Cockeran.
Fitz-Gibbon, Kate and Sandra Walklate. 2018. *Gender, Crime and Criminal Justice.* Abingdon, OX: Routledge.
Stevenson, John. 1984. *British Society 1914-45.* London: Lane.

8

Birth of Richmal Crompton and William Brown

Amidst the domestic turmoil in her sister's marriage, the impact of the war and the additional ravages of the Spanish Flu, Richmal continued to teach at Bromley High School and embarked on her career as a published writer from 1918. Crompton is one of the few women who had a hugely successful career in the early to mid-twentieth century and she is recognised as such by many William fans. There has been limited wider recognition of her achievements. We do not know whether she had an opportunity to marry. It is clear that she was determined to establish herself as a published writer. In pursuit of her ambition, she wrote hundreds of short stories for magazines, including stories about children for adults, like the William stories, a few early romantic stories about love, loss and happiness, other stories about motherhood, families, friendship, and life in a small community, as well as light domestic sketches. In keeping with other women writers of the interwar period, some of her novels and short stories are concerned with women characters who face a choice between marriage or a career.

* * *

Richmal Crompton's earliest known published story to date, 'Thomas, A Little Boy Who Would Grow Up,' appeared in *Girl's Own Paper*, for girls and young women, in January 1918, followed by 'Mrs Tempest' in April of the same year. First published in 1880, according to Mary Cadogan, a previous biographer of Crompton and an expert in children's literature, the *Girls Own Paper* 'addressed itself to both mistresses and servants.'[1] After 1908 it became

© The Author(s), under exclusive license to Springer Nature Switzerland AG 2022
J. McVeigh, *Richmal Crompton, Author of Just William*, Literary Lives, https://doi.org/10.1007/978-3-030-96511-2_8

increasingly liberal, although by 1915 the *Girls Own Paper* remained cautious about what it called, 'the free and militant woman' campaigning for women's suffrage.[2] It aimed to cater for twelve to twenty-five-year-olds.[3] The magazine 'concealed its religious affiliation and avoided over moralizing.'[4] It catered 'both to the majority of girls who expected to become wives and mothers and the growing minority who sought education and careers.'[5] From early in her career, Crompton was writing for a wide age range of readers, albeit in a publication that 'saw girls as supporters of male-inspired ventures, and not innovators.'[6]

'Thomas' tells the story of the moment Thomas decides to grow up and cut off his curls, despite his mother's love of his beautiful curly hair. His friend William decides that he can no longer sit beside him after he has cut off his own curls and has started to wear more grown-up clothes. Thomas fights his friend after William accuses him of looking like a kid. William respects his successful adversary, helps Thomas change his appearance too and his childish curls are no more. Rather than giving up after William had rejected his friendship, Thomas decides to fight for his reputation and to cross over himself into adulthood, even if this means risking his mother's love for 'her curly headed baby.' However, she does not reject him and instead welcomes her more grown-up son into their lives.[7] What it takes to grow up, the struggles to be faced along the way, balancing pressures from friends and family, and the extent to which mothers try to control their offspring's lives, interested Crompton from the very beginning of her writing life.

Richmal was successful with two other stories submitted during 1918, 'The First Arrow' and 'One Crowded Hour,' both written under the name R.C. Lamburn, which appeared in *Woman At Home* magazine for August and September, respectively. 'One Crowded Hour' features Robert Green 'the bad boy of the neighbourhood.'[8] He was always rude, always rough, always dirty, and always greedy, as well as 'disobedient, gloriously, recklessly wicked.'[9] He meets Marie Elizabeth who is the good girl of the neighbourhood and lisps. When she wailed, Robert 'surrendered hastily.'[10] Both Robert and Marie Elizabeth share characteristics of Crompton's more famous William and Violet Elizabeth and read like early prototypes. Despite being lawless and refusing to play with girls, Robert agrees at the end of the story that if he sees Marie Elizabeth in the park some time, he might look at her. He certainly does not promise to play with her.

Then, in February 1919, William Brown was 'born' in 'Rice-Mould,' published in *Home Magazine*.[11] The second William story published the following month, 'The Outlaws,' introduced Ginger, Douglas and Henry, and their meeting place in the old barn. From the very outset, the future of their friendship was laid. The rest, as they say, is history. Crompton received three pounds for 'Rice-Mould.'[12]

Three years after 'Rice-Mould,' Newnes published the first William books, *Just William* (1922) and *More William* (1922), based on collections of the stories that first appeared in *Home Magazine*.[13] Turning briefly to the future, the stories in the William books were initially published individually in magazines until the early nineteen fifties; the last book largely based on previously published stories was *William and the Moon Rocket* (1954).[14] After that, the stories were written for publication in the books. The early stories moved to *The Happy Mag* from January 1923 until May 1940. Crompton did not publish her first novel until 1923, shortly after the William stories moved to the *Happy Mag*. Norman Wright suggests that 'William was far more at home in this family magazine than he had been in the rather high-brow *Woman's Home Magazine* and he soon became one of *Happy Mag's* star attractions.'[15] There is a story that may never be told about why they were moved and whether this had an impact on Crompton's professional reputation. In just a few years, she was established as a popular author, and the stories clearly attracted readers of *Home Magazine*. The move away from this 'highbrow' magazine would have influenced readers' perception about the type of stories she wrote and her status as an author writing for children and adults in the eyes of her peers, as well as gatekeepers such as publishers, journalists and booksellers.

Only six months or so later in 1923, she was fighting for her life having contracted polio while on holiday in Cromer and her sister was short of money in a difficult marriage, after her niece and nephew had been abducted in 1922. She was no longer in a position to write what she wanted after she lost her job in teaching, nor perhaps to negotiate for continued publication in a magazine of her choice, or even to write the kind of fiction she wanted. Crompton needed to earn a living to support at least two adults and two children, as well as herself. Of course, this is conjecture, but her career might have taken a different course if the William stories had not moved away from *Home Magazine*, her family's life had not been traumatic in 1922, and she had not lived with a long-term disability from the summer of 1923. Life can change in key moments with potential opportunities lost forever, although no doubt new ones present themselves too.

As Michael Wace has noted, the twenties was a period 'when children's comics and family and women's magazines flourished; it was these publications which carried much of the contemporary writing for children.'[16] In keeping with the *Girls Own Paper*, they reached readers of all ages. As well as William stories, Crompton published many other short stories in these magazines. These included light-hearted love stories that were not republished in any of her books of short stories and are not her best work, such as 'The Dramatic Moment' and 'Journey's End.' [17] In 1920, Richmal published several stories in *Punch*, again under the name R.C. Lamburn, and several were also published in *Time and Tide*. Her most interesting contribution to the latter is 'The Instinct of Suspicion,' published in 1921. This is a rare opinion piece in which Crompton's voice is clear and critical: 'The ordinary average Englishman and Englishwoman regard everyone they do not know with the darkest suspicion,' she writes. 'We are not inclined to give them the benefit of doubt.... While they are strangers we hate and despise them.'[18] Harsh words indeed. David Schutte suggests that there are many more stories and short humorous pieces published by Crompton in magazines waiting to be rediscovered by researchers, in addition to those that were republished in her ten short stories collections that do not feature William.[19]

During the nineteen twenties, Crompton wrote new William stories for magazines and published ten William books, twelve novels and eight other short story collections. What is clear is that Richmal Crompton was an ambitious, driven and incredibly hardworking author, keen to make her way in literary life, and to earn her living as an author. Her huge output may be one reason why the reputation of her best novels suffered. Some of her short stories are fluffy romances or comic sketches and one senses that they were primarily written for money. Her other writing makes it clear that she was not only creating light stories but, like many authors before and since, she had to make a living to support herself and her family and the quality of her fiction varies at times as a result.

In the five years after her move to Bromley, Crompton established her professional career. As a teacher, Richmal's income was comfortable when she moved to Bromley and, only a year after her move South, this increased considerably as she earned additional income from her writing.[20] Currently we do not know if she had written any of her early stories when she was studying at Royal Holloway or working at St Elphin's, and whether she wanted to publish any before she moved to Bromley, or whether indeed she had; if so, they are lost or lie undiscovered somewhere. At the very least, it is surprising and remarkable that from 1918 she established herself so quickly as a published author, earning her living from her writing when she was also coping with a new job, buying her own home, and supporting her sister and young children financially.

Over the next ten years, her success brought both wealth and responsibility. By 1950, Richmal was still being extraordinarily generous and supportive of her family. Whether her generosity meant that she was always a benign influence on her family's lives, or whether there were some strings attached to her financial contributions, is unclear. Family memory would suggest that her benevolence was indeed benevolent.

* * *

Crompton's growing success and wealth is represented in the homes she bought after her move to Kent. In addition to buying a nice detached home in 1917, she was able to commission a grander new home in 1927, still in Bromley, and in the early thirties she went on to buy a house nearby for Gwen when her marriage broke down.

When she first moved to Kent, Richmal purchased a double-fronted Victorian villa in Bromley Common village. Clara joined her in her new home, and they would live together until Clara's death in 1939. Margaret, Gwen's eldest child, describes visiting Bromley Common village, which had:

> several large farms, extensive orchards, a village school and church hall ... an old rambling vicarage, a market garden, a policeman and a row of small shops ... a butcher, baker, draper, wine merchant and post office. A large part of the local orchards was devoted to cherry trees.[21]

A pond on the corner of Cherry Orchard Road was a favourite haunt for Gwen's children and farms, orchards and a large market garden were in the area, and they had the convenience of a grocery store opposite the house. Nearby was a large Queen Anne-style country house, The Rookery, where most of the charity Sales of Work and garden fetes were held.[22] It is notable that Richmal's status as a property owner was unusual, not least because she was a woman. It was not until 1926 that married and single women could hold and dispose of their property on the same terms as men.[23] In 1918, less than a quarter of UK homes were owner-occupied.[24]

By the end of the nineteen twenties, Richmal Crompton was a successful author of William stories and could afford to build a larger double-fronted home and garden, The Glebe. Built in 1927, the house was designed by architects in a Queen Anne style.[25] They were directed by Clara who, according to her granddaughter Margaret, told them exactly what to do.[26] Richmal's library held books on gardening that feature the care of roses.[27] This does not necessarily suggest that she was particularly fond of roses herself. We learn in one of Edward's letters to his future wife of her love of roses: 'The Rose is your favourite flower, is it not?' he asks her.[28] Roses proliferated in the garden of The Glebe. The tiny detail in Edward's letter suggests that the garden might have been her mother's domain, rather than Richmal's, or at least designed with her preferences in mind. The house was large enough to host regular visits from family travelling south from Bury and other guests.

The Glebe is a grand house sharply symmetrical with a portico in the centre, reached through a short but impressively wide drive, surrounded by walls. It would have been at home in Chesham had Edward and Clara been able to afford a similar house. It is evocative of the Baroque mansions of the eighteenth century, including The Rookery. It is certainly different from the comfortable, smaller, and private house hidden from the road that Richmal bought for herself many years later in Chislehurst, Kent.

* * *

Crompton's writing reflects social changes in property ownership in the nineteen twenties and thirties, and beyond. In 1925, in the William stories, the nouveau riche Mr and Mrs Bott, Violet Elizabeth's parents, are initially tenants of the local Hall, no doubt taking advantage of the property's owners changing fortunes. The Hall is empty most of the year, reflecting the financial struggles of wealthy landowners of the period.[29] By 1964, the Botts own the Hall, 'with its billiard room, library, ten bedrooms, commanding prospect and extensive grounds.'[30]

The style of The Glebe is evocative of larger and grander houses eulogised in fiction by other writers in this period and into the thirties, which British academic Alexandra Harris identifies as a form of romantic modernism: 'If the dream of the 1930s was to recapture a sense of belonging to particular stretches of country, the nightmare was to find these places irrevocably changed.'[31] Harris suggests that 'George Orwell, Evelyn Waugh, Graham Greene: these are very different kinds of writers with very different political vantage points. But related images of the violated landscape recur across their work.'[32] It is a sensibility that Crompton captures in her novels *Roofs Off* (1928), *Chedsy Place* (1934) and *There Are Four Seasons* (1937).

In *Roofs Off* (1928), we meet Martin who has recently moved to a small estate of new houses, built on land previously owned by a wealthy landowner. He acts as an observer of the goings-on around him, like a village *flaneur*, as he moves from house to house getting to know his neighbours. We often see the world through his eyes, as we similarly see the Brown's family and community through William's.[33] In this novel, families who have previously lived on inherited wealth find themselves living beside working people who run shops and other businesses. It is a real social mix of working, middle- and upper-class families. The novel asks questions about what we really value; are money and status more important than friendship and the ability to adapt as the world changes around us?

The novel was published in the nineteen twenties when new housing estates were being built in Kent, Surrey and Hertfordshire: 'These were carefully landscaped, with the houses, often detached villas in substantial grounds, artfully grouped around closes, cul-de-sacs or country lanes,' like the estate in *Roofs Off*.[34] These developments offered both a rural character and access to urban areas. A surge of house building in the UK for private purchase by the middle-class followed in the nineteen thirties when home ownership became the principal aspiration of the bourgeois, which historian Ross McKibbin argues, 'more than anything else defined the character of the English middle classes.'[35]

In *Chedsy Place*, the owner of a large house with grounds opens the house to paying guests for the weekend. His wife looks ahead and hopes their new venture will raise vital funds to support the future of their inheritance.[36] Her husband, and the wealthy landowner in *Roofs Off*, struggle to accept the change in their fortunes.

Readers interested in British society in the thirties and the build-up to war could also read Crompton's *There Are Four Seasons* (1937). We journey through Vicky's ordinary life as she grows up, marries, and has a family. At the end of her life:

> Vicky's thoughts went back again over her life. It hadn't been very eventful, but then few people's lives were eventful. It had consisted chiefly in a gradual shifting of relationships. Andrew [her gardener] was the most stable relationship that life had given her.... The world was very beautiful. It was a pity that people were generally too busy or worried to notice it. She remembered Philip [her husband]—or was it Noel?—reading her a poem that began:

> > Look thy last on all things lovely
> > Every hour....

> You had time, of course, to notice how beautiful the world was when you were old.[37]

The novel ends with this quotation from Walter de La Mere's poem *Fare Well*, published in 1917, as Vicky falls asleep and possibly dies.[38] This novel is more than a journey through an ordinary woman's life, the life of someone who lived in comfort and material wealth in a lovely house with a beautiful garden. Vicky's bond with her garden and her gardener Andrew represents her belief in pastoral and domestic values as the seasons in life come and go on a reassuring cycle. She is not held unwillingly within the gate and walls of her home and finds peace in her garden that becomes her sanctuary and an escape from the harsh realities of life outside. Andrew, the gardener, is her protector and 'would willingly and without question have given his life for her. All feudal England lay at the heart of their relationship.'[39] Is this just a rural saga and the life story of a privileged woman who lives in a rural idyll, marries, has children, and retires to a smaller property in old age supported by her faithful gardener? It promotes a complacent vision of a romantic idyll that is under threat and within which Vicky hides away from the insecurities and fault lines in her life, failing to do anything to protect the world she loves. The novel can be understood as a critique of the complacency of rural landowners at the end of the thirties and the foreboding threat of war. The world she loves will not fare well in the conflict to come.

McKibbin places Crompton firmly within the middle-class world she knew. He suggests that:

> As a writer, in general intelligence and style, Richmal Crompton is in a class by herself ... [the William stories] were exceptionally deft satires of Southern English middle-class life, Crompton's classical training shows: the language is Latinate and not necessarily easy going for younger readers.
>
> William's social origins are carefully kept indistinct. It is never quite certain what sort of middle-class William's family is; they are 'comfortable' and Mr Brown is a 'businessman'; but they are not grand, and easily intimidated by those who are.... Their own house begins as a modern semi-detached, but at some point detaches itself. Nor is it quite certain what kind of school William attends.... Crompton's middle class is more like Agatha Christie's: comfortable, reticent, domesticated, garden loving.[40]

On the one hand, Crompton's world does seem safe, conventional, middle and mainstream, but just look below the surface and her satire often sheds much of this veneer. However, in some of the novels that lack her comic touch and more explicit satirical eye this is easy to miss.

* * *

Home can be a sanctuary and a bolthole where we plot and experience our most exciting adventures, as William knows only too well. The Outlaws have their own special home from home, a barn, which is quite separate from the houses where they live with their families. The barn is the castle where William rules supreme and the Outlaws plan their adventures. It is the venue for many of William's most rousing speeches and many of their activities. In one story, Douglas gloomily remarks that they cannot hold a circus in the barn because it is not much of a place:

The old barn was certainly a ramshackle affair. The roof leaked; the floor was generally three or four inches deep in mud; the windows were broken and the walls consisted chiefly of ventilation. The place was dear to the Outlaws hearts, but they felt that as a show place it was hardly worthy of them. They felt that it might both figuratively and literally have a damping effect upon a circus.[41]

In another later story published in 1966, the Outlaws fear that the barn itself is in danger of being knocked down to make way for a new housing development. Their fears are unfounded, but they are really upset by the thought of losing it:

It partook of the nature of home for them even more than those neat dwellings where they ate and slept and conformed - in a greater or lesser degree - to the rule of Authority. They had taken all this for granted. They hadn't thought about it - till today. And today - faced by the monstrous possibility of its loss - they were dumbfounded and appalled.[42]

The barn is the meeting place for knights of the square table, a venue for a political husting, an exhibition hall, a theatre, a den for kidnappers and a nightclub. It is the place where the Outlaws meet to plot and plan, perform, and gloomily reflect on the persistent inability of the adult world, often in the form of their parents, to understand them. It is the site that symbolises, despite interruptions from the annoying Violet Elizabeth Bott, the boys' comradeship. It is their castle which they will defend undauntingly against the incursions of anyone who seeks to attack it or gain access. Well, almost anyone. Violet Elizabeth, who we will meet in a later chapter, always manages to gain entry no matter how hard they try to raise the drawbridge and keep her out. Violet Elizabeth wants to marry and play 'houth' with William, whilst he would only consider marrying and setting up a home with Joan, the girl who lives next door.[43] Richmal herself did not marry.

Notes

1. Cadogan, with Patricia Craig, 74. Also see other books by Mary Cadogan: *The Woman Behind William* (1986), *The William Companion* (1990) and *Just William Through the Ages* (1994). Also, *Just Richmal* (1986) by Kay Williams.
2. Ibid., 87.
3. Avery, 206.
4. Altholz, 55.

5. Ibid.
6. Cadogan and Craig, 87.
7. See a copy of the story in the *JWSM* 7 January 1999, 4–8.
8. See a copy of the story in *JWSM* 23 Winter 2008, 12–18.
9. *JWSM* 23, 12.
10. Ibid., 15.
11. Schutte, *William – The Immortal*, 10.
12. Wace, *Publishing Tradition*, 252.
13. See David Schutte, *JWSM* 30, 21–26. David Schutte records that from 1925–1942, Crompton sold over 1.8 million William books, which Schutte estimates is a rough average of 100,000 per year (26). Crompton's first William stories are published in *Just William* (1922) - including "The Outlaws" March 1919, "William Goes to the Pictures" April 1919, and "Jumble" June 1919 - and *More William* (1922), including "Rice Mould" February 1919. See Schutte, *William – The Immortal*, 8 and 10.
14. Schutte, *William – The Immortal*, 72. Schutte lists the stories published in *Home Magazine* (February 1919 to October 1922), *The Happy Mag* (December 1922 to May 1940), *Modern Woman* (August 1940 to May 1946), *Homes and Gardens* (June 1943, May 1944, November 1945) and *Home Notes* (January 1947 to September 1954) in his bibliography, 86–91 and 98–99.
15. Wright, 34.
16. Wace, *Publishing Tradition*, 251. See Michael Wace's article on publications by Macmillan in *JWSM* 4. Macmillan published four to seven thousand of each novel from 1932 to 1938, of which the majority were sold to libraries (17). A publication advance of £200 for several of these novels compares favourably with contemporary manager's salaries at Macmillan in the same period (17). Also, see *JWSM* 17 Winter 2006.
17. See copies in *JWSM* 6 and 31 respectively.
18. "Instinct of Suspicion," 1028. Other stories Crompton published in *Time and Tide* are "The Back Garden" 6 April 1923, "I'll Just Have a Look at the Paper" 15 June 1923, "Felicia" 11 July 1924, "Glamour" 19 September 1924 in which a young boy is captivated by Helen during the siege of Troy.
19. Schutte, *JWSM* 31, 39 and 40–43. Crompton published in the *Humorist*, the *Windsor Magazine*, *Pearson's Magazine* and *London Opinion*, among others. Schutte has listed some of the stories that await rediscovering in this article. This is a rich source for future research on Crompton's work.

20. Schutte, *JWSM* 30, 23. Schutte has identified that in 1924, when she had given up teaching, Crompton earnt three times her teaching salary.
21. Disher, M., 71.
22. Ibid., 74.
23. Stevenson, 169.
24. Humphrys, Julian. "A Brief History of Home Ownership in Britain" BBC History Magazine, March 2014. A brief history of home ownership in Britain – HistoryExtra.
25. Disher, M., 103.
26. Ibid.
27. Crompton's library from her last home is held in her archive at the University of Roehampton.
28. Letters that are part of family records.
29. "The Sweet Little Girl in White," 32.
30. Ibid. and "Mrs Bott and the Portrait," 147.
31. Harris, 174.
32. Ibid., 176.
33. The notion of a *flaneur* is discussed in Chapter 14. A *flaneur* or *flaneuse* are most typically found in cities where they wander amidst their contemporaries observing the world around them. Here the idea is being transferred to a village setting.
34. McKibbin, 76.
35. Ibid., 73–74.
36. Chiara Briganti and Kathy Mezei refer to a comparable novel by Stella Gibbon, *Bassett* (1934), in which an Edwardian country house is turned into a successful boarding house. They argue that 'Like so many literary houses, it stands as an effective marker of changing social and economic conditions' (22).
37. *There Are Four Seasons*, 288.
38. Published in *The Sunken Garden* (1917).
39. *There Are Four Seasons*, 287.
40. McKibbin, 502.
41. "William's Mammoth Circus," 107.
42. "William and the Donkey," 55.
43. "William the Match-Maker," 135 and "William and Saint Valentine," 254.

References

Altholz, Josef. 1989. *The Religious Press in Britain, 1760-1900*. London: Greenwood.

Avery, Gillian. 1975. *Childhood's Pattern: A Study of the Heroes and Heroines of Children's Fiction, 1770-1950*. London: Hodder & Stoughton.

Briganti, Chiara and Kathy Mezei. 2006. *Domestic Modernism, the Interwar Novel and E.H. Young*. Hampshire: Ashgate.

Cadogan, Mary and Patricia Craig. 1976. *You're A Brick, Angela! A New Look at Girls' Fiction from 1839 to 1975*. London: Victor Gollancz.

Crompton, Richmal. 1992. First published 1964. "Mrs Bott and the Portrait." In *William and the Witch*, by Richmal Crompton, 145–185. Basingstoke, Hampshire: Macmillan Children's Books.

———. 1984. First published 1925. "The Sweet Little Girl in White." In *Still - William*, by Richmal Crompton, 32–53. Basingstoke, Hampshire: Macmillan Children's Books.

———. 1937. *There Are Four Seasons*. London: Macmillan.

———. 1921. "The Instinct of Suspicion." *Time and Tide*, 28 October: 1028.

———. 1984. First published 1925. "William and Saint Valentine." In *Still - William*, by Richmal Crompton, 236–254. Basingstoke, Hampshire: Macmillan Children's Books.

———. 1993. First published 1966. "William and the Donkey." In *William and the Masked Ranger*, by Richmal Crompton, 53–87. Basingstoke, Hampshire: Pan Macmillan Children's Books.

———. 1984. First published 1925. "William the Match-Maker." In *Still - William*, by Richmal Crompton, 127–152. Basingstoke, Hampshire: Macmillan Children's Books.

———. 1927. "William's Mammoth Circus." In *Wiliam - In Trouble*, by Richmal Crompton, 106–134. London: George Newnes Ltd.

Disher, Margaret. 1990. *Growing Up with Just William By His Sister*. London: The Outlaws Publishing Company.

Harris, Alexandra. 2010. *Romantic Moderns: English Writers, Artists and the Imagination from Virginia Woolf to John Piper*. London: Thomas Hudson.

McKibbin, Ross. 2000. First published 1998. *Classes and Cultures England 1918-1951*. Oxford: Oxford University Press.

Schutte, David. Summer 2012. "Richmal Crompton's Account Books (Part One)." *The Just William Society Magazine 30* 21–26.

———. Winter 2012. "Richmal Crompton's Account Books (Part Two)." *The Just William Society Magazine 31* 38–43.

———. 1993. *William - The Immortal An Illustrated Bibliography*. Stedham, Midhurst: West Sussex: David Schutte.

Stevenson, John. 1984. *British Society 1914-45*. London: Lane.

Wace, Michael. 2002. "From Carroll to Crompton: The work of a children's publisher." In *Macmillan: A Publishing Tradition*, by Elizabeth James Ed., 242–255. Basingstoke, Hampshire: Palgrave.

———. June 1997. "Richmal and Macmillan: Publishing the Novels." *The Just William Society Magazine 4* 16–19.

———. Winter 2006. "William Makes Things Hum." *The Just William Society Magazine 17* 13–14.

Wright, Norman. May 2005. "The William Books of Richmal Crompton." *Book and Magazine Collector* 26–39.

9

More than Aunt Richmal, the Spinster

One of the unanswered questions about Richmal's life is whether before 1922, when the first of her hugely successful William collections were published and she was already thirty-two, she made a choice not to marry and to dedicate herself to a life of writing, which seems unlikely, or whether wider circumstances meant that she did not have the opportunity to do so. Before 1914, the numbers of unmarried women increased following a massive outflow of young male emigrants leaving the country in search of a new life abroad. In 1911–1913, almost half a million young men emigrated.[1] This had a significant impact on young people's marriage prospects.[2] Richmal's brother Jack had joined them. When she was in her twenties and thirties and for most of the interwar period, unmarried women far outnumbered men of the same age group, and 'about one-third of all women who had not married by the age of twenty-nine did not marry during their reproductive years.'[3]

In *Anne Morrison*, a novel that reputedly draws on Richmal's early life, Anne is pursued by Harold, who is killed in the First World War. Anne does not love him: 'He had sent his love to her as he was dying. Anne looked back at her friendship with him with deep regret.'[4] We do not know if Richmal had the chance to marry in this period and whether she loved and lost a young soldier during the First World War, or whether she avoided a potential relationship. She remained unmarried and this was unlikely to change after she entered her thirties in November 1920.

© The Author(s), under exclusive license to Springer Nature
Switzerland AG 2022
J. McVeigh, *Richmal Crompton, Author of Just William*, Literary Lives,
https://doi.org/10.1007/978-3-030-96511-2_9

We read of the experience of single women in novels by women writers in this period, in which the devastation caused by war, the impact of emigration and, perhaps for some, the stigma of being too clever and well-educated, meant marriage was elusive or out of reach.[5] Women's novels in the interwar period did not accept the caricature of an old maid as either a failure or desperate to find a man.[6] These young women wanted to build a life of purpose and self-determination: 'marriage is rejected precisely because it is seen as an imposed rather than a natural condition, a threat to their precious sense of personal autonomy.'[7] In *The Crowded Street* (1924) by Winifred Holtby, Muriel feels that if she marries she would 'have to give up every new thing that has made me a person.'[8] She would rather take her life in her hands to see what she can make of it.

Crompton is also interested in the lives of young women who find their way in life on their own, and whether they do so out of choice or convention, as well as others who decide to marry.[9] Some of her fictional characters go on to have careers, such as teaching or politics, or choose to travel, whilst others choose to marry and bring up a family, despite initial aspirations to follow other dreams and 'see the world.' Others do not marry and yet still have significant responsibilities within their families. These young women realise that many adventures take place in their own homes, if you know where to look for them, and that you can see much of the world from your own doorstep, although several have little choice about whether to stay in the home of a relative and work as unpaid carers and housekeepers.

In *The Ridleys* (1947), Celia becomes a teacher. Early in the novel, Celia challenges her brother who disapproves of her plans to have a career:

> "The reason why men don't like educated women is that they're afraid that if women are taught to use their minds they'll see men as they really are and not as they like to be seen—little tin gods of creation."
>
> "You can talk what nonsense you like. You're not going to college and there's an end of it....
>
> "... Have you read A Doll's House?"
>
> "No."
>
> "Norah says---"
>
> "I don't want to know what Norah or any other blasted fool says," shouted Harold.[10]

In Henrik Ibsen's *A Doll's House* (1879), Nora leaves her husband and children, and says, 'I can no longer content myself with what most people say, or with what is found in books. I must think over things for myself and get to understand them.'[11] Celia and other women characters in Crompton's novels want to have the opportunity to do the same. In another novel published a decade earlier, *Caroline* (1936), Caroline's mother Philippa, like Nora, leaves her husband and young children in pursuit of a new life. Crompton presents her choice as positive and empowering, and she is not punished for her decision.

In Crompton's *Marriage of Hermione* (1932), Helen, Hermione's only sister, is ten years her senior, and so beautiful that everyone predicts a brilliant match for her. Helen has similar aspirations to Celia:

> Unfortunately … she had developed Ideas. Ideas about Education. Looking at the world around her, she had noticed the difference between the education of the two sexes, and it had filled her with a noble frenzy of indignation.… It was scandalous, it was preposterous.… People in general laid the blame on her father. He should not have taught her the classics. Classics, of course, were all right for boys. They were indeed necessary to the Formation of a Gentleman. But for a Young Lady they were unsuitable. They tended to Oddness, and Oddness was the one thing to be avoided.[12]

Richmal was deeply committed to her role as a teacher and as an author whose intellectual and spiritual life inspired her writing. Like Helen, she followed in her father's footsteps, but this might have meant that at times she too was considered odd and, at the very least, a bluestocking. We have the impression that it was in the life of her mind that she found her sense of self and her own way of seeing the world, as she tries in her writing to understand why people behave as they do. Thinking for herself, like Nora, sums up her life as a writer and is at the heart of her identity as a professional woman and as an author. Her mischievous humour and inspired imagination are inherent to her view of the world and live alongside her Ideas.

One of Crompton's short stories is evocative of Virginia Woolf's iconic call for women writers to have *A Room of One's Own* (1929): 'a woman must have money and a room of her own if she is to write fiction,' wrote Woolf, as Crompton must have already known from her own experience.[13] In 'Martin Ford,' published in *A Monstrous Regiment* (1927), Evelyn Ross writes under the pseudonym Martin Ford. She hides her writing life from her husband. The story opens as she 'entered her study, closed the door, and drew a deep breath. The study was her sanctuary. It was the only room in the house that did not reflect her husband's taste.'[14] Evelyn's study is the place where she can be herself, write her successful stories and hide away from her husband's overpowering influence. She is shocked to find out that he is also a famous author and is writing under a pseudonym too. He tells her that he is keen to take over the study now that his authorial identity has been revealed. Evelyn decides that she must conceal hers and yields to his request. She throws all traces of her life as a writer into the fire and, in her case, 'Nothing—nothing was to be left her.... She dared not think of the emptiness that lay before her.'[15] Unlike Bridget, Crompton's main protagonist in *The Innermost Room* who, at the end of the novel, willingly gives up her life as a writer to marry, Evelyn is reluctant and fearful. In these stories, it is not possible to be both a writer and a wife.

Several women in Crompton's novels are unable to marry because of the expectation that as single women they will give up their own dreams for others. On the face of it, Crompton's Millicent Dorrington is unable to take advantage of the opportunities that come her way and she remains single, dedicating her life to her family. In the novel, Crompton uses strong metaphors to give us a sense of how Millicent feels as a single woman who is trapped at home looking after her family after the death of her parents.

Millicent is the only person in her family close to their father and they spend many hours reading together in his study after the death of her mother. She is initially daunted by their new home's high walls and gate, which make her feel shut in.[16] Her father tells her that she can always open the gate and go out, but he wonders if she will. After his sudden death, Millicent gives up a new life with her fiancé to look after her younger sisters. Having decided to take on the role of surrogate mother to her siblings, her brother shuts the gates: 'They shut with a dull reverberating clang of metal.'[17] As she grows older, Millicent tries to escape, but the demands of her siblings and her decision to stay and look after them keeps preventing her from doing so. Like Hero, David Wilding's wife in the Wildings trilogy, she hangs on to the hope of a future career as a professional singer:

> Twice the gates had closed on her, but this key would one day open them and let her out. She must not let her key rust. It must always be there ready. She looked upon her real life as not yet begun.... This was not her life, it was other people's lives—Cecily's, Lorna's, Doris's ... and dearly as she loved them, she yet looked forward with a secret thrill to a life of her own someday.[18]

In the meantime, her father's old study is her refuge, the stronghold, the citadel of the house, which she is never, after all, able or willing to leave. Following her death, her married sisters feel that, as a single woman without children, Millicent has had an empty and wasted life and that fear had held her back and made her turn down opportunities for a career or marriage. Her brother disagrees: 'No one's life is empty unless they deliberately make it so, and Millie didn't.'[19] Another sister, Doris, who is an M.P. and is unmarried herself, argues that there is more to life than sexual relationships and marriage.

Doris believes that the strength of Millicent's instinct to be a mother to her siblings was the explanation of her whole life.[20]

Caroline (1936), published nearly a decade after *Millicent Dorrington*, is another story about the pitfalls of being a surrogate mother to your siblings. Here Crompton takes a more satirical stance and is less sympathetic towards her heroine. Crompton's comedy questions Caroline's selfless sacrifice when she gives up a place at university to support her siblings after her mother leaves home when Caroline is a child and both her father and stepmother die. Caroline's constant support has always surrounded her sister Fay's life, but at eighteen it is suffocating and prevents her doing anything that Caroline disapproves of. Fay guiltily feels disloyal, grudging, and ungrateful. As Caroline tells everyone, she has dedicated her life to bringing up Fay and her older brother and sister. One can almost smell the whiff of a burning martyr. What she does not tell them is that she controls every aspect of their lives, interfering in all their plans for the future. She is stifling Fay, who has been persuaded by Caroline to give up music so that she can pursue the career as a teacher that Caroline had always wanted for herself.

Out of the blue, many years later when the children are all grown up, her mother Philippa asks to come home. Caroline can envisage holding 'out hands of love and pity to rescue her [mother] from the sordidness into which she had inevitably sunk.'[21] She imagines her mother as a wretched broken-down woman falling sobbing into her arms. Her mother, however, has no intention of doing so. She is strong, positive and unrepentant and, much to Caroline's chagrin, everyone thinks she is wonderful.

Philippa and Caroline battle it out, as her mother gradually tries to loosen the chains that restrict the lives not only of Caroline's siblings, but of Caroline too. Can Caroline learn to let go, to give up the patronising control that has dominated all their lives for so long and to develop a life of her own? An astute review of the novel when it was first published captures its poignancy:

> We see [Caroline] gradually developing into a sort of professional, self-sacrificing, always well intentioned, always, in a way, thinking of others and giving herself for them, but, in the long run, breaking them to her own desires, poisoning them with her sweetness, and spoiling their lives by meddling with them in the guise of a narrow minded, purblind, misunderstanding petty providence.... it is an unmistakable lesson for the many over-conscientious would-be doers of good, who end up by being doers of all but irreparable evil. Fortunately, *Caroline* is a romance ... It lightens what might have been tragedy into a species of serious, but not too serious, comedy. *Caroline* might do well on the stage.[22]

So, how do we view the choices made by Evelyn, Millicent, Philippa, or Caroline? *Millicent Dorrington* is a novel of Crompton's early career, whilst *Caroline* has a sharper, more ironic edge and was published when she was in her mid-forties and some of her youthful passion as a writer has faded.

In her novels and short stories, Crompton writes about women and mothers who are faced with the same kind of choices Nora had to make. Some, like Mrs Fowler, choose to stay and can find resolution in life as a mother and wife, others, like Nora, decide to remain single, or leave both their husband and children, such as Philippa. Sometimes Fate takes a hand, as William knows only too well. The impact of emigration, her closeted career at a boarding school for many years, the death of her father, and the tragic loss of young men in the First World War, plus an increasing need to support her family, would have influenced whether Richmal had the opportunity to marry and become a mother. Her friendships with women were important to her, but there is no conclusive evidence to suggest that these reflected her sexuality. Her relationship with her mother, sister and niece were at the centre of her daily life for many years. After she left home at eleven years old, Richmal lived with other women at school, university and at home until she lived alone from her early fifties. Following her move to Kent, she was committed to her professional life as a teacher and an emerging career as an author. Her role as an aunt and the head of her family in Kent lay at the heart of her personal life.

* * *

'It all began with William's aunt,' declares the opening line of the first William book published a hundred years ago in 1922. This particular aunt is in a good temper, which is unusual for any aunt of William Brown's, especially when they are in his company. She gives William some money, one of the main reasons for the existence of any aunt, at least from William's point of view.

In 'A Busy Day,' three aunts stay with the Browns on Christmas Day:

> The aunts sat round the drawing-room fire talking and doing crotchet-work. In this consists the whole art and duty of aunthood. *All* aunts do crotchet-work.... The aunts [are] in the drawing-room discussing over their crotchet-work the terrible way in which their sisters had brought up their children. That, also, is a necessary part of aunthood.[23]

William discovers, as they do, that a busy day is not necessarily a happy day.[24] Aunts cause similar disquiet during another Christmas visit to the Browns:

"Was there ever a family," groaned Robert, "with as many aunts as ours?"... Aunts, of course, varied. Some were better than others.... Some could be bent to circumstances, others bent circumstances to themselves. Some were generous, others were mean. If there had to be an aunt at Christmas (and there generally had) it was as well to know beforehand what sort it was going to be.[25]

William's loyal friends, Ginger, Henry and Douglas, consider the benefits of their aunts, who blight all their lives throughout the William stories. It was a depressing meditation:

All the Outlaws seemed similarly situated with regard to aunts and aunts' gardens.

"I never *meant* to fall through her old greenhouse," said Ginger. "I was only jus' trying to climb over it, an' ever since then she's not even let me go inside her gate."

It appeared that Henry, having been asked recently by his aunt to post a letter, had forgotten all about it, and it had stayed in his pocket for a week. It had been, according to Henry's aunt, a most important letter.... and they were now not on speaking terms, while William, after an unsuccessful attempt to graft one of her new apple trees on to another, according to some instructions that he had read in the paper, had been forbidden by his aunt ever to enter her garden again.

"We do have rotten luck in aunts," said William, wistfully. "The only ones I have that are nice to me an' give me things are the ones I never see. Seems sort of queer."

By strange coincidence the others were in the same plight. The only aunts they had who were really nice to them were the ones they never saw.[26]

Nevertheless, some aunts can enjoy a visit to William and his family. Great-Aunt Jane wants to give William a treat, but William thought that the presence of Great-Aunt Jane 'would be enough to dispel the hilarity of any treat.'[27] She agrees to take him to the local fair. She has never in her blameless life entered a place of entertainment before. The fun of the fair goes to Great-Aunt Jane's head, and she relishes her turns on the Helter Skelter, which she sails down with squeaks of joy. On returning to the Brown's home, she thinks that William enjoyed himself, but it was quite impossible that she had.[28] Another Great-Aunt Jane has a positive experience as the rough and tumble of William's behaviour bounces her back to health: 'You're too priceless to be true, William,' she said, which is, of course, true.[29] There are many different versions of aunts in the William stories.

Aunts are everywhere in Crompton's work and they feature in her novels. They may bring up their nephews and nieces, taking on the role of surrogate parents. In *David Wilding* (1926), Aunt Flossie is the most trying of David's aunts; she is 'tremulously eager, tremulously garrulous, tremulously over-dressed, with a floating squadron of scarves and frills and necklaces accompanying her maypole-like form…. Her hat was crooked. Her coat's buttonholes embraced the wrong buttons, as indeed they generally did.'[30] Aunt Flossie might be endearing, but other aunts in Crompton's novels are stern and formidable and often misunderstand, as they do in the William stories, that the reason for their existence is to support the young people in their care.

* * *

As an aunt herself, Richmal was warm, a caring listener and a 'good sort.' She attended her youngest niece's and nephew's school functions, where they could count on her to do the right thing. Margaret reflects on Richmal's character, recalling:

> We all thought of Richmal as a lovely kind aunt who was always amusing and invariably interested in whatever we were doing. Without exception she put others first and herself last. To this day I cannot assess to what extent she covered her true feelings by exercising strong self-control…. On the rare occasions that she became angry, it was always in defence of someone else who had been unjustly treated.[31]

Aunt Richmal kept much of her private thoughts to herself, whilst outwardly she was gregarious and fun to be around. Margaret remembers that she 'loved ridiculous situations and people and noticed every detail of odd behaviour.'[32] She recalls that Richmal was an observer and had an intense curiosity about other people. In her writing, Crompton draws on her observations of people in public places, and she would focus on tiny details that many people would never have noticed, entertaining her companions with witty asides and caricatures.[33] Margaret's aunt would often make an absurd statement accompanied by a totally serious face and, when she was talking to some of the people she knew, her conversations were rarely serious.[34] She had a positive outlook on life and saw opportunities when problems arose. Richmal told her family that she had a much more interesting life as a writer than as a teacher, a career she had to give up in 1923 when she contracted polio.[35]

Richmal Disher (most commonly known by her married name, Richmal Ashbee), her sister Gwen's youngest daughter, was much closer to her aunt than Margaret and was a hugely important person in her aunt's life. They saw each other frequently and often several times a week when Richmal Disher was a child and after her marriage. During her childhood, unlike Margaret, Gwen's youngest daughter went to a local school in Bromley and went on to study history at Westfield College, a college for women students and part of the University of London. Richmal invited Gwen and her children to live with her at times, particularly when Thomas Disher left his family for long periods to live abroad. After Richmal Disher was born in March 1929, the thirties were a period of instability for Gwen and her children, followed by five years of war. In 1949, Richmal Disher met her future husband Paul Ashbee, who was eleven years older, through her involvement with the university's archaeological society. In the future, her aunt's support was to become more important than ever.

For Richmal Ashbee's children, Kate and Edward, their great-aunt Richmal, who was known as Ray or Auntie in the family, was a constant presence in both their lives. They saw her almost every week at their home and, whilst their mother was working, she collected them from school, played with them at her home and took them on outings. Each of Richmal's literary successes were celebrated with a trip to London to a show or ballet. Richmal also enjoyed more serious plays and loved the theatre.[36] Kate remembers:

> I saw a lot of her as a child.... We used to spend a lot of time at her house in Chislehurst and she used to come to all our school plays and fetes. She had a bay window, with a curtain which drew straight across it, where we could perform plays for her. She was very hands-on. We would go and play cowboys and Indians or Custer's last stand on the edge of Chislehurst Woods, and she would stand there with her walking frame, playing Custer.... She loved children and was on the same level as them. I think she just understood people whatever their age.[37]

In 1968, when he was fifteen, Edward was seriously ill in hospital and she visited him every day, bringing him home whilst his parents were away on a dig. Their father Paul Ashbee was by then a well-known archaeologist. Edward and Kate remember their great-aunt as a constant, stable presence and a calming influence in their lives; she was a 'rock of stability' holding the family together.

Later in life, Richmal described herself as a surviving example of the Victorian 'professional' aunt and constructed a public image of herself as a rather conventional middle-class woman and an aunt whose work was outside the literary canon.[38] She had little interest in portraying her personal life to anyone outside her family and friends. In 1961, Crompton writes to a young fan from Bury, where she was born. She lets him know that she does not think she will write an autobiography, adding that her 'bent is more towards fiction than the presentation of facts and I have spent a very uneventful life!'[39] This biography is a story about someone whose private life lies hidden behind this idea of the uneventful life of a professional staid, ineffectual aunt. It is the view of her that the world saw and continues to see. However, sometimes we can glimpse Ray peeping out from behind her shoulder.

* * *

In the six years when she was teaching at Bromley High School (1917–1923), Richmal's life was replete with creativity on the page, as well as on and off the stage at school. She brought to Bromley High School her love of performance and drama. In the summer term 1921, the Dramatics Society performed Shakespeare's *A Midsummer Night's Dream*. A pupil remembers that 'thanks to the timely aid of Miss Lamburn during the last week of rehearsals, and the keenness of all concerned' the play was a great success. Richmal became 'a most indefatigable "coach" and stage-manager.'[40] In 1922, we also catch a glimpse of her performing in a school play herself, the farce 'Between the Soup and the Savoury' (1910).[41] This one-act comedy by Gertrude E. Jennings was popular in the nineteen twenties, appearing on BBC Radio from 1924–1929.[42] The three cast members are a cook, a parlour maid and a kitchen maid, and Miss Lamburn played the cook.

At the end of the summer term 1923, she was busy directing a successful performance of *The Merchant of Venice* and organising a meeting of the Debating Society that debated whether a prohibition would be beneficial for the country. It was unanimously defeated.[43] Richmal was not averse to making fun of herself on occasions. She remembers priming her class with arguments for use during meetings of the Debating Society and fixing 'them with a stern eye till they had actually made these prepared contributions to the discussion.'[44] Once again, we can glimpse an extrovert young woman enthralled by performance and debate, drawn to tragedy or comedy, and a natural leader.

The performance of *The Merchant of Venice* became her swansong at the school. At school and university, Crompton brought her knowledge of dramatic performance and writing to her fiction. She would return to the stage a decade later in the nineteen thirties, when her own plays appear in London, but in the summer of 1923, her life was about to change forever.

Notes

1. Stevenson, 22.
2. Ibid., 148.
3. Joannou, 77–78.
4. *Anne Morrison*, 183.
5. Historian John Stevenson notes that, 'The pre-war years had been marked by a considerable "excess" of women of marriageable age because of the massive outflow of emigrants. When this drain of young men was checked by the Great War, possibilities of more women being married were opened up and led to a greater percentage of women of all age groups marrying between the wars than before 1914' (148). However, by 1918 Richmal was twenty-eight at a time when women over thirty were less likely to marry.
6. Joannou, 84.
7. Ibid., 86.
8. Holtby, 270.
9. Eight of her novels feature the name of the main female protagonist in the title. *Anne Morrison* (1925), *Millicent Dorrington* (1927), *Naomi Godstone* (1930), *The Odyssey of Euphemia Tracy* (1932), *Marriage of Hermione* (1932), *Caroline* (1936), *Matty and the Dearingroydes* (1956), *Mrs Frensham Describes a Circle* (1942).
10. *The Ridleys*, 108.
11. Ibsen, *A Doll's House* Act III, 115.
12. *Marriage of Hermione*, 5.
13. Woolf, 3.
14. "Martin Ford", 67.
15. Ibid., 75–76.
16. A contemporary reviewer also notes the power of this imagery. See *Hull Daily Mail*, 18 August 1927, 3.
17. *Millicent Dorrington*, 213.
18. Ibid., 246.
19. Ibid., 463.
20. Ibid., 464.
21. *Caroline*, 27.
22. *Belfast Newsletter* 27 August 1936, 10.
23. "A Busy Day," 20.
24. Ibid., 13.
25. "William and the Vanishing Luck," 139.
26. "What's in a Name," 35.

27. "Aunt Jane's Treat," 76.
28. Ibid., 88.
29. "The Cure," 43.
30. *David Wilding, 15.*
31. Disher, M., 207.
32. Ibid., 137.
33. Ibid., 24.
34. Ibid.
35. Ibid., 200.
36. Ibid., 138.
37. *The Mail on Sunday* 19 December 2010, 47.
38. Ashbee, Paul, 6. Also, *The People* 28 November 1954, 2.
39. Bury Libraries and Archive. Letter to Thomas Hope Floyd, 29 May 1961.
40. *Bromley High School Magazine* 1922, 14.
41. *Bromley High School Magazine* 1922, 13 and 1923, 5.
42. The play was broadcast on 29 February 1924, 29 April and 4 May 1925, 25 September 1928, and 20 September 1929. Source BBC Genome Project.
43. *Bromley High School Magazine* 1924, 22–23.
44. Bridge, 37.

References

Ashbee, Paul. 2007. *'Auntie': Richmal Crompton As I Knew Her.* The Just William Society.

Bridge, Marie Ed. 1983. *Schoolgirl Voices, Bromley High School 1883–1983.* Dorchester: Henry Ling.

Crompton, Richmal. 1959. First published 1922. "A Busy Day." In *More William*, by Richmal Crompton, 13–32. London: George Newnes Ltd.

———. 1925. *Anne Morrison.* London: Jarrolds.

———. 1953. First published 1924. "Aunt Jane's Treat." In *William - The Fourth*, by Richmal Crompton, 75–88. London: George Newnes Ltd.

———. 1936. *Caroline.* London: Macmillan.

———. 1926. *David Wilding.* London: Hodder & Stoughton.

———. 1932. *Marriage of Hermione.* London: Macmillan.

———. 1927. "Martin Ford." In *A Monstrous Regiment*, by Richmal Crompton, 67–76. London: Hutchinson & Co.

———. 2017. First published 1927. *Millicent Dorrington.* London: Bello.

————. 1961. First published 1923. "The Cure." In *William Again*, by Richmal Crompton, 30–43. London: George Newnes Ltd.

————. 1947. *The Ridleys*. Howard Baker: London.

————. 1984. First published 1938. "What's in a Name." In *William - The Dictator*, by Richmal Crompton, 22–54. Basingstoke, Hampshire: Macmillan Children's Books.

————. 1987. First published 1939. "William and the Vanishing Luck." In *William and the Air Raid Precautions*, by Richmal Crompton, 139–165. Basingstoke, Hampshire: Pan Macmillan Children's Books.

Disher, Margaret. 1990. *Growing Up with Just William By His Sister*. London: The Outlaws Publishing Company.

Holtby, Winifred. 1987. First published 1924. *The Crowded Street*. London: Virago Press.

Ibsen, Henrik. 2013. First published 1879. *A Doll's House*. London: Sovereign.

Joannou, Maroula. 1995. '*Ladies Please Don't Smash These Windows*'. Oxford: Berg.

Stevenson, John. 1984. *British Society 1914-45*. London: Lane.

Woolf, Virginia. 2000. First published 1929 and 1938 respectively. "A Room of One's Own." In *A Room of One's Own/Three Guineas*, by Virginia Woolf, 3–103. London: Penguin Classics.

10

Polio in Summer 1923

Following the publication of the first two William collections in 1922, 1923 heralded two significant, but less well-known, turning points in Richmal's life and career. Her first novel, *The Innermost Room*, was published and she contracted polio whilst on holiday in Cromer with her mother:

> Polio was one the diseases that defined the twentieth century. Its transformation from a grumbling endemic curiosity to explosive outbreaks that left thousands paralysed occurred at different times in different regions: the 1910s in the United States, the years after the Second World War in Great Britain and Europe, and the 1960s in Russia. The worst times for the Western world were during the decade leading up to the introduction of the first effective polio vaccine in the mid-1950s.[1]

At the moment when her writing life was on the point of taking another exciting direction, Richmal became seriously ill and we lose sight of the woman immersed in the life of her fellow students and in her caring, extrovert role as a teacher. After a life surrounded by people, many social activities, and a challenging and stimulating career in education based on the study of classical literature and language, and an emerging profile as an author, Richmal Crompton Lamburn largely disappears in the mid-twenties behind the front door, gates and walls of her home. She re-emerges in her local community in the late twenties and in London's literary life in the early thirties. Throughout this period Richmal Crompton continued to write and publish William stories, books of other short stories and novels.

© The Author(s), under exclusive license to Springer Nature
Switzerland AG 2022
J. McVeigh, *Richmal Crompton, Author of Just William*, Literary Lives,
https://doi.org/10.1007/978-3-030-96511-2_10

From 1924, Richmal had to come to terms with the lifelong consequences of impaired mobility and recurring pain. Richmal did not see herself as a victim of polio and we should not do so. What is also significant are the unintended social consequences of her disability. We have no direct evidence that other writers, publishers, reviewers, journalists and associated professionals in the literary world, treated her differently. Nevertheless, we can say, given society's attitudes towards disabled people at the time, that it is likely that they would have done so.

Society held firm views about normalcy; public and social policy was geared towards keeping disabled people out of the public eye, literally and metaphorically, and away from mainstream society. For much of the early to mid-twentieth century, many disabled people continued to live in institutions, and were treated as second-class citizens, out of sight and out of mind. There was significant intolerance towards anyone who did not conform to society's expectations about how everyone should look and behave. The eugenics movement was influential until the end of the Second World War. In the first half of the twentieth century, Barry North comments that many factors 'conspired to place disabled people at a disadvantage,' based not only on places and buildings that were inaccessible but also on attitudes that ranged from 'overt prejudice to pity or ignorance.'[2] After her illness, the professional view of Richmal Crompton held by those who knew her and had the power and influence to promote her work is likely to have changed, but Crompton was defiant and continued to pursue her career. She wrote about characters with disabilities in her novels and was active in organisations raising the profile of disabled people's experience.

* * *

In 1923, on their return from the US, Gwen and her family were barred from entering Richmal's home because she was very seriously ill. For over a week, it was not clear if she would live or die.[3] The right side of Richmal's body was paralysed. Gradually the use of her hand and arm returned. Gwen's children Margaret and Tommy helped her with exercises. Eventually, she had full use of her arm, but the damage to her right leg was permanent. Gwen, Margaret and Tommy moved back in with her whilst she was recovering from her initial illness, helping her with exercises that were part of her rehabilitation, until she was writing again. Margaret recalls:

> [Aunt Richmal's] right side was paralysed but the use of her hand and arm gradually came back. We helped her do exercises to get the muscles working and were thrilled when she could once again hold a pen and write. She kept

reassuring us that as long as one finger was working she would be able to type, although we knew that most of her writing was typed by someone else. In the end her right arm worked just as well as the left, yet it seemed that nothing much could be done for her leg. For a long while she had to use crutches, then she graduated to two sticks and eventually to one, but she was to drag her leg for the rest of her life.[4]

Richmal broke her legs several times as she grew older. Until the end of her life, she was unable to walk unaided and always needed someone's arm or her stick when she was out. The walking frame she used at home and when she was with her family was kept away from public view.

For colleagues and pupils at Bromley High School, 'it was a great shock to find in September 1923 that Miss Lamburn was seriously ill and unable to return to School.'[5] Shortly after her illness, Richmal went back to the school by taxi three times a week to support a small group of girls who were planning to go to university, 'teaching them more than Latin by her courage and cheerfulness.' In later years, some ex-pupils visited her at home to 'talk about everything under the sun.'[6] After she left, according to one ex-pupil, Richmal 'treated her disability in such a matter-of-fact way that one almost forgot it existed and when it occasionally led to falls and broken limbs it was an education to hear her infectious laughter as she ridiculed her own clumsiness.'[7]

In 1968, she told one journalist: 'After having polio I decided to do what I could with writing. I had got enough of a foot in with writing for *Punch* and various magazines.'[8] When she gave up teaching, Richmal was faced with securing an income to support herself and her mother, as well as contributing what she could to help her sister. It must have been a great relief to all of them that her success as an author provided a regular and comfortable income. The prospect of adequate help, financial or otherwise, from her absent brother-in-law would have seemed extremely unlikely.

In the late nineteen twenties, Richmal became more independent and mobile when she bought a car, with hand controls.[9] Richmal was driving until the end of her life. She noted in an appointment diary that her driving licence expired on 4 July 1968 and with that her freedom to go where she pleased could have been taken away. Her family, however, remember that she was driving to the end of her life, although she died a mere six months later in January 1969.[10]

Richmal loved travel and considered it a challenge to her disability. She travelled as much as possible in Europe. There was always the risk that she might be injured, so she usually went away with one or two friends or relatives. She would have faced significant practical challenges, even on shorter journeys. There are of course other ways to 'see' the world. Millicent Dorrington had '"never been out of England," she admitted, "I've done all my travelling in print. It's really quite a thrilling way of doing it."'[11] No doubt Richmal's extensive reading took her to far off places too. She did have a holiday in Rome and saw the glories of its ancient civilisations but was 'disappointed not to reach more of the lands of her classical studies.'[12]

* * *

After the Second World War, changes in social policy had a significant impact on the lives of the public. The Beveridge Report, published in 1942, laid the foundations for the welfare state in Britain to address what became known as the five giants of need: want, ignorance, squalor, idleness and disease. In a story first published in 1944, William wrongly decides that the report is merely concerned with the needs of grown-ups: 'I don't see why grown-ups should get everything an' us nothin',' he declares to the Outlaws.[13] They decide to write a report of their own:

> Outlaws Report
> Habby. Ass. Corpuss.
> Magner Carter.

1. As much holidays as term.
2. No afternoon school.
3. Sixpence a week pocket munny and not to be took off [in the event of Outlaw misdemeanors].
4. No Latin no French no Arithmetick.
5. As much ice creem and banarnas and creem buns as we like free.
6. No punnishments and stay up as late as we like.[14]

The Outlaws consider that they would be freed from want if these demands were met. However, the boys decide, after some misadventure, that 'a pantomime in the hand is worth a dozen Acts of Parliament in the bush.'[15] Crompton places William once again at the heart of national events.

New government legislation followed Beveridge and heralded the establishment of the National Health Service in 1948, provided some financial assistance for people who were out of work, and required that every child should receive an education. As social welfare improved, from the nineteen fifties there was also a move to reduce the number of people living in institutions and to provide services that enabled disabled people to remain living at home and within their local communities.[16] Richmal was active in organisations that supported this change.

Richmal not only supported charities for disabled people with regular donations, but she also appeared in radio appeals as her celebrity status grew from the mid-nineteen forties. On 28 December 1947, Richmal recorded a BBC radio appeal for funds on behalf of the Infantile Paralysis Fellowship, now the British Polio Fellowship.[17] In 1949, she also made a brief appearance in a public health film, *His Fighting Chance*, about rehabilitation for people who had contracted polio.[18]

It was a disease that had seasonal rises in the summer months when outbreaks usually occurred. This happened in the UK in 1926, 1938 and 1940, but in 1947, when Richmal made her appeal, polio had reached the level of an epidemic in the UK, which lasted until 1950.[19] By the fifties, polio was a major public health problem in England and Wales.[20] In the context of the pandemic seventy-five years later, it is salutary to note that there was no polio vaccine available in 1947. The first vaccine did not become available in the UK until the mid-fifties. There were localised epidemics in areas such as Belfast, Coventry and Hull amongst others in 1957–1958. These were the last major epidemics of polio in the UK. The vaccine rollout was slow and did not really have an impact until years later. Polio was not eradicated in the UK until 1985.[21] Richmal had clearly been called upon to help at a critical period when the disease was on the increase and the work of the British Polio Fellowship was more important than ever. As well as raising much-needed funds for the charity, North records in a history of the charity that her broadcasts 'did sterling work in lifting the profile of the Fellowship. Just about everybody in Britain knew about polio but not so many knew that there was an organisation dedicated to helping those whom it had affected,' he writes.[22]

On 12 February 1950, Crompton broadcast another appeal, this time on behalf of the Central Council for the Care of Cripples.[23] This patronising and inappropriate title changed whilst Richmal was a member of the organisation. In the nineteen fifties, Crompton became Vice-President of the Council.[24] In 1960, staff carried out a local survey in Kent, Richmal's own county, and found that many disabled people were isolated at home. They had little contact with other people, or access to transport that would enable them to take part in community activities.[25] One of the aims of the organisation was to listen to disabled people and develop services to meet their needs. A fragment of paper, on which she made notes for her writing, is taken from the minutes of one of the organisation's meetings.[26] It comes from the minutes of the Annual General Meeting of the Council held on 9 May 1962 in County Hall, London. The fragment shows notes of a discussion about changing the name. One speaker, not Crompton herself, comments:

I think this old name is not 1918 but almost Dickensian. I think we should accept a new attitude of mind ... and as a disabled person I would beg you to vote for this with an overwhelming majority.[27]

The charity's name was changed to the Central Council for the Disabled, based on a survey of members.[28] A symbolic new name was not going to lead to a sea change in social and public attitudes overnight, but it was a significant moment as part of a wider drive to inform public policy. However, the new name is patronising too. The name of many organisations have subsequently been changed to remove the stigma of labels that stereotype disabled people, who are individuals first and foremost, not an anonymous homogenous group with the same experiences, hopes and expectations, as Crompton herself already knew and expressed in her writing.

*   *   *

Before 1945, Crompton writes about disabled people in several novels. They do not feature in the William stories, or in her first three novels.[30] As we shall see in a later chapter, Nicholas in *The Inheritor* (1960) is the only character with a disability to feature in a 'lead' role in any of her novels. Crompton considers how disabled people are treated within society.[31]

In *Millicent Dorrington* (1927), Millicent Dorrington's sister Lorna loses her leg following a cycling accident and her fiancé immediately abandons her. He feels that her wings have been broken and she 'had lost what he had loved in her, and with it his love was gone. He had shrunk from maimed and diseased things all his life. His horror was too great even to admit of pity.'[32] His love is superficial, embodied in Lorna's physical appearance, and the harsh language describing his attitude highlights his prejudice against her. When she eventually recovers from her heartbreak, Lorna's life is full of ability:

> There was nothing disconsolate or pathetic about Lorna despite the artificial leg. It had rather seemed a challenge to her. She had set herself to conquer her disabilities in the spirit of joyous adventures she had brought to bear in the old days on feats of skill and daring. She cycled, she walked, she played golf—not, of course, as she had done in the old days, but passably well. She had had to give up tennis and dancing, and in the active pursuits which she could still carry on the satisfaction lay, not in the old joy of speed and movement, but rather in the dogged baulking and defying of the mysterious It who was responsible for her affliction.[33]

We are not told who or what 'It' might be, but this conjures up an unidentifiable force or power that prevents us from doing the things we hoped to in life,

Fig. 10.1 Richmal Crompton Lamburn late nineteen twenties[29]

Fate perhaps. Many of us have certainly said 'It is not fair,' and Fate often is not. Lorna finds that she is patronised by her ex-fiancé and her brother, both young men who cannot see beyond her disability. She marries an older man who loves her for herself, as does Millicent, and has a family of her own. Unlike Millicent, she is able to leave her childhood home.

Many disabilities are hidden or misunderstood. In *Steffan Green* (1940), Mrs Turnberry's son Frank steals from her to buy drink. He was fond of her and would help her out in the house, scrubbing, scouring and cooking, and during these private, domestic activities they would be as happy as if he was a little boy again, which is how his mother describes his childlike qualities.[34] Frank has a poor memory, cannot pass the simplest exam, or concentrate on even a paragraph of print.[35] His mother is terrified that he will be sent away:

> I'd rather die than let them take Frank from me. ... Oh, it isn't anything wonderful – mother love or anything like that. I don't know that I even like him. Sometimes I'm almost sure that I don't like him, but – he's all I've got, and I'm all he's got. He'll never marry. He doesn't care for women.... I don't know what he'd do without me, and I don't know what I'd do without him. We're company for each other. And he's fond of me.[36]

Like many other mothers, Mrs Turnberry is self-effacing and gives without expectation. Her son needs her, and she needs him, so that is It.[37]

Other disabled people fail to find anyone who can see beyond their disability. They meet other people whose care and support are misconceived and who lack self-awareness. In *Chedsy Place* (1934), Mr Fielden is blinded in the First World War and his girlfriend promptly leaves him. Whilst in hospital he meets Maud, a nurse:

> He had turned to Maud for everything, as if he had been a child. It was she who took him out, guiding his footsteps, describing the things and people they passed.... He didn't actually fall in love with her, but he became so dependent on her that he literally could not contemplate life without her. He felt that no one else would ever know just how and when he needed help. And she, on her side, was in love with him.[38]

By the time they arrive at Chedsy Place to stay for the weekend, their relationship has soured. Mr Fielden feels stifled and patronised by Maud. His need for her has become one of his grievances against her, whilst Mrs Fielden moans in her plaintive voice that he is selfish and ungrateful given all that she has done for him. Her love for him is not based on equality, but his dependency.[39] He wants to become part of a wider world in which his disability does not define his identity:

> He avoided other blind men, and he refused to learn Braille. Both seemed somehow to emphasise the disability that he was determined to ignore, seemed to brand him as an exile from the normal world to which he was determined, in spite of everything, to belong.[40]

However, his ability to do so is impeded by other people's ways of seeing disabled people. Here Crompton challenges what the nature of a so-called 'normal' world might be, and who defines it. Society sees Mr Fielden's disability first and foremost, not someone who has significant abilities and who just happens to have a disability.[41]

How carers and others support people with complex needs is a concern in Crompton's novels. Caring is a responsibility that deserves recognition, but not all carers are able to see beyond their own needs. Millicent's sister Bunny, and Agnes in *The Holiday* (1933), are supported by their mothers—Millicent is a surrogate mother in Bunny's case—and they need help with every aspect of their daily lives. Bunny has 'a clouded intelligence.'[42] Agnes walks 'awkwardly with shambling, unsteady footsteps. Her head dropped forward, and as she came nearer they saw that her mouth hung open ... and that her blue eyes were fixed vacantly in front of her.'[43] Both mothers support the girls to take part in social gatherings, but other people who meet them can be less sympathetic and feel uncomfortable when they are in their company. Another Agnes, in *Merlin Bay* (1939), needs support too: she 'was a large loose-knit girl of eighteen who had not developed beyond childhood. She was not, as many people described her, an 'idiot.' She was affectionate and sensitive, but utterly without control over mind or body.'[44] The girl needs to be cared for 'as if she were indeed a child,' and her mother seldom leaves her 'even for a moment.'[45] Agnes in *The Holiday* and Bunny need care with every aspect of their lives and it is given without remorse or bitterness by their mothers.

In *The Holiday*, Agnes's father tries and fails to love his child, whom he sees as a wedge between himself and his wife. He does not know how to cope with his daughter's erratic behaviour. In one scene, his hands are clasped together so tightly that the knuckles show like bare bones:

> "It's criminal that she should have to be kept in the world," he burst out jerkily. "How can one believe in God when such things happen? ... "You saw my wife the other day. She looks fifty and she's only thirty-five. Since the child was born, she's devoted herself to her day and night. She's sacrificed her whole life for the child."[46]

His wife barely speaks to him and cannot forgive him for his attitude towards their daughter. He is in danger of losing his family if he cannot accept and love his daughter for who she is.

In *Merlin Bay*, Miss Hinkley, who is eighty, impoverished and lives alone, arrives on holiday to stay with Agnes's mother and offers to help:

> [She] had been a poor relation all her life and had brought it to a fine art.... She lived, as it were, on the very fringe of life—her food a bare sufficiency, her clothes always made for and worn out by somebody else before they reached her—but to that fringe she clung with limpet-like endurance.[47]

Miss Hinkley spends much of her time edging her way into other homes for brief stays, which reduces the pressure on her income and gives her a chance to stay in more comfortable surroundings than she would otherwise be able to afford. She is happy to offer to help her hosts in return for her board and lodging. She tells Agnes a story about a world of chocolate in the sea. Agnes is enthralled by the story:

> Agnes was tired and still a little over-excited. "She jumped right into the sea," she kept telling [her family], "and she didn't even get wet, and the merman met her and took her into the palace, and she had doughnuts and cream and chocolates and red jelly and iced cakes and plum pudding and roast chicken, and she ate them all and she wasn't sick. She jumped right into the sea." She told them the story over and over again in her loud harsh voice, the words jumbled up together so unintelligibly that even Mrs. Bevan [her mother] could hardly understand her.[48]

Mrs Bevan thanks Miss Hinkley for all the time she has spent with Agnes:

> Miss Hinkley loved Agnes in return with a love that she had seldom given to anyone in all her life before.... talking to Mrs. Bevan about her, gave her the purest thrill of happiness she had known for years. It melted away the hard shell of loneliness, which had enclosed her heart so long that she now hardly realised it was there.[49]

Agnes jumps into the sea to find the palace and drowns. We empathise with Miss Hinkley's loneliness, and she genuinely tries to help, but she is not a suitable carer for Agnes. In her relationship with Agnes, she is thinking of herself rather than trying to consider Agnes's point of view. In 'Flotsam,' a story in *A Monstrous Regiment* (1927), Crompton describes another character with learning disabilities, Miss Crockett, who lives an isolated life on her father's estate. He has died and the property is now owned by her brother, who hates her. He has decided to sell the estate and put his sister 'under proper restraint.'[50] In his view, 'it's a scandal that that she should be about at all.'[51] Miss Crockett overhears him: 'Misty though her brain was, it had understood.'[52] She drowns herself in the lake on the estate. The attitudes of Miss Hinkley and Miss Crockett's brother are different, of course, but they are both unable to recognise that people with learning disabilities should be given the right to be treated on their own terms and as people who are adults, with their own way of looking at the world. These stories question why disabled people are treated like children.[53]

Agnes and Miss Crockett die because others who were meant to care for them have not been able to understand life from their point of view. In *Merlin Bay*, her family does not realise that Agnes would take Miss Hinkley's story literally. This is not Agnes's problem, although she must bear the consequences, but that of her carers who fail to care for her on her own terms, rather than their own. To think of someone else as having childlike qualities can be patronising if we cannot see the world from their point of view as adults. Crompton's novels explore disabled people's experience and ask why it so difficult for them to be accepted and understood on their own terms. She has not previously been known as an author who deals with social issues from the early to mid-twentieth century. Her novels that feature the lives of women, changes in the structure of local communities and, at the very least, those that feature disabled characters, suggest that this perspective deserves re-evaluation.

* * *

For Sandra, a fan, 'reading William stories lifts my spirits.' Looking back in 2021, she remembers her own aunt who became permanently disabled after an accident in childhood and years of inadequate treatment and botched operations. In the nineteen twenties and thirties, her aunt was patronisingly known as 'a cripple with a limp and her disability affected the way that people saw her,' Sandra said. Also, 'as a single woman she was not expected to achieve very much.' She believes that, like her aunt, Richmal was pigeon-holed both as a disabled person and because she was unmarried. 'Perhaps if she had lived later in the twentieth century, she would have received the recognition she deserved,' Sandra said.[54] Quite so, although it is by no means certain that she would have done.

Her niece Margaret and other members of the family remember that Richmal made jokes about her disability and never complained.[55] She rarely discussed it in interviews for the media and was not disempowered by it. By keeping it out of the public eye, and making light of it within her family,

Richmal tried to ensure that it was not the main feature of her life that defined her identity as an aunt, a sister or as an author. From 1924, she entered the most prolific period in her career as a writer and she was writing until her death forty-five years later. In the year Violet Elizabth Bott was born, she decided 'I can,' and she did indeed pursue her flourishing career as well as supporting her family, in a period when disabled people struggled to find suitable mainstream employment and to live as they chose.

Notes

1. Williams, 26.
2. North 2012, 362, 363.
3. Disher, M., 50.
4. Ibid., 51.
5. *Bromley High School Magazine* 1924, 2.
6. *Schoolgirl Voices*, 41–42.
7. Ibid., 42.
8. Francis, 4.
9. Disher, M., 109.
10. UoR RC/2/12. Appointment diary 1968.
11. *Millicent Dorrington*, 415.
12. Disher, M., 199.
13. "The Outlaws Report," 113.
14. Ibid., 117.
15. Ibid., 126.
16. Significant legislation included the Disabled Persons Employment Act 1944, the Education Act 1944, the Family Allowances Act 1945, the National Insurance Act 1946, the Children Act 1948 and the Mental Health Act 1959. The Piercy Committee Report in 1956 was also influential.
17. North 1999, 54.
18. *His Fighting Chance* is available online from the British Film Institute (BFI).
19. Martin, W.J. "Poliomyelitis in England and Wales, 1947–1950." *British Journal of the Society of Medicine* (1951), 5, 236–246. Polio was endemic in England and Wales since 1912, when formal notification began, but in other years it had 'the nature of a sporadic disease with a seasonal rise [in the summer] rather than that of an epidemic disease' (236).
20. North 2012, 366.

21. Information provided by the British Polio Fellowship.

22. North 1999, 54.

23. BBC Written Archive. Card index card on Crompton scripts.

24. National Archives, MH55/2243.

25. National Archives, MH55/2244.

26. UoR RC/1/1/1/1/4.

27. UoR RC/1/1/1/1/6.

28. National Archives, MH55/2244.

29. UoR RC/3/17/023.

30. Characters with a disability feature in *Millicent Dorrington* (1927), *The Holiday* (1933), *Chedsy Place* (1934), *Merlin Bay* (1939), *Steffan Green* (1940), and *Narcissa* (1941).

31. Linett, 1–18. Linett argues that in literary studies that encompass disabled characters: 'The goal ... is not just to discover how a character is depicted by its author, but also how that depiction affects the overall workings of the text and what it tells us about how embodiment was understood in particular times and places' (5). Further studies of Crompton's fiction featuring disabled people could address this issue in greater depth.

32. *Millicent Dorrington*, 333. Also, see Roger's attitude towards his wife Faith in *Blue Flames* (1930).

33. Ibid., 352.

34. *Steffan Green*, 70.

35. Ibid., 73.

36. Ibid., 196.

37. As Jenny Kendrick notes, a novel contemporary to Crompton's work is William Faulkner's *The Sound and the Fury* (1931), which features Benjy who has learning disabilities. In the novel, other characters 'fail to understand or to care about one another and display a self-centredness far outweighing any lack in Benjy's character.' Kendrick argues that a lack of an equal place in a novel's cast list fails to acknowledge disabled people as integral to a novel, rather than only of significance in relation to themes about disability. She argues that 'In order to be a signifier not merely a vehicle of significance, a character with learning disabilities, like his or her real-life counterpart, has to take equal place in the cast list: to be in the plot, not isolated from it.' Disabled people play a significant role in Crompton's fiction, although *The Inheritor* is the only novel in which a disabled character has a central role.

38. *Chedsy Place*, 87.

39. Ibid., 183.

40. Ibid., 89.
41. See Maren Tova Linett's discussion of Henry Green's novel, *Blindness* (1926) about a young man's experience of being blind and his search for independence (66–73).
42. *Millicent Dorrington*, 264.
43. *The Holiday*, 51.
44. *Merlin Bay*, 39.
45. Ibid., 40. Mermen are the male equivalents of mermaids.
46. *The Holiday*, 93.
47. *Merlin Bay*, 68.
48. Ibid., 91.
49. Ibid., 160.
50. "Flotsam," 272. This story is published in Crompton's collection *A Monstrous Regiment of Women* (1927). This saying comes from a pamphlet published by John Knox in 1558, *The First Blast of the Trumpet Against the Monstruous Regimen of Women*, which is a diatribe against women in senior positions who have authority over men.
51. Ibid.
52. Ibid.
53. Teresa Michals exposes the dangers of seeing disabled people as the 'eternal child': 'In eliminating all growth, the figure of the eternal child also rules out the possibility of uneven development. That is, rather than recognising that a given person possesses different levels of mental and physical disability in different areas at a given moment, differences that may or may not change over time, this way of thinking rounds down all discrepancies.' This concern is reflected in Crompton's writing about her disabled characters' experience. They are treated like children, rather than accepted on their own terms as adults.
54. Based on a conversation in 2021.
55. Disher, M., 51.

References

Crompton, Richmal. 2015. First published 1934. *Chedsy Place*. London: Bello.
———. 1927. "Flotsam." In *A Monstrous Regiment*, by Richmal Crompton, 267–273. London: Hutchinson.
———. 1939. *Merlin Bay*. London: Macmillan.
———. 2017. First published 1927. *Millicent Dorrington*. London: Bello.
———. 1940. *Steffan Green*. London: Macmillan.

————. 1933. *The Holiday*. London: Macmillan.

————. 1989. First published 1945. "The Outlaws Report." In *William and the Brians Trust*, by Richmal Crompton, 112–126. Basingstoke, Hampshire: Macmillan Children's Books.

Disher, Margaret. 1990. *Growing Up with Just William by His Sister*. London: The Outlaws Publishing Company.

Francis, Sue. 1968. "Just William Creator Still Busy at 78." *Yorkshire Evening Post*, 6 December: 4.

Kendrick, Jenny. 2004 (24.1). "Images of Learning Disability in Fiction for Children." *Disability Studies Quarterly* https://dsq-sds.org/article/view/846/1021.

Linett, Maren Tova. 2017. *Bodies of Modernism: Physical Disability in Transatlantic Modernist Literature*. Ann Arbor: University of Michigan Press.

Michals, Teresa. 2018 (38.2). "'Oh, Why Can't You Remain Like This Forever!': Children's Literature, Growth, and Disability." *Disability Studies Quarterly* https://dsq-sds.org/article/view/6107/4914.

North, Barry. 1999. *'Something to lean on' The First Sixty Years of the British Polio Fellowship*. South Ruislip, Middlesex: British Polio Fellowship.

————. 2012. "The British Polio Fellowship: Its Contribution to the Development of Inclusivity for Disabled People." *Dynamis 32 (2)* 361–390.

Williams, Gareth. 2013. *Paralysed with Fear: The Story of Polio*. Basingstoke , Hampshire: Palgrave Macmillan.

Part III

(1924–1938)

11

Birth of Violet Elizabeth and Introducing William-Lite Characters

In 1924, Violet Elizabeth Bott was born. There are two girls in William's life who are in many ways two sides of the same coin: the caring, conventional Joan, who always makes William feel better about himself, and the abrasive, unpredictable Violet Elizabeth, who makes him feel ill at ease and shares his sense of adventure. They influence William's life for good and ill. Crompton had the energy, sense of purpose and ambition of both William and Violet Elizabeth that drove her to achieve her dreams as a writer, whatever was happening in the rest of her life. Other short stories experiment with older versions of William and Violet Elizabeth style characters, but they fail to capture our imagination in the same way.

Violet tells William that, "'F you don' play houth with me. I'll thcream n' thcream till I'm thick. I can," she added with pride.'[1] Violet Elizabeth is a powerful role model for any reader, especially girls, when she retorts confidently, 'I can.' This two-word follow up to her most famous saying is where the real power in her threat lies. She can, and she will. What is so liberating about Violet Elizabeth is not that she just feels like screaming, it lies in the fact that she does it, with confidence and aplomb.

We first meet her in 'The Sweet Little Girl in White,' first published in *The Happy Mag* in 1924, and then in *Still William* (1925). Like William, she is a heroic warrior against Authority, represented by Mr Brown, the Outlaws' fathers and all equally unreasonable adults. On one occasion, William is horrified when his father metes out a punishment for some, at least in his view, perfectly reasonable incident that his father objects to:

© The Author(s), under exclusive license to Springer Nature Switzerland AG 2022
J. McVeigh, *Richmal Crompton, Author of Just William*, Literary Lives,
https://doi.org/10.1007/978-3-030-96511-2_11

William glared furiously at the logs. Had chopping the logs been forbidden, William's soul would have yearned to chop them. Had the chopping been an act of wanton destruction it would have appealed immeasurably to William's barbarian spirit. But the chopping was a task enjoined on him by Authority. So William loathed it.[2]

As Crompton's narrator indicates here, this seems perfectly reasonable to William and is, of course, how many of us would respond as adults to a similar situation when we are asked to do something over which we have no control. Violet Elizabeth is equally dismissive of Authority and has none of Joan's gentle acquiescence:

Violet Elizabeth was six years old. She possessed bobbing curls, blue eyes, a lisp, and an imperious temper, and she had, without invitation, or even encouragement, attached herself to the Outlaws. The Outlaws had tried to shake her off by every means in their power, but she possessed weapons (chiefly the weapons of tears and pertinacity) against which they were defenceless. Violet Elizabeth, following them wherever they went, weeping tears of rage and screaming screams of rage whenever they attempted to send her away, had broken their nerve. They now accepted her presence as an inevitable evil.... She accepted their lack of cordiality as part of their charm, and was inordinately proud of her position.[3]

Violet is prim and condescending towards William on their first meeting, sharing the aloofness of Estella greeting Pip in Charles Dickens's *Great Expectations* (1861). The first thing Violet says to him is 'Good Afternoon,' followed by: '"Come along, boy," said Violet Elizabeth at last, holding out a hand.'[4] In *Great Expectations*, Pip thinks to himself when he meets Estella: 'Though she called me "boy" so often, and with a carelessness that was far from complimentary, she was of about my own age.... and she was as scornful of me as if she had been one-and-twenty, and a queen.'[5] On another occasion, Estella beckons to him:

'Come here! You may kiss me, if you like.'
I kissed her cheek as she turned it to me. I think I would have gone through a great deal to kiss her cheek. But, I felt that the kiss was given to the coarse common boy as a piece of money might have been, and that it was worth nothing.[6]

Estella lets Pip kiss her, but William is more reluctant to kiss Violet Elizabeth. He is being pursued by her, rather than the other way round. In a small detail, which might be of interest to Crompton's fans, in the collection in which

Violet Elizabeth first appears, Miss Hatherly features in a story called 'The Haunted House.' She is a member of the Society for the Encouragement of Higher Thought. Miss Haversham in *Great Expectations* is equally haughty.

In an earlier story, published in 1918, some of Violet Elizabeth's famous attributes are displayed by Marie Elizabeth, whose lips quiver as she wails plaintively to get what she wants.[7] Violet more famously goes on to do more than wail and screams for years to come. As Crompton tells us:

> She cultivated and used for her own purpose a scream that would have put a factory siren to shame and which was guaranteed to reduce anyone within ten yards of it to quite an expensive nervous breakdown. It had never yet been known to fail. William dreaded and respected Violet Elizabeth Bott.... She cherished an affection for the Outlaws which was not reciprocated though they were helpless against her weapons.[8]

She also displays an 'air of superior knowledge which the Outlaws always found so maddening in one of her extreme youth.'[9] Violet is quite prepared to resort to crime when necessary to achieve her ends and in one story proceeds to steal a young man's wallet: "'I've thtolen it," she said, "I'm a crim'nal."'[10] She usually can and does what she wants; we envy her confidence and inimitable directness.

William and the Outlaws usually fail to divert her from her chosen purpose, and she is immune to their disdain. When asked by William who asked her to come to the barn she says, without hesitation and with dignity, that she asked herself[11]:

> William had the feeling he so often had in his dealings with this redoubtable child, a feeling of being stripped of his authority and ousted from his position as chief—and that with a sweetness and apparent pliability that gave him no handle against her.[12]

Violet Elizabeth uses William's own methods of argument against him, which he finds disarming. It is a form of logic that is attractive to many of us, if only we had the same supreme self-assurance to use it. She tells him sternly, 'you've not bought the world, have you? People can be in the thame plathe ath other people, can't they? There'th no law againth it, ith there?'[13] The Outlaws stare at her helplessly.[14]

In another story, childhood reading plays a part.[15] The Outlaws have been reading *Robin Hood* and Violet Elizabeth suggests that they should take things from rich people to give to poor people:

The suggestion was received in silence. The Outlaws looked at William, the leader. William screwed his freckled countenance into a thoughtful frown.... His contempt for the proposer (which was almost a point of honour with him) struggled hard with his secret delight at the proposal.[16]

William's life is plagued by this strong and worthy opponent, his nemesis, Violet Elizabeth Bott, who has a rare ability to outsmart him.

Violet Elizabeth's parents, Mr & Mrs Bott, live in the local Hall with many rooms and extensive grounds. Mr Bott has made his money in business and despite their wealth the landowning upper classes fail to accept the nouveaux rich couple. Mrs Bott has a painful relationship with women from the aristocracy, who she calls the 'high-ups.' They look down on her and ignore her overtures: 'There were times when she accepted this state of things. There were times when she rebelled against it and returned to the fray.'[17] Mrs Bott decides that it is, 'Funny how stiff some of these Society people were. Really difficult to entertain. Nothing to say for themselves.'[18] Similar social climbers are mercilessly pilloried by Crompton in other writing.

In *The Ridleys* (1947), Harold's wife Janet relishes her husband's obnoxious materialism and social climbing, which she did not care for before they married. As one onlooker comments, 'Read your Pirandello, my dear. If you wear a mask long enough, it grows into you.'[19] The Italian writer Luigi Pirandello suggests that people in society mislead themselves and others: 'there is in us, we do not know how, or why or whence, the necessity of constantly deceiving ourselves with the spontaneous creation of a reality ... which from time to time we discover to be vain and illusory.'[20] It is such illusions that fascinate Crompton. Harold is a man of business and has little time for the highbrow. Art must mean something and appeal to the emotions, 'Not like those meaningless splodges that your impressionists turn out,' he declares.[21] No doubt Mrs Bott would not like the splodges either.

* * *

Of the two girls in William's life, Joan is the only girl he could contemplate marrying. William is quite certain that he is misunderstood and undervalued, and the adult world certainly fails to understand life from his point of view. But in Joan, the girl who lives next door, he finds a loyal supporter: 'All his life, William had accepted Joan's adoration and homage with condescending indifference.'[22] She adores him because he does such exciting things:

Joan was the only girl whose existence the Outlaws officially recognised.... Joan was admitted to all such games as required the female element. The others she was graciously allowed to watch.[23]

In one story, Joan has been visiting an aunt (no-one in the William stories ever seems to have just one aunt):

> Though she did not accompany them on their more dangerous and manly exploits she was their unfailing confidante and sympathiser and could be always counted on to side with them against a hostile and unsympathetic world. She was small and dark and very pretty and she considered William the greatest hero the world has ever known.... She firmly believed that William could do anything in the world better than anyone else in it.[24]

No doubt a sentiment William shares. Joan, in the spirit of J.K. Rowling's Hermione, puts a spell on Mr Galileo Simpkins hoping to turn him into a donkey, which he seems to resemble in many ways already. The narrator enters and informs the reader: 'And now comes one of those coincidences without which life and the art of the novelist would be so barren.'[25] When Mr Simpkins is called away without their knowledge, the Outlaws find a donkey in his place. Joan's spell has apparently been successful. The donkey looks as if it is reading Mr Galileo Simpkin's book. Chaos, as one might imagine, once again ensues.

Joan, like Ginger, is a loyal follower, rather than an equal. Violet Elizabeth, on the other hand, is his nemesis and challenges William's leadership far more than Hubert Lane and his gang ever can. Her resplendent challenge to Authority is a rallying cry to any girl or boy who wonders if they can too.

* * *

From 1922, as the success of William in regular magazines and books grew apace, Crompton remained committed to writing short stories, some of which include comparable characters to William and Violet, although they have never secured a faithful following of fans. Over the five years 1926–1931, Crompton published nine collections of other short stories, and a further collection was published in 1936.[26]

In one of these collections, *A Monstrous Regiment* (1927), the stories are concerned with the lives of women, several of whom are unsympathetic characters. The stories question the nature of love, particularly within families, when duty comes at a price and some family members' lives are controlled by the bullying duplicity and narcissism of others. Of Crompton's remaining short story collections a range of character types struggle with the ups and downs of daily life. One contemporary reviewer commented that in "The Family," from *The Middle Things* (1928): 'one finds the essence of a long novel; a family group in miniature, each member defined clearly as in a larger portrait, and simple details given the significance of great drama. These little masterpieces are fascinating.'[27] Several are tightly structured stream of consciousness pieces that focus on a moment, such as a hairdresser washing and drying a woman's hair, or a mother worrying about her family when they are all out of the house on a Saturday afternoon. In *Ladies First* (1929), Crompton explores barriers between the classes as her characters strive to move between them or find themselves pigeon-holed as either from this or that social group. She is interested in the lies we tell each other in the process. These stories also explore how many people perform a role in life that seems very convincing but is built on sand. We can love someone and live with them for many years, without realising that we do not know them at all.

Three of the short story collections are arguably based on characters who bear some similarities to William and Violet Elizabeth, although they are older. They are featured in amusing sketches that lack the outstanding sparkle and bite of the William stories. Both *Kathleen and I, and, of course, Veronica* (1926) and *Enter Patricia* (1927), were written in the same period as E.M. Delafield's popular *Diary of a Provincial Lady* (1930).[28] They are story collections about a married couple in which the character of the husband narrates the stories. In *Felicity Stands By* (1928) a teenage girl, who can be almost as adventurous as William or Violet, is the central character.[29]

In *Enter Patricia*, the male lead, and first-person narrator, is at first suitor, fiancé and then Patricia's husband. He is a comic character who is always making a mess of things and his patient wife acts as a foil to his exploits. In one story, which is evocative of the William stories, he bemoans yet another of the mishaps that plague his life:

> I went downstairs and took the envelope out of my raincoat pocket. And it wasn't addressed to Tutt [the coal merchants] at all. It was addressed to Mrs Jones-Smythe. It was a refusal to a party that Patricia had given to me to post weeks ago. I *had* posted the letter to Tutt's—and Tutt's were sending the coal [which I had meant to cancel]. And Fleming's were sending the coal. And Black's were sending the coal. And our shed only holds two tons.[30]

Each company was sending two tons each. He decides to depart the scene as all three coal deliveries arrive at the same time and to take 'a good long walk.'[31] He is clearly a man with William's habit of misadventure and advantageous exit.

The opening of *Kathleen and I* notes that the stories in the book are drawn from short comic sketches about married life published initially in *Punch*, as well as in *The Humorist* and *London Opinion*. These stories are based on the family life of Kathleen, her husband, John, and their daughter Veronica, who finds that, 'Grown-ups are such inexplicable things.'[32] John is the first-person narrator.[33] He is a writer himself and has published several books.[34] In stories reminiscent of William, his cousin Archie Fenton is an artist and he has aunts called Emily, Martha and Mathilda. John makes unsuccessful New Year resolutions, pretends that he is too ill to go to work, has his coat sold at a local bazaar and uses someone else's shoe cream on his hair. The echoes of the William stories inherent in these plots will be obvious to any William fan. John settles down to write and reflects on his art: 'Nothing happens in my stories. I dislike things happening to me, and I credit my characters with the same tastes. Now some editors like that sort of thing and some don't.'[35] Had Crompton ever been told that nothing much ever happens in her novels? It is possible. Aspects of these two collections are arguably adult William-lite versions of William, created, as ever, by a dry, sardonic Crompton, who cannot bring them to life with quite the same sharp-edged satirical tone that lies at the heart of her genius in William.

Crompton creates a young female comic protagonist in *Felicity Stands By* (1928), a collection of stories or sketches based on the antics of sixteen-year-old Felicity. She is from the upper classes and lives at the Hall with her sister Rosemary, her grandfather Sir Digby Harborough, his secretary Franklin, who is in love with Rosemary, and Moult the butler, with occasional visits from Felicity's brother Ronald and aunt, Lady Montague. The book is held together by a loose plot that revolves around Franklin and Rosemary's relationship and Felicity herself as she grows up. In the first story, Felicity has just left school and by the last story, she has cut off her plaits and had her hair shingled for her coming-out party. By the end of the collection, both Ronald and Rosemary are engaged, the latter, of course, to the poor but adorable Franklin. Felicity's 'familiar demon of mischief' inspires all sorts of adventures based on meddling, misunderstandings, and mistaken identity.[36] For Felicity, 'Real life is very disappointing.'[37] William and Violet Elizabeth would no doubt sympathise with her plight, although it is adults they find disappointing, not life itself, which always seems to hold endless adventure. In Crompton's novels, young people find life disappointing too, but their experience is viewed from a more sanguine and less light-hearted perspective.

$$* \quad * \quad *$$

It is worth pausing to consider that the publication dates of Crompton's books and stories in the nineteen twenties might not reflect the pace of her writing life. *Anne Morrison* (1925), published in the same year as the first novel in her trilogy, *The Wildings*, ends shortly after the First World War. It is tempting to consider whether it, as well as other early novels, could have been written several years before 1923 and the publication of her first novel, *The Innermost Room* (1923). This conjures up a biographer's vision of Richmal travelling between St Elphin's and Bromley, where her mother had moved after the death of her father in 1915, and subsequently from 1917 to 1923 flashing past on her bicycle between Bromley High School and her new home in Kent, clutching a writing box, or at least a battered leather satchel, full of manuscripts, akin to Jane Austen.[38] Her evenings could have been spent writing short stories at an incredible rate, preparing her lessons and marking her pupils' work, as well as writing her early novels. If this was not the case, from the age of thirty—Anne Morrison's age at the end of her third novel—over ten years from 1921, Crompton wrote and published an astonishing fifteen novels, in addition to thirteen William books based on stories published in magazines from 1919. Nine other short story collections were published from 1926 to 1931, including four in 1928 alone. In addition to the William stories, she was also publishing other stories that appeared in magazines but were not included in the book collections. All one can say is that it would not be surprising if Crompton had written early versions of novels, as well as her short stories, during the long evenings when she was teaching at St Elphins and Bromley High School from 1914, or at least in the five years after she moved to Bromley in 1917 when she had 'a room of her own,' in her home in Kent.

In 1968, she explained that she was indeed writing throughout her youth. She told journalist Madeleine Harmsworth:

> At school she was always writing little stories, and continued the habit through a Classics course at [Royal Holloway College] London University, and when she became a schoolmistress at the Bromley High School for Girls.
>
> "I wrote heaps of short stories about all sorts of things, and started submitting them to magazines. They all got sent back, but I couldn't stop. I decided to be philosophical. I thought I would regard my writing as a hobby, like others had golf or stamps. Only I had an advantage. My hobby wasn't so expensive."
>
> "Gradually I started to get accepted, but I kept it all a secret—I don't know why. I'd always wanted to hide away from my writing."
>
> "I felt it was incongruous that the me who wrote wasn't the me people thought they knew. At school I was always Miss Lamburn, so it was easy to keep it quiet."[39]

Here Crompton the author is hidden behind Miss Lamburn. No doubt the private life of Ray was hidden away too.

Crompton brought her experience of children, younger and older adults from school, university, and home into her writing. The adventures of their everyday world from both a child or adult perspective is a feature of her writing. Some people like Patricia's husband struggle to make the transition from childhood into adult life.

Notes

1. "William the Match-Maker," 135.
2. "William the Bold Crusader," 196.
3. "William the Philanthropist," 158.
4. "The Sweet Little Girl in White," 35.
5. Dickens, 48.
6. Ibid., 78.
7. "One Crowded Hour," 179.
8. "All the News," 83.
9. Ibid., 92.
10. Ibid., 103.
11. "William the Philanthropist," 159.
12. "Only Just in Time," 91.
13. "William and the Little Strangers," 30.
14. "William and the Haunted Cottage," 148.
15. In another story, Crompton writes about a six-year-old girl in a version of the fairy tale *Little Red Riding Hood*. Her parents ignore her as they enjoy a social whirl of golf, lunches, dances, and the theatre. The girl runs away and finds herself in some wood. A pretty cottage entices her in and the old grandmother who owns the cottage finds the girl asleep in her bed. The girl hopes she is a kind witch, and the grandmother believes that the girl is a reincarnation of her dead grandchild. A local vicar breaks the spell and reunites the girl with her parents, who vow to become a real mother and father to her in future. In this allegorical tale it is the girl's parents who need to join the real world and become better parents. "How April Found Her Fortune" *The London Magazine*, February 1925. Reprinted in *JWSM* 36, 22–29.
16. "William the Philanthropist," 162.
17. "William and One of Those Things," 91.
18. "William the Philanthropist," 171.
19. *The Ridleys*, 123.
20. Quoted in Mariani, 9.
21. *The Ridleys*, 127.
22. "The Rivals," 91.

23. "Henri Learns the Language," 16.
24. "The Terrible Magician," 24.
25. Ibid., 33.
26. *Kathleen and I, and, of course, Veronica* (1926), *A Monstrous Regiment* (1927), *Enter Patricia* (1927), *The Middle Things* (1928), *Felicity Stands By* (1928), *Sugar and Spice and Other Stories* (1928), *Mist and Other Stories* (1928), *Ladies First* (1929), *The Silver Birch and Other Stories* (1931), *The First Morning* (1936).
27. *Dundee Courier*, 28 July 1928, 8.
28. Delafield's popular novel takes a satirical look at the life of an upper-class married woman.
29. *Enter Patricia* is part short story collection and part novel. The structure is loosely based on the courtship and marriage of Patricia and her husband, whilst each chapter stands alone as a vignette.
30. *Enter Patricia*, 79.
31. Ibid.
32. "An Original Holiday," 260.
33. John in *Kathleen and I* is named in "The Donkey's Head" (158) and "The Burglar" (211).
34. "Fame," 250.
35. "The Story of a Story," 281.
36. *Felicity*, 139.
37. Ibid., 116.
38. In 1801, when Jane Austen moved to Bath with her family she took early manuscripts of her novels, "First Impressions" and "Elinor and Marianne," with her. The novels were not published until many years later, and after her move to Chawton, with revised titles, *Pride and Prejudice* (1813) and *Sense and Sensibility* (1811) respectively.
39. Harmsworth, 17.

References

Crompton, Richmal (Lamburn R.C.). September 1918. "One Crowded Hour." *Woman at Home*, 174–179.

———. 1927. "All the News." In *William - In Trouble*, by Richmal Crompton, 80–105. London: George Newnes Ltd.

———. 1926. "An Original Holiday." In *Kathleen and I, and, of course, Veronica*, by Richmal Crompton, 257–260. London: Hodder & Stoughton.

———. 1927. *Enter Patricia*. London: George Newnes Ltd.

————. 1926. "Fame." In *Kathleen and I, and, of Course, Veronica*, by Richmal Crompton, 249–252. London: Hodder & Stoughton.

————. 1928. *Felicity Stands By*. London: George Newnes Ltd.

————. 1984. First published 1925. "Henri Learns the Language." In *Still - William*, by Richmal Crompton, 1–15. Basingstoke, Hampshire: Macmillan Children's Books.

————. Summer 2015. "How April Found Her Fortune." *The Just Wiliam Society Magazine 36* 22–29.

Crompton, Richmal. 1992. First published 1934. "Only Just in Time." In *William - The Gangster*, by Richmal Crompton, 83–105. Basingstoke, Hampshire: Macmillan Children's Books.

————. 1947. *The Ridleys*. Howard Baker: London.

————. 1959. First published 1922. "The Rivals." In *More William*, by Richmal Crompton, 80–90. London: George Newnes Ltd.

————. 1926. "The Story of a Story." In *Kathleen and I, and, of Course, Veronica*, by Richmal Crompton, 281–286. London: Hodder and Stoughton.

————. 1984. First published 1925. "The Sweet Little Girl in White." In *Still - William*, by Richmal Crompton, 32–53. Basingstoke, Hampshire: Macmillan Children's Books.

————. 1984. First published 1927. "The Terrible Magician." In *William - The Outlaw*, by Richmal Crompton, 18–51. Basingstoke, Hampshire: Macmillan Children's Books.

————. 1991. First published 1956. "William and One of Those Things." In *William and the Space Animal*, by Richmal Crompton, 84–108. Basingstoke, Hampshire: Macmillan Children's Books.

————. 1992. First published 1952. "William and the Haunted Cottage." In *William and the Tramp*, by Richmal Crompton, 1–36. Basingstoke, Hampshire: Macmillan Children's Books.

————. 1990. First published 1937. "William and the Little Strangers." In *William - The Showman*, by Richmal Crompton, 20–48. Basingstoke, Hampshire: Macmillan Children's Books.

————. 1930. First published 1926. "William the Bold Crusader." In *William - The Conqueror*, by Richmal Crompton, 179–197. London: George Newnes Ltd.

————. 1984, First published 1925. "William the Match-Maker." In *Still - William*, by Richmal Crompton, 127–152. Basingstoke, Hampshire: Macmillan Children's Books.

————. 1930. First published 1926. "William the Philanthropist." In *William - The Conqueror*, by Richmal Crompton, 157–178. London: George Newnes Ltd.

Dickens, Charles. 1992. *Great Expectations*. London: Wordsworth Classics.

Harmsworth, Madeleine. 20 November 1968. "William and the Old Lady of Beechworth." *Daily Mirror*, 16–17.

Mariani, Umberto. 2008. *Living Masks: The Achievement of Pirandello*. Toronto: University of Toronto Press.

12

Growing Up

In several Crompton novels, we see characters grow up, or at least grow older, unlike William or Violet Elizabeth. We follow some of them over the years when they return to the same place where they have stayed before, perhaps for a holiday. As in the William stories, many of Crompton's novels are based on episodes and scenes in which we capture her characters at specific moments, enjoying one kind of domestic adventure after another, or facing a turning point in their lives as they grow older. We do not necessarily get close to them, but we come to know what happens to them and how their lives are changed as a result. *The Innermost Room* (1923), *Anne Morrison* (1925), *The Four Graces* (1929), *Blue Flames* (1930), *Quartet* (1935) and *Frost at Morning* (1950) are all novels about growing up, what we become as the years pass, how we see ourselves at different stages in our lives, and whether we could have become other than we are. In other novels, Crompton focuses on a specific moment in time and what happens to several characters over a day, weekend or on holiday, in a structure that is comparable to the episodic William stories.[1] Her stories about growing up and the William stories have been read by older children and adults. They look at the world in a way that encompass perspectives that mean something to her readers whatever their age.

Crompton cares about the extent to which our childhood influences our sense of identity and worth. Some people can never set aside the disadvantages of their youth altogether, but they might learn to live with and learn from what has happened, especially if they find someone who can help them

J. McVeigh, *Richmal Crompton, Author of Just William*, Literary Lives, https://doi.org/10.1007/978-3-030-96511-2_12

come to terms with their experience. In several novels, Crompton portrays young people growing up without the support of their parents or anyone else who could advise them with their best interests in mind. Aunts may be involved in bringing them up, but they might not be a positive influence.[2]

The Innermost Room (1923) and *Anne Morrison* (1925) follow a young girl as she grows up. In *The Hidden Light* (1924), her heroine finds love and marries, whilst Anne chooses to turn down offers of marriage and is happy to live as she chooses on her own. However, the ending is clichéd. Anne can only make this choice because she receives a surprise inheritance. *Anne Morrison* was sent to potential publishers in the early nineteen nineties. They turned it down. It is a pity that they were not sent any of her more clear-sighted early novels from the nineteen twenties, such as the Wildings trilogy, *The Wildings* (1925), *David Wilding* (1926), and *The Thorn Bush* (1928), or *Millicent Dorrington* (1927) and *Roofs Off* (1928).

The Innermost Room (1923) is a coming-of-age novel, also known as bildungsroman, written from ten-year-old Bridget's point of view. She introduces us to her older brothers, Robert and Derek, and her sister Gloria. Gloria is beautiful and loves shopping for clothes to show off her appearance, whilst Bridget is clever and prefers reading and observing people. She feels that she has little to show off about. Aunt Valentine agrees with her, shaking her head when Bridget does not listen to her words of advice during a shopping trip: "'It's all right," she said, "I won't trouble Bridget as she takes no interest in things. Not like dear Gloria."'[3] It is her characters who lack this interest in things, in possessions and how much they cost, rather than people, that Crompton values.

This novel is also a story about an emerging author who gives up writing for love and marriage and about a girl and young woman who feels isolated from the world of adults. She seeks solace in her fiction. At fifteen, Bridget starts writing poems and stories, which are part of her inner sanctuary; what she calls her innermost room. 'Everybody had an innermost room…. Nobody knew anybody really' and as a young woman it is Bridget's refuge, the room of her own.[4] Bridget has a vision of the maze of rooms she has built up within herself to protect her from being hurt and to hide her true nature. Before she goes to college and meets her friend Susan: 'No one came into the innermost room. Bridget's little soul dwelt there—impregnable, aloof and remote.'[5]

In Elizabeth Bowen's *Death of the Heart* (1938), Portia is another young protagonist, and we see the world through her frightened eyes too as the world around her seems to have a sense of certainty and confidence that she does not possess:

Portia could see it going on everywhere. She had watched life … with a sort of despair – motivated and busy always, always progressing…. She could not believe there was not a plan of the whole set-up in every head but her own.[6]

In Bowen's novel most of the adult characters are unsympathetic and rarely have Portia's best interests at heart. In its portrayal of adult duplicity, it has even more in common with Crompton's later novel, *Frost at Morning* (1950). Maroula Joannou argues that in *The Death of the Heart*, the 'acquisition of grown-up status is a central theme.'[7] Portia's innocence and emotional connection with the world is challenged when she meets the dry and worn cynicism of adults around her. Her childlike view of the world peers out onto all that is new to her and as readers we look on with dismay at the bitter view of the world we see through her eyes. Bridget also looks outwards with confusion at times. She and other young characters in Crompton's novels show us the world seen through their younger eyes too.

When she grows up and falls in love, Bridget is initially frightened of giving up her freedom to write and never belonging to herself anymore.[8] Yet she chooses marriage over a life as an author and gives up her novel and the sanctuary of the room where she wrote it. She gives up her room of her own full of 'things … things … things … shadows she'd mistaken for substance.'[9] Other women in Crompton's novels make a different choice.

The Four Graces (1929) is the story of four sisters, Helen, the eldest, Patricia, who is known as Peter, Joanna, and Gabriel, the youngest. Their father gave them all the same middle name, Grace.[11] At the opening of the novel, they have lived with their Aunt Bertha for ten years since the death of their parents. Helen comes of age and asks her aunt to leave. Bertha persuades herself that this is exactly what she had wanted to do anyway. Helen and her sisters are keen to escape their aunt's interference. The sisters learn to rely on each other more than anyone else, and Helen takes charge of the household.[12] When they are young adults, Helen's and Peter's lives are blighted by the cruelty of other people who claim to love them. The pursuit of selfish ends by those who purport to care for them has tragic consequences. Crompton's writing style has a light touch, which belies the tragedy in this novel. In 1929, a contemporary review of *Four Graces* suggests that it will appeal directly to younger readers: 'The novel sparkles with lively dialogue, with comedy, pathos and tragedy intermingled.'[13] This novel in part reflects Crompton's concern in other stories with difficult relationships between women friends, including those who are teachers, and the extent to which power imbalances between them can suffocate one of their lives.

Crompton is interested in bullies who draw someone so close to them that there is no aspect of their life that they do not control. In *Chedsy Place*,

"RICHMAL CROMPTON."
· Author of "The Four Graces."

Fig. 12.1 Richmal Crompton Illustrated London News 1929[10]

Miss Kimball realises that she must not hurt her younger companion Sidney 'beyond healing':

> She could not live now without Sidney's freshness and youth and adoration. It was more necessary to her than her drug. She was at the zenith of her beauty, her hard charm, her exquisiteness, but it wouldn't last much longer…. She must have Sidney with her for her middle age, for her old age…. She wouldn't share Sidney with anyone. Not with anyone. Ever.[14]

Whilst in 'The Beast,' from *A Monstrous Regiment* (1927), Pauline is Jennifer's boss at the school where they teach, and they live in the same hostel.

Pauline expects to be able to control every aspect of Jennifer's life and once their ties are firm and fixed, Pauline starts to criticise her in public and belittle her private life. Similarly, in *The Four Graces* Peter is in awe of her colleague Vere, who enjoys lying in the sunshine; the older woman is 'conscious of this child's passionate devotion, teasing her with just a touch of cruelty ... administering just the right amount of flattery.... It was a game she'd always loved, a game which lent to life the zest without which it would be unbearable.'[15] She drives a wedge between Peter and her sisters and ultimately ruins her life. Crompton is interested in friendships between women based on subservience, possessiveness and control. For some people it is not possible for them to see anyone except as an adjunct to themselves. Her most fiendish representation of a possessive woman who is overpowering and frightening is in *Narcissa*, as we shall see in a later chapter.

In *Blue Flames* (1930) we follow three brothers over four decades in scenes set at ten-year intervals from 1899, when they are children, ending in 1930 when the innocence of youth has been eroded and bitterness has taken its place. *Quartet* (1935) similarly follows four siblings, two girls and two boys, as they grow up and captures their lives in 1900, 1910, 1919 and 1929. In the formal staged structure of these two novels, we capture these characters at significant moments in their lives, rather than following them as they grow up more slowly over a number of years. It is an anecdotal style that is reflected in the episodic nature of the William stories too. *Four Graces* is more nuanced, and we care about what happens to these young women.

Crompton has a tendency to return to similar themes in later novels from 1950 in which the youthful passion of her earlier novels is lost. In several a more mature perspective successfully takes its place. In *Frost at Morning*, children grow up without the support of their families. It asks what happens when a child grows up in a second family after a divorce, both parents are absent, or when a mother prefers drinking, parties and flirtation to domestic chores and family life.[16] Three unrelated young children are living away from home in a vicarage. During her short life, Monica has been sent to many similar places. Her parents are divorced and often send her away: 'She knew things that children should not know, that she must not mention to other children, things that lay like a fog over her spirit, giving her a sense of fear and, strangely, of guilt.'[17] Geraldine knows that her real parents do not want her, and her adoptive parents have now sent her away to have a baby of their own. Her adoptive mother, Grace, tries to love her but struggles to do so. Philip returns home to find that his father has remarried and that he now has a stepbrother. He feels excluded and alone within a new family to whom he does not belong. Amidst their anger and sense of isolation, Philip and

Geraldine miss the chance to become friends. This is a story about searching for a sense of belonging despite the lack of any special place, home or family and how the disadvantages of our childhood can be overcome.[18]

As well as stories about growing up, in other novels, Crompton is interested in what it means to behave in a grown-up way, whatever age her characters might be. In *Merlin Bay* (1939), Jessica's husband Brian drinks, but she remains loyal to him: 'He's kind and generous, like a child, and irresponsible like a child.... Each time he says he's learnt his lesson and it will never happen again, and each time he absolutely believes it.'[19] He goes on hurting his wife, oblivious to the impact that his actions have on her and the rest of his family. In *The Ridleys* (1947), Edward is unhappy in his marriage to Babette, who is 'one of those people who've never really grown up ... She was happiest as a school-girl, and she's fixed there permanently for the rest of her life.'[20] Being childlike as an adult is a form of innocence that harkens back to childhood. However, it can also mean that these characters never grow up to accept responsibility for themselves and those close to them, becoming more and more selfish and unable to form meaningful relationships. People close to them are hurt and left to shoulder responsibilities on their own.

What happens to us as we grow up, and childlike qualities in some adults, fascinates Crompton. She does not consider growing up merely on the basis of age. In her writing, she is concerned with what it means to behave in a mature and considerate way whatever age her characters might be. She recognises that many adults struggle with the implications of growing up and the responsibility to take a wider view of the world that is concerned with people other than themselves. And in doing so, she considers how relationships can turn on moments in life when people could have treated each other better. She has learnt the lesson her father taught her and Gwen when they were children themselves.

* * *

These novels, suitable for both younger and older readers, consider the perspective of children and young adults as they grow older. William is a complex character. In his stories, there is a child's perspective and a narrator's wry eye on the inability of some adults to grow up and behave in a considered way that puts other people first. Also, William is an ageless touchstone who has moments that almost seem to be touched by maturity, although he is unlikely to recognise them as such. As we shall see in a later chapter, he is a flawed hero who helps us to see ourselves more clearly. He has an innocence mixed with a hint of guile when he is trying to achieve something he wants. In common with other heroes, he can be egotistical at times. However, he rarely does anything that will deliberately hurt or undermine another person. When he does so, it is usually to draw attention to pomposity, greed and hubris. We can see in his antics a reflection of our own less than mature flaws and misdemeanors.

It is both their childlike self and a more mature perspective that many readers bring to the William stories. The William stories from the twenties and thirties were written for adults and are popular with adult readers. As mentioned in the first chapter, in the nineteen fifties, Crompton looks back and feels like a wolf in sheep's clothing when she is considered as a children's writer. The William stories were first published as stories for adults about children and did not find their way onto the shelves of children's books until after the Second World War. She believes that 'the fact that the "William" stories were originally written with no eye on a child-reading public has helped to make them popular with children.'[21] Crompton does not think:

> that there is any hard line of demarcation between writing for children and writing for adults (except, of course, in the case of very tiny children). A child and an adult dwell side by side in most of us. The normal child has a keener insight into the adult world than we realize, and the normal adult is nearer his childhood than he would admit.[22]

She is describing here a form of double address from her perspective as an adult with a conscious concern not to write down to children. As British academic Peter Hunt has suggested, anyone 'interested in exploring the elusive borderland between children's and adult books can do no better than to look at the work of Richmal Crompton.' He describes the William stories as situation comedy, which operate as double narratives, 'addressing two audiences simultaneously but separately, and the adult audience primarily.'[23] Crompton's narrator addresses the many readers of differing ages who love the situation comedy in the stories and Crompton's wry tone. William's popularity with adults is based on more than nostalgia for childhood reading.[24]

The satirical style and vocabulary in the William stories are sophisticated.[25] American academic Betty Greenway argues that the narrative viewpoint is the most important factor in dual-audience texts by Crompton and Dylan Thomas. She suggests that Thomas was influenced by Crompton in his stories for young people, such as *Portrait of the Young Artists as a Young Dog* (1954). In their stories we hear the voice of the adult narrators, 'who are aware of things the child protagonist does not know.... Crompton's narrator is a wise, understanding, and humorous commentator on the specific action,' Greenway writes, and 'there is an adult's recognition of the meaning behind a childhood perception.' In William, stories are told through action set in a series of scenes, rather than in descriptive narrative, and this means the reader has 'the opportunity to reflect on the disparity between what the protagonists think has happened and what really has.'[26] David Buckingham agrees that there is both a child-centred perspective and a style attractive to adults in William and that the stories have a dual address. He argues convincingly that the:

> vocabulary is often quite elevated, and there are elements of social satire and irony that most child readers would probably find obscure. Many of the descriptions of adult eccentricities … refer to aspects of adult life that would be beyond the grasp of many children….
>
> Perhaps more significantly, the narrative often requires the reader to be more knowledgeable than William himself…. The humour depends upon us recognizing William as a loveable fantasist, whose plans cannot conceivably work.
>
> Likewise, William frequently misunderstands adults' ideas and intentions, even as he exposes their hypocrisy: he often imagines sinister and melodramatic explanations for their behaviour (such as international espionage) that invariably prove wide of the mark…. While it easy to see how these ironies might appeal to adult readers, there is no reason to assume they are not accessible to children as well…. The reader, we might say, has to read as an adult, and not only as a child.[27]

Finally, Ralph Stewart also suggests that in the stories from the nineteen twenties the 'point of view [of the narrative] is ostensibly adult…. overt appeals to the reader are sometimes made over William's head,' whilst being told from his point of view. He adds, complementing Greenway and Buckingham, that the 'satire in the William stories … is a natural result of juxtaposing two worlds with different standards' and 'the relative sophistication of the style implies lack of condescension to child readers.'[28] These articles contribute to our understanding about why William has attracted a dual audience and the crossover characteristics in Crompton's writing. As she wrote in *The Writer* in 1952, encouraging children to read material originally intended for adults respects them as readers. In the stories, adult readers can look at their own doubleness in a gentle form of self-mockery. Children and adults can live in and empathise with the worlds created in the William stories in which style and tone is more important than plot and the stories appeal to both our past and present selves.[29]

Author Philip Pullman, whose *The Dark Materials* trilogy is read by older children and adults alike, describes Crompton's narrative voice similarly, or what he prefers to call *stance*—'not quite the same as voice, not quite the same as *point of view*, it's a mixture of where the camera is, so to speak, and where the sympathy lies.'[30] He suggests that, in the William stories, 'it's a matter of being *with* the characters but not entirely *of* them, and it's a stance that works very well with [her] mixed audience.'[31] It is this ability to be *with* both child and adult readers, to understand the perspectives of both, even though William's world may be different from his readers, and to appreciate that in some ways we never grow up so much that we leave our childhood selves behind us altogether, that helps to explain why Crompton has such an insight into a child's view of the world. Her study of mankind embraces her readers whatever their age.

* * *

The literary merit in her writing lies in the language, style and tone of the narrative that speak to both adults and children, although some, but not all, children may miss Crompton's wry eye reflecting on the absurdities of the adult world. In 'William Goes Shopping' from *William's Happy Days* (1930):

> William had spent a happy morning roaming the countryside with Ginger, Douglas and Henry…. they had discussed at length that insoluble mystery— why a morning passes so much more quickly in holiday than in term time.[32]

Time passes more slowly in 'work time' too. There is an edge to much of the farce in the story that a dual audience can enjoy. His mother asks him to go shopping for her, even though it is the first afternoon of the holidays. He seeks to dissuade her: 'William had an unexpectedly delicate hand at bargaining.'[33] On this occasion, he is rewarded for his expression of unselfish devotion and sets off moodily and with 'gloomy reverie' into town.[34] After an inevitable misadventure, he is trying to escape capture when he finds himself posing as a wax model in a shop window. A little girl describes his face as ugly to her mother. They do not suspect that he is a fraud. William is relieved, 'a relief that was tempered with indignation at the strictures that had been passed upon his appearance,' although this is clearly not how he would have described the situation himself.[35] On his escape, he jostles with a bus conductor, who also has a 'septuagenarian clergyman' as a passenger.[36] The conductor tells William that the circus at Hadley had performing monkeys:

> "I thought they'd have kept you for that."

William replied breathlessly but with spirit:

> "Oh no. They said they weren't doin' much business. The people in Hadley'd seen you so often that the performin' monkeys seemed quite or'din'ry."[37]

During a series of adventures, which have nothing to do with the purpose of his outing, William has forgotten that he has been sent on an errand to buy some fish for his mother. He tries to find a way out of his predicament:

> The idea of pretending to have acted from humanitarian principles because he thought it wrong to kill fishes occurred to him, but was dismissed as untenable in view of the fact that he spent the larger part of his holidays angling for fish in the village stream with a bent pin on the end of a string.[38]

Fate saves him on this occasion and his mother is apologetic. She has forgotten that the fishmongers are closed for the afternoon. He sets off to buy Christmas presents with some unexpected funds, although 'he wasn't going to spend more than he could help on [his] presents. Everyone said that it was the *thought* that mattered not the actual value of the present, so he'd jolly well take them at their word.'[39] This story reminds us how we all might feel in similar circumstances, uses language and vocabulary uncommon in many children's stories, and even includes a sitcom style joke.

One of William's adventures in this story is an opportunity to learn how to make a wooden whistle:

> Life seemed to stretch before him—one long glorious opportunity for whistle making.
>
> He gathered breath and blew a piercing blast—a paean of exultation and triumph and joy of life.[40]

This moment is one of the joys William's readers share with him. His indefatigable sense of hope is one of his most important qualities, if not the most significant. Whatever happens William always has hope that everything will turn out for the best, even when it has not, because he convinces himself that it has. This is a quality that many adults long for at moments when hope has faded, and life is not going at all well.

This William story encapsulates the performative, dramatic quality in Crompton's fiction and it is just one example amongst many others. It is not surprising that, in the nineteen thirties, Crompton's writing was reimagined for the stage, although her plays for the radio after the war would prove far more successful and much of the satirical nuances of her prose is 'lost in translation' in the stage productions.

Notes

1. These novels include *The Holiday* (1933), *The Old Man's Birthday* (1934), *Chedsy Place* (1934), *Merlin Bay* (1939), and *Four in Exile* (1954).
2. These novels include *The Innermost Room* (1923), *Millicent Dorrington* (1927), *The Four Graces* (1929), *Naomi Godstone* (1930), *Caroline* (1936).
3. *Innermost Room*, 42.
4. Ibid., 223.
5. Ibid., 84.
6. Bowen, 59.
7. Joannou, 139.
8. *Innermost Room*, 197.
9. Ibid., 280.
10. [c] Illustrated London News/Mary Evans Picture Library.
11. *Four Graces*, 69.
12. Also see *Millicent Dorrington* (1927) and *Caroline* (1936).
13. *Aberdeen Press & Journal* 4 March 1929, 2.
14. *Chedsy Place*, 137.
15. *Four Graces*, 89.
16. Crompton draws on poetry in her novels. This title resonates with Samuel Coleridge's poem "Frost at Midnight" (1798) about his own childhood.
17. *Frost at Morning*, 3.
18. In *Four in Exile* (1954), four children also spend time away from their family while their mother is in hospital. On their return they are outwardly unchanged, yet they have grown up. The children are unaware of the extent to which those who took them in temporarily have been changed too by the time they return home.
19. *Merlin Bay*, 168.
20. *The Ridleys*, 191.
21. UoR RC/1/1/2/3. *The Writer*, October 1952, 4.
22. Ibid., 5.
23. Hunt, 54. Barbara Wall describes dual address for a dual audience of both children and adults in which: 'Their narrators address child narratees, usually covertly, but often openly … either using the same 'tone of seriousness' which would be used to address adult narratees, or confidentially sharing the story in a way that allows adult narrator and child narratee a conjunction of interests. Concern for something other than

purely children's interests dominates their stories: pride in the artist's craft perhaps, or commitment to an idea; in the case of the greatest of all writers for children, the Charles Dodgson of the *Alice* books, a delight in language and logical problems' (35). Crompton is certainly committed to addressing ideas and values in her stories and her delight in language is clear.

Also see David Galef on the work for adults by A.A. Milne in "Crossing Over: Authors Who Write Both Children's and Adults' Fiction" *Children's Literature Association Quarterly 20.1* (1995).
24. Greenway 2001, 133.
25. Greenway 2002, 105.
26. Greenway 2001, 137–138.
27. Buckingham 2017.
28. Stewart, 181–184. Hunt similarly argues that William's continuing popularity has been maintained 'despite or because of the ambivalence of the narrative voice, which seems often to privilege the adult view of childhood while endorsing childhood's victories over the adult' (56).
29. Greenway 2001, 137–138.
30. Pullman, 137. The novels in the trilogy are *Northern Lights* (1995), *The Subtle Knife* (1997), *The Amber* Spyglass (2000). Pullman cites as an example the ending of the story in which William and the Outlaws meet and are outwitted by Violet Elizabeth, "The Sweet Little Girl in White": 'There is a very subtle and fluid mixture here of sympathy and satire, of affection and mockery, of cool knowledge and the memory of what it is not to have it,' he writes (138).
31. Ibid., 138.
32. "William Goes Shopping," 1.
33. Ibid., 3.
34. Ibid., 6.
35. Ibid., 20.
36. Ibid., 23.
37. Ibid.
38. Ibid., 25.
39. Ibid., 26.
40. Ibid., 26.

References

Bowen, Elizabeth. 1998. First published 1938. *The Death of the Heart.* London: Vintage.

Buckingham, David. 2017. "Just William: 'The Most Popular Boy in Fiction.'" *Growing Up Modern: Childhood, Youth and Popular Culture Since 1945.* Online at: https://davidbuckingham.net/growing-up-modern/just-william-the-most-popular-boy-in-fiction/

Crompton, Richmal. 2015. First published 1934. *Chedsy Place.* London: Bello.

———. 1950. *Frost at Morning.* London: Hutchinson.

———. 1939. *Merlin Bay.* London: Macmillan.

———. October 1952. "On Writing for Children." *The Writer 10.4* 4–5.

———. 1927. "The Beast." In *A Monstrous Regiment*, by Richmal Crompton, 208–242. London: Hutchinson & Co.

———. 1929. *The Four Graces.* London: Hodder & Stoughton.

———. 1926. *The House.* London: Hodder & Stoughton.

———. 1923. *The Innermost Room.* London: Andrew Melrose.

———. 1947. *The Ridleys.* Howard Baker: London.

———. 1999. First published 1930. "William Goes Shopping." In *William's Happy Days*, by Richmal Crompton, 7–28. Basingstoke, Hampshire: Macmillan Children's Books.

Galef, David. 1995. "Crossing Over: Authors Who Write Both Children's and Adults' Fiction." *Children's Literature Association Quarterly 20.1* 29–35.

Greenway, Betty. 2001. "The Influence of Children's Literature—A Case Study: Dylan Thomas and Richmal Crompton." *Children's Literature Association Quarterly 26.3* 133–139.

———. 2002. "William Forever: Richmal Crompton's Unusual Achievement." *The Lion and the Unicorn 26.1* 98–111.

Hunt, Peter. 2001. *Children's Literature.* Oxford: Blackwell.

Joannou, Maroula. 1995. *Ladies Please Don't Smash These Windows.* Oxford: Berg.

Pullman, Philip. 2020. *Daemon Voices: On Stories and Stoytelling.* Oxford: David Fickling.

Stewart, Ralph. 1988. "William Brown's World." *Children's Literature Association Quarterly 13.4* 181–185.

Wall, Barbara. 1991. *The Narrator's Voice: The Dilemma of Children's Fiction.* Basingstoke, Hampshire: Macmillan.

13

On Stage and in Literary London

It is hard to find many traces of Richmal's life in the fifteen years from 1924. We do not know how long it took her to adjust to her disability after she contracted polio or the extent to which she lived with ongoing pain. In the midst of her writing and other literary activities, as well as dealing with the long-term consequences of polio, Richmal developed breast cancer in her forties. She had a mastectomy and was nursed, as before, by her mother, who had already suffered from the same disease.[1] Yet, her experience of disability and serious illness did not define her life or her writing.

The thirties took Crompton beyond the bounds of Bromley on to the London stage and into modest literary circles. In 1931, her brother returned to England, and she also knew her brother-in-law's brother, Maurice Willson Disher. We can see aspects of Crompton's comic artistry in stories that feature William's brother Robert, and comparable young male characters are reinvented in other stories that are less well-known. As William's fame grew, Crompton experimented with new stories featuring William as first-person narrator.

Whatever else was happening in her personal life, Crompton's writing continues unabated, and she was publishing at a furious pace in this period. One version of her in these years is of a calm, unruffled, ambitious, consummate professional working hard to support her family. In another, she is as vibrant, mischievous and sardonic as ever, performing on the page and writing dramatic scenes of comedy and more serious drama in other fiction.

* * *

J. McVeigh, *Richmal Crompton, Author of Just William*, Literary Lives, https://doi.org/10.1007/978-3-030-96511-2_13

During the thirties, Crompton was moving tentatively within literary London. There was another writer in the family, whom Richmal came to know after her sister's marriage and who was more familiar with this territory. Maurice Willson Disher (1893–1969), Thomas Disher's younger brother, was a journalist and writer. His wife, the artist Eve Disher, moved amidst the fringes of Bloomsbury circles. By the age of eighteen, Maurice became a sub-editor for *The Evening Standard*, working on music hall reviews, following an apprenticeship for a local paper. By 1912, he became the newspaper's deputy dramatic critic, and the principal critic nine years later. He went on to be a critic for *The Observer* and *The Daily Mail*.[2] Willson Disher also produced and broadcast programmes on BBC radio about old music halls, comic operas, theatre composers and comic songs, and he wrote extensively about clowns, pantomimes and music halls.

Maurice's overriding interests were the circus and Victorian music hall. Margaret remembers that family life in the thirties included many outings with Aunt Richmal and Clara, including those with Uncle Maurice. He knew many well-known stage stars and artistes, authors and painters and lived on the fringe of London's bohemian life. She recalls that,

> wherever Uncle Maurice went, all eyes would turn to look at him. He used to wear a dramatic black hat (almost compulsory for theatre critics) and had a pronounced limp owing to a childhood illness; he had to use a stick for walking… Maurice was married to a talented artist – Eve Disher – but they lived in separate flats, visiting each other from time to time…. She was described as 'the last of the Bloomsbury Set', who had shared a house with the Stracheys [and she shared a studio with the artist Vera Cunningham for a time]. But sometime after the war, Maurice found himself a delightful second Eve and they lived happily ever after, the last years of his life in Spain.[3]

Maurice and Richmal had much in common. Richmal loved performance, and often visited the theatre locally and in central London. One of Maurice's legs had been impaired since childhood, so both had experience of disability. Whether they talked about this, or reticence prevented them from doing so, we do not know. Perhaps a cache of letters between them will surface one day. In the thirties, plays based on a couple of Crompton's stories briefly appeared on the London stage and Maurice would have been a useful contact during this period.

* * *

The theatrical and performative are central to the William stories. Meetings or hustings, shows, lectures, musical performances and plays feature throughout and often set the scene for some of the funniest stories. William is a theatrical figure, performing on and off the stage in anecdotes staged within each story. The stories are dramatic in design and content. Each one is made up of a series of scenes, with William at their centre. They have a carnivalesque quality in which the fun is overlaid with a satirical eye that allows us to look at the day-to-day world from a different perspective.[4] In his writing about clowns and pantomime, Maurice Disher argues that for the showman 'laughter is directly related to emotion,' although it is an emotion that the audience can disassociate from real life, because they know that what is being presented to them is make-believe.[5] As a result, this 'imperfect sympathy enables the playgoer to see comedy in happenings which he would take seriously outside a theatre.'[6] As Disher suggests, the imperfect sympathy of Crompton's readers allows us to see a truth about people and society in the stories, whilst suspending disbelief about the veracity of William's world.

This dramatic quality in the William stories is reflected in many of Crompton's other short stories and novels and is a feature of her writing as a whole. For example, in novels set within a specific place, such as *Roofs Off* (1928) based on a new housing estate, and *Chedsy Place* (1934), vignettes are strung together in a series of episodes about different characters. In the latter, a country house is reinvented as a hotel. Guests arrive for the opening weekend, and we learn about each of them in a snapshot of their lives. How did they get to where they are and where are they going? Living rooms, hotel rooms, dining rooms and gardens all provide ideal settings for turning points in life, love and loss. A few of Crompton's novels use a village as the theatrical setting for a dramatic tale in which the 'stage' is set across a number of houses where different characters live within families, or in a group of friends. In three novels about life in a village, *Leadon Hill* (1927), *Abbots' End* (1929) and *Steffan Green* (1940), Crompton moves on to 'the stage' a range of characters who perform a series of vignettes that hang together loosely, as we move from family to family, house to house, to watch and stare. These novels offer a plethora of character types in a composite of staged scenes but without a strong overarching plot. It is hard to really care about many of them. We do not know them well enough to get under their skin, but their behaviour, and those of others who know them, tells us something about the values that Crompton cared about. They feature pomposity, selfishness and pettiness, as well as suffocating control by parents or amongst friends and the search for personal freedom. Values and allegories, not complex characterisations, lie at the heart of these stories.

In her plays, or those written by others, much of the depth found in her novels is missing. In Crompton's comic play, *In Mrs 'awkins' Kitchen*, a couple of working-class women gossip about the murder allegedly perpetrated by Mrs Hawkins's husband.[7] It was performed at least once in an afternoon matinee organised for members of the Royal Society of Arts at the Everyman Theatre in Hampstead in 1931.[8] The play has a strong oral quality based on Crompton's wordplay on Mrs Hawkins's working-class accent and might have done better on radio. The comedy is light, and the plot is simple. The main quality of her writing is in the language and the banter and pace in the women's conversation. This could have been lost in a stage production, which might have accentuated the character's physical appearance, rather than nuances in their accent.

Miss Tracy, a play written by Ireland Wood and based on Crompton's *The Odyssey of Euphemia Tracy* (1932), was performed at the Shilling Theatre, Putney Bridge London in October 1934.[9] Aunts Emily and Agnes live with their brother Henry and cantankerous mother in another play, *Charity Begins* (1936), also written by Ireland Wood, based on a short story by Crompton, 'Up the Garden Path.'[10] The play focuses on their sister Catherine who fled the family home as a young woman. She returns to live with them many years later, in common with Philippa in *Caroline* (1936).[11] *Charity Begins* was performed at the Aldwych Theatre, London in January 1936.[12] Rex Harrison, well-known on stage and screen in the early to mid-twentieth century, played a cad and a bounder in this production. In July 1937, Margaret Rutherford, another star of stage and screen in this period, appeared in a performance of the play at the Embassy Theatre in London and, in 1934, she was also a member of the cast for *Miss Tracy*.[13] Trevor Howard, who starred in the iconic film *Brief Encounter* (1945) with Celia Johnson, performed in a production of the play in Colchester in October 1939. There were further performances of *Charity Begins* by local theatre companies into the nineteen fifties.[14] The comedy in both plays is light. The loss of Crompton's touch found in *The Odyssey of Euphemia Tracy* and other novels weakens the plot and the comedy in these plays is frothy, rather than pithy. Crompton's presence in London's theatres was short-lived and she was not destined to become a well-known playwright for the stage. Nevertheless, some of the greatest actors of this era performed in her plays.

* * *

Crompton knew about the activities of literary societies at first hand as an active member of the London Lyceum Club, particularly the Writers' Section. The Club was established in 1902 to bring together women with an interest in the arts. In 1934, Crompton gave a talk to the writers' group on 'Laughter in Literature.'[15] She attended social events for over a hundred guests, speaking at one event about 'Why do I write?' In a debate held in 1938, she opposed the proposition that 'The woman novelist is less reticent than her male co-writer.' The proposition was lost. In 1936–1937, she was Secretary of the Writers' Section and was subsequently elected Vice-Chairman in 1938.[16] Authors such as Dorothy Sayers, Rose Macaulay and Walter de la Mare gave talks at their meetings. In the thirties, a survey of eight hundred children living in the east end of London identified William story collections as their most popular books.[17] Crompton was a hugely successful, popular writer by this stage in her career and one wonders how these other authors thought of her in the thirties and whether they accepted her as an equal.

Members of literary societies are pilloried in William stories. Professor Golightly is hiding from his aunt, and he meets William who is doing likewise. The Professor does not want to speak at the local literary society. He loathes literary societies and William nods understandingly, although as the Professor is grown-up William does not understand why he cannot just go and tell his aunt that he does not want to go. The Professor admits that he is a bit scared of her, something that William would have struggled to understand, knowing no fear.[18] They both agree that women are wearing:

"They're a bit of a nuisance, women, aren't they?" said William.
   "They are indeed," said the Professor. "They can't take "no" for an answer. It's – wearing."
   "Yes, it wears me, too," said William.[19]

William of course has no idea what he is saying, but his adult readers will. Whether anyone felt scared at any of the meetings Richmal arranged is unlikely. She spoke about writing at a few meetings of the Lyceum Club but, sadly, what she said on these occasions remains hidden in an archive somewhere or is lost.[20]

Moving beyond the thirties, in common with other authors, Crompton knew people associated with the world of books in London who were part of her professional circle. She kept in touch with Fred Bason, a bookseller who was keen to develop his connections with writers and collected their autographs. They met in the early nineteen fifties, although Bason had asked for her autograph many years before in 1929. Bason gave her a copy of the 1947 edition of *The Saturday Book*, which included a handwritten inscription:

Christmas 1929 I take an hour to hand paint a Christmas card & write a friendly fan mail letter to my favourite authoress. Winter 1951 we meet for the 1st time. Aug 1952 at my birthday party I show her the autograph she sent to me 1929 – still as fresh as the day she sent it! Who dare say I am not loyal and faithful. Fred Bason[21]

They kept in touch until she died and Bason visited her at home several times. He was a friendly literary acquaintance keen to keep in contact with her rather than a close friend.

She also knew Jill Anne and Nancy Bowden who, like Bason, moved on the fringes of literary London. They often sent Richmal books and discussed their reading with her. From 1950, Jill Anne and Nancy worked in the book-shop owned by Cyril Beaumont (1891–1976) at 75 Charing Cross Road in London. Jill Anne helped Beaumont close the shop in 1965. Beaumont was a well-connected bookseller and publisher, specialising in classical dance, and was known by leading figures in the ballet and dance world. He knew members of the Diaghilev Ballet Company and many other leading dancers, including Lydia Lopokova, Ninette de Valois and Marie Rambert.[22] Both Jill Anne and Nancy worked as his assistants on some of his books. In a hand-written dedication in a copy of his memoirs, *Bookseller at the Ballet* (1975), Beaumont thanks Nancy for all her support: 'To My very dear Friend Nancy, But for whose constant encouragement this book might never have been achieved.'[23] A fragment of a letter found inside this copy is from Nancy. She believes that 'Richmal's art of story-telling will be taken more seriously as time passes, and that William will be regarded as one of the great twentieth century literary creations.' Quite so.

Nancy's work in the bookshop brought her into contact with contem-porary poets. Beaumont published early poems by Walter de la Mere and Edmund Blunden, amongst others and he knew the Sitwell family. As part of her job, Nancy was in touch with some of them, including John Masefield and Walter de la Mere. Nancy supported Masefield by delivering material from his home near Oxford to an exhibition to celebrate his work in London in 1958 on the occasion of his eightieth birthday.[24] She may have under-taken many similar tasks in her role at Beaumont's bookshop. In a letter to her, Walter de la Mere encourages her to continue writing and wishes they could meet again.[25] Jill Anne and Nancy also shared their own poems with Richmal, which reflect their Christian faith. A love of poetry sustained Crompton and it is one of the inspirations for some of the allegory that underpins much of her work.

After the war, Crompton's celebrity took her to further literary events and more illustrious circles. Her profile grew significantly as William's fame spread following his regular appearances on BBC radio from 1946. At a Foyles lunch at the Dorchester hotel in 1948, attended by celebrities including come-dian Arthur Askey and actor John Mills, she sat next to author Compton

Mackenzie, who was the guest of honour.[26] Mackenzie was a popular and influential Scottish author of novels, autobiography, biography and history. In 1949, his novel *Whisky Galore* (1947) was made into a successful film.

Crompton had known Askey for several years, at least since the end of the war. In March 1946, she joined him as a panellist on a BBC radio quiz show, *Call Yourself a Detective*. He fears they were lousy as detectives.[27] The BBC may have agreed, and it has not been possible to trace any evidence that she ever appeared on another panel show.

Paul Ashbee recollects that 'Auntie talked from time to time about the events of her busy literary life. There had been a Foyle's lunch, attended by [the archaeologist] Sir Mortimer Wheeler ... and meetings with various writers of fiction, one of whom was Agatha Christie,' he remembers.[28] She was surprised that her niece Richmal and her husband Paul, who was himself an archaeologist, knew Christie's husband, Max Mallowan, who had been a Chair of the London Institute of Archaeology. Crompton knew other contemporary children's writers, including Anthony Buckeridge and Arthur Ransome, and had met Enid Blyton and W.E. Johns, but none of them were close friends.[29] Richmal's great-niece Kate remembers going to the Royal Ballet with her great-aunt in the mid-nineteen sixties and Enid Blyton was also there. By this time, both were hugely successful authors for children.

* * *

In 1931, Richmal's brother John, who was known in the family as Jack, returned to England after eighteen years living abroad. As she became more successful as a writer, Richmal was always keen to stress that William was not based on the character or antics of her brother, younger relatives or any one particular boy. She told one journalist that:

> There never was an actual William, but he was a composite boy based partly on my brother, and lately on my nephew, boys in the choir (my father was a vicar), and all the boys I've ever known.[30]

There is no reason to think that her relationship with her brother was especially influential. Like tens of thousands of boys and young men of his generation and since, Jack no doubt shared some characteristics with William.

In his youth, Jack was a boy in search of adventures, and he wanted to escape from a career in the church. He was not the scholar his father had hoped for. In 1913, at the age of twenty, Jack abandoned his studies in Manchester, leaving the country to join the Rhodesian Mounted Police.[31] His search for adventure was not out of kilter with the adventure sought by many of his peers. He was one of a flood of young, unattached men who emigrated shortly before the First World War.[32] After the war, Jack went to China as an employee of a merchant and shipping company.[33] In 1931, after a long and adventurous career in China, which took him on the kind of perilous journeys and into the remote places that William dreamed of, he retired in his early forties. He went to live with Richmal and her mother Clara until he married.

Jack turned to writing and he published nine novels as John Lambourne, mainly in the nineteen thirties. After the Second World War, as John Crompton, he turned to natural history, including books about bees, ants, spiders, wasps and snakes.[34] In a letter to her niece Richmal Ashbee in February 1954, Crompton notes that her brother's book on ants has just been published. She is pleased because there are, 'Two Crompton books out in one week.'[35] Their father would have been delighted with their success.

* * *

In *Anne Morrison*, Anne's brother Paul is a young boy in search of adventure. Anne is in awe of him and his 'gang' of friends. William is rarely in awe of his brother, who in turn finds his younger brother's existence a source of persistent annoyance. In this novel, at times the boys portray William-like behaviour. On one occasion, Paul and his friends were at first brushed, clean and silent, 'But the jelly and blancmange and iced cake charmed away their shyness.'[36] Also:

> Strange noises proceeded from Paul's bedroom when they were there—thuds and bangs and whoops. Their chief pastime was wrestling matches, and [Paul's mother] sometimes feared for her ceilings when they were in Paul's bedroom.[37]

After reading a book about smuggling, the boys ceaselessly hunt for smugglers, hoping to find their den.[38] Anne is excited to join them in their games, much to Aunt Susannah's dismay. She is the kind of aunt who brings disappointment and disapproval into the lives of William Brown and the Outlaws. Aunt Susannah epitomises aunts who taunt children with stern admonishment: 'She had a way of pressing her lips together and sniffing when she said anything disagreeable, and she often said disagreeable things'[39]:

> "In a girl of your age, Anne," said Aunt Susannah with grim disapproval, "this horseplay with boys is more than unsuitable. It's fast."
> Anne stood silent. Her brightness fell from her suddenly. She felt icy cold, horror-struck. Fast-Fast-a terrible thing.[40]

Nevertheless, Anne is not deterred by her aunt and loves what her younger sister calls 'adventure walks.'[41] She was never content to accept things as they were and had to 'spin a web of romance or terror over them.'[42] Many young girls in the interwar period and after loved carefree, rough-and-tumble adventures too, whilst stern relatives reminded them to behave properly. There is no reason to think that in her youth Richmal was any different. Crompton was a keen observer of families and young people. As she grew up, like Anne, Jack was one of many boys she played with at home. There were young relations, Jack's friends, or boys from Bury Grammar School who came to stay and study with Edward. The spirit of William and Violet Elizabeth lives on in the childhood of many girls and boys.

As she grows up, we see different sides to Anne's character:

There were two Annes. One was shy, elusive, imaginative and sensitive…. That was the usual Anne. But under the stimulus of excitement that Anne disappeared and another Anne came – daring, excited, laughing, flushed and bright-eyed, full of quick wit and provocativeness.[43]

Crompton's portrayal of Anne, and of other characters, such as Mrs Fowler in *Family Roundabout*, remind us that there are at least two versions to anyone's character and often many more. Richmal, like Anne and William, was no doubt daring, quick-witted and provocative too.

* * *

As her success grew exponentially, Crompton started a new venture that features William as the first-person narrator. William chats away about his life and his beliefs in tirades that will be familiar to readers of the traditional William stories. In his role as narrator, William comments in 'School is a Waste of Time' that he has been told that everyone should want to be educated, 'so as to become a fine and noble character when he grows up.' However, he notes sardonically, 'You have only got to look at the grown-ups around you to see that [education] does not do that.'[44] He reflects on lessons delivered by one history teacher, who made the boys act out scenes from the past:

In his first lesson he taught us about King John signing the Charter, and I was King John. Ginger wanted to be the Charter, but [the teacher] wouldn't let him be.

The scene did not end exactly as it ends in the history books because the unruly barons became so unruly that I had to get up and smack their heads, and Douglas upset the ink and the scene ended in confusion.[45]

In the traditional William stories, we can hear the unruly, misspelt banter between the boys and enjoy the comic eye of Crompton as narrator, who captures the tone and comedy of any scene where the Outlaws are brought together. And we hear their shared misconceived versions of history in these stories too.

In one story, the Outlaws are discussing the general election, although they are not sure about the role of different national leaders. Their understanding of history is playful and surprisingly accurate, and yet:

> "Like the man they have in It'ly called the duck?" said Douglas anxious to air his knowledge.
> "You're thinking of the dog," said Ginger scornfully, "the man we had in history what ruled a place called Venice an' was called a dog."
> "I'd have called myself somethin' better than a dog or a duck if I was goin' to be a ruler," said William. "I'd be called a lion or an eagle or somethin' like that."[46]

William is equally bemused by the history portrayed in pageants: "'If a man comes on in a crown, wearin' a rose, it'd be Charles the First in the War of the Roses, or somethin' like that,'" he says confidently. Henry tells him that he does not think it was Charles the First, so William decides that it must have been Charles the Second:

> "An' if someone comes on an' puts a coat over a puddle it'd be that man who put his coat down for Queen Elizabeth. The Black Prince, wasn't it?"
> "Sir Walter Raleigh," murmured Henry.
> "Yes, I knew it was either him or the Black Prince," said William.[47]

William careers across the centuries failing to remember anything without Henry's help. In another story, William's mother's understanding of history is little better than her son's. She too remembers that Queen Elizabeth walked across the mud on someone's coat. She is not interested in the fact that he helped defended England against the Spanish Armada, but is concerned about the state of his clothes:

> "I don't care *what* he did, dear," said Mrs Brown firmly. "I think it was most inconsiderate to walk on that poor man's coat. I can never think of her without seeing that poor man brushing away—and I'm sure he never got it off. I know what I've gone through with Robert's football shorts."[48]

Despite his sporting attire, Robert, William's older brother, is faultlessly tidy and smart.

* * *

Robert is seventeen, although fan Terry Taylor has identified that Robert ages at times in the stories: 'William always stays at eleven and Ethel seemingly at nineteen, Robert's age varies from seventeen to twenty-one,' he writes.[49] In the traditional William stories, when we first meet Robert his superficial values are quickly exposed. He runs his hands wildly through his hair during an ecstatic declaration of love for the latest in a long line of his girlfriends: '"It's so important, how one looks. She—people *judge* you on how you look,"' he tells his mother.[50] A never-ending procession of young females pass through Robert's life, and he declares eternal fidelity to each one. It is difficult to keep pace with them. Robert is 'no Don Juan. He was earnest and simple-minded, and each specimen of youthful glamour for which he fell was to him the One Great Love of his Life.'[51] William follows Robert's girlfriends with interest. William contemplates that 'A handle against Robert was useful and more than once Robert's love affairs had afforded useful handles.'[52] Robert rarely appreciates his efforts.

For one thing, William fails to meet Robert's standards for behaviour and dress. He declares wildly that, '"At every crisis of my life that boy turns up and always in something ridiculous. He's—he's more like a nightmare than a boy."'[53] Robert wonders why four grown-ups in the same household cannot keep a boy like William in order: '"You'd think he wouldn't be allowed to go about spoiling people's lives and—and ruining their bicycles."'[54] When Robert meets the current One and Only Love of his Life, William manages to ruin the romantic lunch Robert has carefully planned. Robert angrily declares to his brother that:

> when William met with the One and Only Love of his Life he need look for no help or assistance from him (Robert), because he (William) had dashed to the ground his (Robert's) cup of happiness ... he hoped he (William) would realise, when he was old enough to realise, what it meant to have your life spoilt and your happiness ruined ... Whence it came that William, optimist though he was, felt that any appeal to Robert for funds would be inopportune, to say the least of it.[55]

The narrator's use of indirect speech when Robert is talking highlights his ludicrous hyperbole and heightens the comedy. Repetition as ever in William heightens the comedy too. We can imagine William's not-so-innocent face looking up at his brother in shocked disbelief. The final sentence is a beautifully crafted punchline in this sad old-fashioned tale of William's harassment by yet another grown-up.

Not only does William destroy Robert's love life, but, according to Robert, he humiliates him in public too. William has ruined a play and Robert's dramatic scene within it:

> William, said Robert, had disgraced him—Robert—for ever. Never again, he said, would he hold up his head. His whole life was ruined. Nothing awaited him but a dishonoured old age brought upon him prematurely by William. Nobody, said Robert, would ever talk about anything else for the rest of his life.... It was no use doing anything at all with his life now. It was ruined. Absolutely ruined.[56]

This brilliantly sums up this young man's conviction that the world revolves around him and his terror of breaching social conventions. Some of us convince ourselves as we grow older that the world is not laughing at us when we make mistakes or are made to look a fool in front of others, although one wonders if we are ever totally convinced about this. Crompton knows this and it is the truth that lies at the heart of this scene and so many others in the William stories. We laugh gently at Robert's foolish self-centred nature. William cares for him whatever happens and we, perhaps, understand some of the missteps of Robert's youth.

In another story, William meets a young man who is a kindred spirit, unlike his brother. He is staying with his aunt who has serious doubts about her nephew's sanity, which can only be an advantage from William's point of view; after all, 'The young man, unlike most grown-ups, knew how to make himself comfortable in a wheelbarrow.'[57] From their respective wheelbarrows, they share stories about being an international crook (the young man), and a Scotland Yard detective (William). William forgets that their stories have been made up and decides that he would like to join the young man's criminal gang. William lives on the cusp of the boundaries between the mundane in real life and the made-up world of his adventures. He is drawn to those, like his friend in a wheelbarrow, who are also able to live in these parallel worlds.

William is a good friend of Archie, Ethel's hapless suitor, another young man who shares William's tenuous hold on everyday life and another well-known character in the stories. Ethel occasionally finds time to be kind to him in the intervals between her swiftly changing romantic entanglements.[58] The Outlaws feel at home in the perpetual disorder and disarray of Archie's home.[59] He struggles with social conventions and has dreadful manners:

> Archie Mannister, the vague and impecunious artist who lived in a tumble-down cottage at the other end of the village, was, as it seemed to William,

in the adult world but not of it. He didn't worry about the things that other grown ups worried about. Tidiness, method, routine meant nothing to him. He lived on old picnic-like meals. He never put anything away. Nothing he arranged ever turned out right. Everyone laughed at him and most people disapproved of him, but William had an odd, protective feeling towards him. The fact that Archie was hopelessly and desperately in love with William's sister Ethel ... lent Archie the final touch of pathos in his eyes.[60]

Archie and William have a certain amount in common: 'Both were driven by vaulting ambitions that life had as yet failed to satisfy, and fate had a way of landing both of them in strange and unexpected situations.'[61] In many ways, Archie is more innocent than William, who manages to turn the innocence of youth to his own considerable advantage on occasions.

In less-well-known stories, Crompton creates other young men whose ineptitude similarly hampers their progress through life. They share the qualities of both Robert and Archie.

The seventeen-year-old boy Charles Anthony Mostyn, aka Robert Brown, appeared in print in the late nineteen twenties. He has a chance encounter with a young woman whom he thinks is his neighbour's maid and might be a shoplifter; he later discovers she is a film star. He planned to marry the maid, but the film star is out of his reach, and he falls for one of his sister's friends instead.[62] Charles misunderstands every circumstance, wallows in his own glorious future, and sees the world exclusively through his own eyes. He is depressed, like William, because he has wasted his life and, unlike Julius Caesar, Napoleon or Alexander the Great, he seems to have done nothing of note. He cannot think what has happened to all the bolting horses in real life:

> In books they were all over the place. It was so easy to be a hero in a book. People fell over themselves to be rescued. There was always someone drowning in a river, or hanging from a precipice, and you could plunge in or climb up – always before the admiring crowd – a dozen times a day.[63]

Charles felt that he was intended to be a hero, but, sadly, his life of seventeen years was devoid of heroic achievement.[64] Charles sees Mr Bloggs coming up the road; he is rich and lives in a large house with lots of servants but, 'Mr Bloggs was Excelsior Pickles, and Charles despised Commerce. It lacked glamour and romance.'[65] He meets Mr Stair, who is a famous novelist. Charles decides that he wants to embark on a new career and become a novelist, instead of a businessman.[66] That evening, Charles starts to write about his hero who feels dauntless in any 'emmergency, emergensy, emmergensy, emergency.'[67] Charles does not have a dictionary and the road to becoming an author seems full of insuperable obstacles.[68]

In other stories, Henry Augustus Bradley, another Robert-like character, is also seventeen and loves his motorcycle until he meets the girl of his dreams. If he cannot be with her his whole future life will be blighted, but he decides that 'Fate could not be so cruel as that.'[69] Fate, aka Richmal Crompton, as we shall see in a later chapter, can be cruel indeed and has a pervading influence over William's life.

* * *

In November 1938, shortly after her forty-eighth birthday, twenty years after the publication of her first magazine story and ten years after she had moved into The Glebe, Richmal's career took another huge leap forward on the cusp of war. She received her first film offer. *Just William* the film appeared in 1939 based on six existing stories, published in *Just William: The Story of the Film* (1939).[70] She decided to hold a lavish cocktail party in London to celebrate. Her niece Margaret remembers the event:

> [She invited] all the people she had met during radio interviews and stage productions, also Mr and Mrs John Watt, her agent and his wife, many personal friends, and several branches of the family. The ones I remember best were Leon Davey, a well-known scenery designer who later married Gracie Fields's secretary, the actor Ireland Wood who was well known to our family [and wrote the plays *Miss Tracy* and *Charity Begins*, based on Crompton's stories] ... and another family friend of longstanding, Stanley Rowland [who had taught with her father at Bury Grammar School]. Our cousins the Wrigleys, the Lamburn family and the Dishers all stayed on for dinner at the Kensington Park Mansions.[71]

It would be surprising if Gwen's brother-in-law, Maurice Disher, and her cousin John Wrigley, who played a leading role as a civil servant in coordinating the movement of evacuees from London, were not present at the party. Maybe Rex Harrison and Margaret Rutherford, who had performed in Crompton's plays a few years before, were there too. They were both famous actors.

Stanley Rowland had been a young classics master at Bury Grammar School when Richmal's father was teaching there. She had remained friends with Stanley for twenty-five years after he left Bury. Stanley, born in June 1877, was twenty-five when he joined Bury School for boys in 1902, leaving in July 1914 to go to Mill Hill School in London. He stayed at Mill Hill until

1919 and by 1926 he was Senior Classical Master at Strand School, Brixton, London. In 1938, he was sixty-one and no doubt retired from teaching.[72]

In *Anne Morrison*, Sandy is a colleague of Anne's father and visits the family often. When Anne becomes a teacher herself and is already thirty, he asks her to marry him, acknowledging that he is no longer a young man. He can offer her companionship as she faces life on her own. She decides to turn him down. After all, she was still the 'captain of her soul, the master of her fate.'[73] There is no direct evidence that Sandy is based on anyone from Richmal's own life.

Looking ahead briefly into the last decade of her life, for another expensive event in 1960, Richmal took her niece and the Ashbee family to the famous Ivy restaurant in London to celebrate the publication of one of Paul Ashbee's books, where Paul observed that the service was adroit 'as Auntie was well-known.'[74] She clearly enjoyed entertaining and social occasions where we can briefly glimpse the outgoing and lively Richmal of her youth, and an ambitious professional networking amidst London's literary and cultural community from the nineteen thirties.

* * *

Crompton is an observer and commentator on the world around her at home and in the circles she knew. The caricatures of young men discussed in this chapter are another illustration that she is often at her strongest when writing comedy and allegory about human foibles. Apart from her family sagas, readers of her fiction may be disappointed if they look for real people in her work. It is recommended that they suspend disbelief, look for comedy, satire and even tragedy, sometimes of the most subtle kind, consider the values underpinning her allegory, enjoy her language and pay attention to her tone. Robert's glorious hyperbole is absent in her other fiction, but some of her best characters are those who live on the fringes of the real, like William; their own foibles, or those they see in others, seem human, all too human.

Notes

1. Cadogan, 21–22.
2. Disher, T., 52. Also, Maurice Willson's obituary in *The Times*, 29 November 1969, 8.

3. Disher, M., 140.
4. See Mikhail Bakhtin's theory of the carnivalesque in *Rabelais and His World* (1965). In his study of medieval culture, Bakhtin discusses the universal qualities of laughter in medieval carnival, which sanctions the freedom to laugh at other people and society in a way that would be unacceptable outside it and exposes truths about the world; such laughter becomes 'the social consciousness of all the people' and an escape from fear (92). William sanctions laughter at other people that many would shun in polite society.
5. *Clowns and Pantomimes,* xiv and 7.
6. *Clowns and Pantomimes,* 7.
7. UoR RC/1/1/2/2/3.
8. *Journal of the Royal Society of Arts* No 4077, 19 January 1931, 181. Another play, *The Christmas Present*, is based on a short story published in *Truth* magazine on 21 December 1931. Copies of both *Mrs 'awkin's Kitchen* and *The Christmas Present* are held in the Richmal Crompton Collection (UoR RC/1/1/2/2/3).
9. An acting edition of the play by Ireland Wood is owned by the author. Please see the next chapter for a discussion of this novel.
10. Wood also contributed to the dialogue for the film *Just William* (1939). Actor and writer John Ireland Wood was born on 31 October 1899 and died in London in April 1980.
11. UoR RC/1/1/2/2/3. There is a similar plot in another play by Crompton in which a woman returns to her family after many years, *Alive, Alive, Oh* (1931). She has trained as a doctor since she left her family's home. Like Philippa, she leaves her young children behind when she leaves. The manuscript is held in her archive at the University of Roehampton.
12. An acting edition of the play by Ireland Wood is owned by the author.
13. Review in *The Times* 7 July 1937, 14.
14. See *Middlesex County Times* 24 October 1936, 2 and 9 January 1937, 4; *Advertiser & Gazette* (Uxbridge) 21 January 1938, 8; *Evening News* 22 October 1949, 2; *The Guardian* (Morecambe) 16 April 1937, 8; *The Advertiser* (Croydon) 27 January 1939, 8; *The Lancashire Daily Post* 19 April 1937, 1; *Aberdeen Press and Journal* 28 April 1938, 8; *The Scotsman* 31 October 1936, 14; *Perthshire Advertiser* 17 October 1942, 12; *Nottingham Evening Post* 15 November 1941, 1; *Gloucestershire Echo* 18 January 1938, 3; *The Era* 15 January 1936, 12 and 1 July 1937, 19.
15. London Lyceum Club Executive Committee minutes, January 1935.
16. London Lyceum Club monthly journal May 1935, March and December 1936, January, April, and June 1938.

17. "The One Best Book," *Manchester Guardian* 17 November 1938, 10.

18. "William Meets the Professor," 62.

19. Ibid., 65.

20. London Lyceum Club Newsletter, July 1934, 5. Richmal was interested in spiritualism and mysticism, and her library includes books on this subject, as well as Christianity, philosophy and Greek literature. Her intellectual and literary interests were eclectic and wide ranging. Spiritualism was not an unusual interest amongst her contemporaries. Members of the London Lyceum Club in the thirties had meetings on the subject.

21. *The Saturday Book* 1947, 48. In the 1968 edition of *The Saturday Book*, Bason inscribed a piece about literary life in the nineteen twenties: 'When one grows old memories are precious! Very sincerely Fred Bason 1968.' Held in the Richmal Crompton Collection. This was an annual miscellany on British cultural life published from the forties until 1975.

22. See articles by Katherine Sorley Walker: "Cyril W. Beaumont: Bookseller, Publisher, and Writer on Dance Part Two" *Dance Chronicle* Vol. 25, No. 2 (2002), 265–301 and "Cyril W. Beaumont: Bookseller, Publisher, and Writer on Dance Part Three" *Dance Chronicle* Vol. 25, No. 3 (2002), 447–476.

23. Personal copy held by the author.

24. I am grateful to Philip W. Errington of the John Masefield Society for this information about the exhibition.

25. De la Mere, 12 May 1947, Coll-1848/18–0117/1 University of Edinburgh.

26. See: https://www.britishpathe.com/video/boys-will-be-boys-1/query/Richmal+Crompton.

27. UoR RC/6. Letter to Richmal Crompton from Arthur Askey 16 March 1946.

28. Ashbee, Paul, 6.

29. Evidence from family archives and interviews and UoR 2010/6 (1) photograph of the panel at the 1949 *The Sunday Times* National Book Exhibition. In the summer 1943, Arthur Ransome sent Crompton's niece Richmal Disher a postcard from Coniston in Cumbria, which is six miles from Bowness in Windermere. Ransome draws attention to the connection between Bowness in Windermere and his Swallows and Amazon novels on the card. Held in family papers.

30. Kitchener, 4.

31. Disher, M., 56 and 65.

32. Crompton's early novels feature a young male character who leaves to work in Africa or other far-flung places. For example, *The Innermost*

Room, Anne Morrison, Millicent Dorrington and the Wildings trilogy. Literary critics have noted that novels of home and family by women writers 'rarely refer to family members or friends serving abroad or incorporate issues of migration' (Briganti and Meze 29), but Crompton is one of the few who do.

33. Disher, M., 66.
34. British Library Add MS 89,262/2/18 Letter from A. P. Watt to Macmillan 8th March 1940.
35. UoR RC/2/1/2/3. Letter to Richmal Ashbee 5th February 1954.
36. *Anne Morrison*, 51.
37. Ibid., 14 and 77.
38. Ibid., 67.
39. Ibid., 12.
40. Ibid., 50.
41. Ibid., 76.
42. Ibid., 72.
43. *Anne Morrison*, 51.
44. "School is a Waste of Time," 55.
45. Ibid., 59.
46. "William, Prime Minister," 62.
47. "The Battle of Flowers," 123.
48. "William Tries the Films," 39.
49. *JWSM 29*, 22.
50. "William the Intruder," 35.
51. "William Among the Chimney Pots," 60.
52. "William Spoils the Party," 191.
53. "William's Extra Day," 193.
54. "William the Intruder," 56.
55. "The May King," 137.
56. "Mistakes Will Happen," 54.
57. "William and the Young Man," 65.
58. "William and the Returned Traveller," 107.
59. "Archie has a Party," 214.
60. "William and the Cottage," 54.
61. "William and the Holiday Task," 82.
62. "Amateur Knight Errant," 337.
63. "The Literary Career of Charles Anthony Moston," 305.
64. Ibid., 306.
65. Ibid., 306.
66. Ibid., 308.

67. Ibid.
68. See also "The First Day.".
69. "The Old Love," 349.
70. The six stories were: "The Outlaws and Cousin Percy," "William to the Rescue," "The Outlaws and the Triplets," "William and the Wonderful Present," "The Outlaws and the Fifth," and "William Enters Politics." The stories and the script of the film were published in *Just William: The Story of the Film* (1939) by George Newnes.
71. Disher, M., 142.
72. I am grateful to Mark Hone from Bury Grammar School and Peter Elliott from Mill Hill School for providing me with these details.
73. *Anne Morrison*, 253.
74. Ashbee, P., 8.

References

Ashbee, Paul. 2007. *'Auntie': Richmal Crompton As I Knew Her.* The Just William Society.

Bakhtin, Mikhail. 1984. First published 1965. *Rabelais and His World.* Bloomington, IN: Indiana University Press.

Cadogan, Mary. 2001. *Richmal Crompton and Her Bromley Connections.* Folkestone, Kent: Lilburne Press.

Crompton, Richmal. 1925. *Anne Morrison.* London: Jarrolds.

———. 1990. First published 1952. "Archie Has a Party." In *William and the Tramp*, by Richmal Crompton, 214–230. Basingstoke, Hampshire: Pan Macmillan Children's Books.

———. 1985. First published 1933. "Mistakes Will Happen." In *William - The Rebel*, by Richmal Crompton, 51–70. Basingstoke, Hampshire: Macmillan Children's Books.

———. 1990. "School Is a Waste of Time." In *What's Wrong with Civilizashun and Other Important Ritings*, by Richmal Crompton, 55–61. Basingstoke, Hampshire: Macmillan Children's Books.

———. 1990. First published 1950. "The Battle of Flowers." In *William - The Bold*, by Richmal Crompton, 121–144. Basingstoke, Hampshire: Macmillan Children's Books.

———. 1959. First published 1922. "The May King." In *More William*, by Richmal Crompton, 126–143. London: George Newnes Ltd.

———. 1928. "The Literary Career of Charles Anthony Moston." *The Red Magazine*, 29 June: 305–315.

———. 1928. "The Amateur Knight Errant." *The Windsor Magazine*, 7 May: 330–340.

———. 1927. "The First Day." *The Windsor Magazine*, 12 September: 94–102.

———. 1925. "The Old Love." *The Windsor Magazine*, 16 February: 347–354.

———. 1991. First published 1958. "William Among the Chimney Pots." In *William's Television Show*, by Richmal Crompton, 109–135. Basingstoke, Hampshire: Macmillan Children's Books.

———. 1992. First published 1962. "William and the Cottage." In *William's Treasure Trove*, by Richmal Crompton, 53–76. Basingstoke, Hampshire: Macmillan's Children's Books.

———. 1975. First published 1965. "William and the Holiday Task." In *William and the Pop Singers*, by Richmal Crompton, 76–104. London: Armada.

———. 1990. First published 1952. "William and the Returned Traveller." In *William and the Tramp*, by Richmal Crompton, 106–131. Basingstoke, Hampshire: Pan Macmillan Children's Books.

———. 1951. First published 1931. "William and the Young Man." In *William's Crowded Hours*, by Richmal Crompton, 57–83. London: George Newnes Ltd.

———. 1990. First published 1952. "William Meets the Professor." In *William and the Tramp*, by Richmal Crompton, 37–72. Basingstoke, Hampshire: Pan Macmillan Children's Books.

———. 1984. First published 1925. "William Spoils the Party." In *Still - William*, by Richmal Crompton, 184–207. Basingstoke, Hampshire: Macmillan Children's Books.

———. 1990. First published 1922. "William the Intruder." In *Just - William*, by Richmal Crompton, 33–56. Basingstoke, Hampshire: Macmillan Children's Books.

———. 1987. First published 1940. "William Tries the Films." In *William and the Evacuees*, by Richmal Crompton, 34–61. Basingstoke, Hampshire: Pan Macmillan Children's Books.

———. 1951. First published 1930. "William, Prime Minister." In *William - The Bad*, by Richmal Crompton, 61–84. London: George Newnes Ltd.

———. 1953. First published 1924. "William's Extra Day." In *William - The Fourth*, by Richmal Crompton, 175–194. London: George Newnes Ltd.

Disher, Margaret. 1990. *Growing Up with Just William By His Sister.* London: The Outlaws Publishing Company.

Disher, Maurice Willson. 1925. *Clowns and Pantomime*. London: Constable & Co.

Disher, Thomas Frederick Rhodes. 1954. *Sixty Odd Years.* London: Clerke & Cockeran.

Harmsworth, Madeleine. 1968. "William and the Old Lady of Beechworth." *Daily Mirror*, 20 November: 16–17.

Kitchener, Pamela. 1958. "William's Misdeeds." *Western Mail*, 14 February: 4.

Taylor, Terry. Winter 2011. "Will the Real Robert Brown Stand Up?" *The Just William Society Magazine 29* 22–30.

14

Richmal Crompton, the Wanderer

Crompton wanders amongst us, observing, sometimes judging and always keen to guide. She casts her satirical eye over families, local communities and the social world she knew, part of it and yet maintaining her privacy. She listened to other people closely, often writing down some of the phrases and colloquialisms she overheard on scraps of paper, using them later in her writing. Crompton was a wanderer, protecting many of the details about her private life, amidst a world in which she loved to roam.

In *Roofs Off* (1928), Martin wanders amidst his new neighbours on a modern housing estate. Some of the residents meet and discuss what is happening to their area and what it was like in the past. One of them recalls that local children used to play a game:

> She gave us each some building bricks and a little red cardboard roof and a handful of dolls and furniture from her doll's house and we had to build little houses and arrange the dolls and furniture inside and then put on the little red cardboard roof and then Susan would blow on her little whistle and say, 'Roofs Off!' and we had to take off the cardboard roof and Susan would come round and judge whose dolls were doing the most interesting things....
>
> "I wonder," said Martin dreamily, "which would be the most interesting thing in Woodlands Avenue if someone said 'Roofs Off!'"
>
> Mrs Glendower shot him her quick smile.
>
> "They'd all be incredibly dull," she said.
>
> "I doubt it," challenged the doctor. "I believe that there isn't such a thing in the whole world and never has been such a thing as a dull life. What you

© The Author(s), under exclusive license to Springer Nature Switzerland AG 2022
J. McVeigh, *Richmal Crompton, Author of Just William*, Literary Lives,
https://doi.org/10.1007/978-3-030-96511-2_14

see of it may be dull but you only see a part of the pattern or a back side of the pattern. If you could see the whole you'd be amazed. You'd be thrilled. A life may be sad or even uneventful, but it can never be dull."[1]

In her novels and stories, whatever the theme, Crompton similarly wanders like a *flaneuse* across the life of middle-class England lifting the roof on the life of her peers. She certainly never finds them dull.

William similarly wanders through the lives of his family and local community lifting the roof, observing and judging too and, when he seeks to guide events, they invariably cause chaos. He has a childlike sense of wonder and an awe about the most trivial of everyday things; an awe we often lose as we grow older but find again in his stories. Whilst his home is in a village, he is close to a town and his father commutes into the city each day. His habitat is closer to Surrey and Kent than rural communities much further from London. William lives amidst jumble sales, sales of works, afternoon teas and literary societies, as well as the fields owned by Farmer Jenks. He careers through middle-class society in search of adventure, whilst drawing attention to the flawed adults who inhabit his home and his local area, as well as the best qualities of his friends and some of the other people he meets. We look at the world through his eyes, an adult world he is convinced is mad, and we see it from his perspective.

Crompton's knowledge of classical Greek society and literature pervades her fiction. In *The Wildings* (1925), following their marriage David and Hero Wilding live in the same lodging house as Mr Canford, who is in awe of Greek society and in despair about modern proclivities. He declares scornfully that, 'we've left behind beauty and restraint and culture.... We know a million things that the Ancient Greeks didn't, and how are we happier ... how are we better?'[2] He believes that life is dull because the 'greatest tragedy of our civilisation is the loss of the sense of wonder. There's nothing left to wonder about. We know everything.'[3] William's sense of wonder is a quality that, as adults, we too have lost, but we are reminded of it when we read about William's antics.

A few of Crompton's novels, published in the thirties, have a central character who, like William, rubs up against the conventional boundaries of middle-class life, living on the fringes of a world to which they do not fully belong. We look at this world through their unconventional eyes. They too have dreams, optimism, confidence and hope. These characters serve as a catalyst for sub-plots laden with social commentary and are the pivot, like William, around which much of the allegory in these novels revolves. They are either an observer, moving amongst different groups of people reflecting on how they behave, or someone who is integral to the action and acts as a foil against which the behaviour of others is judged.[4] These are not realistic novels in which believable people come to life, but carefully structured comedies. The drama is staged in different scenes where we meet a range of characters. They serve the values underpinning each of these novels, which focus on how to live a 'good life.' A life that has a purpose, no matter how every day and ordinary it might seem; that is always interested in other people and the community in which they live; and that they continually try to improve. The characters in these novels are not people we come to know. They have a role to play within the overall plot that considers their way of life and values, for good or ill. In some cases, a moment of recognition offers them the opportunity to become other than they are.

* * *

In *The Odyssey of Euphemia Tracy* (1932), Euphemia can at last break free from her abusive, bullying father after his death. Both her parents were servants for an aristocratic family. Since her mother's death, Euphemia has been trapped at home, her life subsumed by her father's demands. She travels to London seeking a new life and quickly finds herself in a ladies' residential club, the equivalent of a hotel or lodging house for women who cannot afford a home of their own. The owner is dismayed that Euphemia is not a gentlewoman of the appropriate class, but we soon learn that she is gentle and kind with childlike qualities of wonder and excitement: 'A hunger for life—life so long denied her—filled every fibre of her being.'[5] Her passion for life lies in other people and she is entirely uninterested in herself.[6] She believes that 'it's only other people that make one exist, somehow.'[7]

Euphemia's odyssey takes her to a range of housekeeping jobs, during which people are changed when her actions or advice touches their lives. She is both down to earth and ethereal, too good to be true, and wise and comforting. She is forty, but feels much younger, full of vitality and yet she has a calming and spiritual nature. She brings out the best in people and offers them hope. She believes that one 'must learn to love without wanting to possess.'[8] Something that some of Crompton's characters who are mothers fail to understand.

Euphemia is not someone that we are ever likely to meet, not in this world at least, although, unlike Lolly, in Sylvia Townsend Warner's novel *Lolly Willowes* (1926), she could not be described as a witch. Lolly Willowes feels trapped in her role as Auntie Lolly, dependent on her relatives for food and board and living with them as an unpaid servant. She is no longer seen by her relatives as Laura, her first name: 'she had become two persons, each different.

One was Aunt Lolly, a middle-aged lady, light-footed upon stairs, and indispensable … The other was Mrs Willowes … But Laura was put away.'[9] She decides to escape her life as a spinster aunt and discovers her vocation as a witch. Her life is now full of adventure. Lolly lives on the boundaries between her everyday life, and another filled with her own private sense of herself in a world beyond the real.

In *Matty and the Dearingroydes* (1956), published over twenty years after The Odyssey, Matty, like William, is accused of being crazy. Like Euphemia and Lolly Willowes, she is a servant to other people's wishes, and a fiercely independent spirit. When the novel opens, she owns a shop selling second-hand books, clothes and other bric-a-brac. Like William and Euphemia, Matty relishes with a child-like wonder the adventures she imagines in the lives of the people she meets. She roams the streets in search of secondhand goods to buy and sell, like a buccaneer on a voyage of discovery.[10] People tell her that she should stop at her age, an indeterminate late middle age.[11] She becomes a housekeeper to several families to whom she is related. She is a *flaneuse*, sharing some qualities with E.H. Young's *Miss Mole* (1930), who is a housekeeper too.[12] Both characters are employed in families whose antics they often observe with dismay.

Matty's relatives treat her like a servant, but she is richer in love and integrity than they will ever be. Their lives too are touched and, in some cases changed for the better, by her influence. She brings a spirit of optimism into their lives, although she is more life-like than Euphemia and a more obvious comic character. Mathilda, Matty's alter ego, is very well read, devouring with equal enjoyment Montaigne, Chaucer, Rabelais and Samuel Johnson's *Lives of the Poets*, as well as adventures about the Wild West by Zane Grey.[13] Like Mrs Fowler in *Family Roundabout*, she can play her part as Mathilda, who has gentle speech and irreproachable manners, alongside Matty whose buoyancy is sustained by a lightness of heart.[14]

In *The Old Man's Birthday* (1934), another of Crompton's more accomplished novels, Matthew is fiercely independent following his adventurous life travelling the world. He is keen to hide his heart condition from his daughters in case they treat him like an invalid. It is the early nineteen thirties, and he is celebrating his ninety-fifth birthday today. The novel follows him throughout the day, arguably the most important of his life. Matthew reflects on the character of his children, grandchildren and great-grandchildren whom we meet during the course of the day.

His grandson, Harold, is pompous, and his daughter, Catherine, is fierce in her protection of family conventions and traditions, looking down on anyone who is in any way different. Helen, Harold's wife, comes to realise that a previous relationship was based on a physical passion, not love based on trust and understanding. Enid, Matthew's granddaughter, is forty-two and single. She has the chance of passion and an affair with a married man. Fortunately, she wakes up to his lies and the indignity of her position should she succumb. Another grandson, Paul, is married to Lilian who is consumed by jealousy and his relationship with his first wife which has the power to 'sweep over her and turn her into a devil.'[15] Some might consider that Matthew's son, Richard, has wasted his life in comfort and laziness:

> He would awake in the morning and see it stretching out through its placid hours of reading, writing, gentle constitutional, to the mellow glow of the evening—the excellent dinner perfectly cooked … and then those three hours of lighter reading … with which his day always ended— those three hours in which the blissful somnolence, induced by the excellent dinner, merged gracefully into the equally blissful somnolence that marked the approach of night.[16]

In a more serious example, Philippa, one of Matthew's great-grandchildren, is horrified at the slovenliness of her mother and their home, in which the 'the lack of care and method … lay like a blight over the whole house.'[17] At times, a 'sudden wave of anger surged over her.'[18] Her father, Arnold, is worse and he 'sometimes flew into grotesque rages and hit out at them savagely while they dodged his blows as best they could.'[19] Matthew's family members are in turn proud, envious, greedy for food and other superficial pleasures, lazy, driven by sexual passions, and angry; their seven sins abound.

Matthew's grandson Stephen has been living 'in sin' for two years with Beatrice, much to his daughter Catherine's dismay. The couple are to join them for Matthew's birthday dinner party. Beatrice is both young and old, her voice is clear and musical 'with something appealingly childish in it'[20]:

> Her hair was thick and glossy, falling about her ears in soft curls, but it was silvery white; her skin was fine and delicate, of a clear transparent pallor as if a light burned through alabaster; her eyes were the deep blue of cornflowers, widely spaced with dark sweeping lashes; her lips curved into a faint enigmatic smile. Oddly enough, the white hair emphasised instead of detracting from her youth.[21]

Beatrice has a spiritual, ethereal appearance, like a goddess or an angel.[22] Serenity surrounds her like an atmosphere, and warmth and light seemed to steal from her over Matthew's soul.[23] As a young man Matthew fell in love with Hope, a young and innocent girl whom he met only once.[24] She is the love of his life. When he meets Beatrice, Hope, or rather what she has meant to him throughout his life, returns to him. Hope is the quality that both Matthew, in *The Old Man's Birthday*, and William share, encouraged in turn by Beatrice and Crompton.

As the time for his dinner party approaches, Matthew reads the poet, Frederic Manning (1882–1935). He opened the book at random and reads his poem 'Kore':

> She passed as shadows pass amid the sheep,
> While the earth dreamed and only I was 'ware
> Of that faint fragrance blown from her soft hair.[25]

Beatrice has the ethereal qualities of Kore. Judith Little argues:

> Certainly, one of the most famous and widespread myths of the ancient world is that of the Kore maiden, or the descent-and-ascent pattern of the combined stories of maid (Persephone, Kore) and mother (Demeter).... In both stories the dying and rising god can be read as a symbol for transformation, or rebirth, of the self.[26]

Both Euphemia and Beatrice encourage this sense of transformation and rebirth in others. Their transformation is achieved when they rise above poverty and the limitations imposed on the working class in Euphemia's case and despite sexual transgression in Beatrice's. In *Caroline* (1936), Philippa too has transgressed by leaving her husband and children, but her role as an influential mother is reinstated when she returns to her family and contributes to her daughter Caroline's chance to transform her life. In Crompton's work, women characters who are not conventional are influential and valued. In common with other contemporary women writers of the early to mid-twentieth century, she wrote both to reinforce and challenge the world she knew.

As each of Matthew's family meets Beatrice, several face their fears, their sins, and she guides them towards a different direction in life, with Matthew's help. Crompton's Christian faith, her love of poetry and her classicism are brought together in this powerful allegory in which a spirit of goodness embodied in Beatrice brings redemption at the end of Matthew's life.

* * *

Euphemia and Beatrice have other-worldly qualities and, like William, are part of the day-to-day world and yet not quite belonging to it. Matty, in a novel published in the thirties when Crompton was older, is a more down-to-earth messenger. All three live on the boundaries of harsh reality and a life full of hope and optimism; we can laugh with them at the foolishness they meet. In their travels, they help us to see other people more clearly and from another perspective.[27] William too is quite confident that he makes the world a better place and he has one foot in daily life and another in his daydreams, but he is never ethereal.

Crompton their creator has Mathilda and Matty like qualities and is hard to know:

> William was a great judge of character. He could tell at a glance who was likely to object to him, who was likely to ignore him, and who was likely definitely to encourage him. The last was a very rare class indeed. Most people belonged to the first class.[28]

Crompton belongs to this rare class and is a great judge of character, although the childlike wonder that we can see in some of her characters and that is part of William's charm, diminishes as she grows older. Nevertheless, in several of her novels of the late forties and into the fifties, Matty and Mrs Fowler still harbour a self-awareness that keeps their hope and optimism alive. By the time she reaches her sixties, some of Crompton's vibrant imagination fades in the later William stories, but her comic touch remains sharp in her portrayal of Matty and in *The Gypsy's Baby* (1954). But first, during the Second World War, when she was in her early fifties, she wrote some of her most thought-provoking novels and her life, like everyone else's, was dominated by the war.

Notes

1. *Roofs Off*, 197.
2. *The Wildings*, 138.
3. Ibid., 211.
4. *Roofs Off* (1928), *A Portrait of a Family* (1931), *The Odyssey of Euphemia Tracy* (1932), *The Old Man's Birthday* (1934), *Matty and the Dearingroydes* (1956) are like this, as are her comic novels *The Gypsy's Baby* (1954) and *Journeying Wave* (1938).
5. *The Odyssey of Euphemia Tracy*, 83.
6. Ibid., 226–227.
7. Ibid., 220.
8. Ibid., 286.
9. *Lolly Willowes*, 61.

10. *Matty*, 2 and 33.
11. Ibid., 2.
12. Briganti and Mezei argue that in *Miss Mole* (1930) by E.H. Young (1880–1949), an unmarried housekeeper becomes 'an occasional *flâneuse* of a provincial town' (105).
13. *Matty*, 12.
14. Ibid., 30.
15. *The Old Man's Birthday,* 215.
16. Ibid., 189.
17. Ibid., 118.
18. Ibid.
19. Ibid., 123.
20. Ibid., 37.
21. Ibid., 36.
22. Whether Beatrice and Hope bear comparison with Danté's 'Paradiso' in *The Divine Comedy* I leave others to consider.
23. Ibid., 37.
24. Ibid., 42.
25. "Kore" by Frederic Manning (1882–1935).
26. Little, 18.
27. Flora in Stella Gibbon's *Cold Comfort Farm* (1932) is another central female figure who intervenes in the lives of the rural Starkadder family, although she is from the upper classes, resoundingly down to earth and has little else in common with Euphemia or Matty.
28. "The Fête-and Fortune," 42.

References

Briganti, Chiara and Kathy Mezei. 2006. *Domestic Modernism, the Interwar Novel and E.H. Young*. Hampshire: Ashgate.
Crompton, Richmal. 2012. First published 1956. *Matty and the Dearingroydes*. Edinburgh: Greyladies.
———. 1928. *Roofs Off*. London: Hodder & Stoughton.
———. 1953. First published 1924. "The Fête - and Fortune." In *William - The Fourth*, by Richmal Crompton, 42–58. London: George Newnes Ltd.
———. 1932. *The Odyssey of Euphemia Tracy*. London: Macmillan.
———. 1934. *The Old Man's Birthday*. London: Macmillan.
———. 1925. *The Wildings*. London: Hodder and Stoughton.

Little, Judith. 1983. *Comedy and the Woman Writer: Woolf, Spark and Feminism.* London: University of Nebraska Press.

Townsend Warner, Sylvia. 1993. First published 1926. *Lolly Willowes.* London : Virago Press.

Part IV

(1939–1945)

15

On the Home Front with William and Richmal

In 1939, war brought inevitable changes to Richmal's own life. Not surprisingly, the extent of her writing is reduced in these years, and she never returns to the extraordinary pace of the twenties and thirties. In March, a local newspaper looks forward to Crompton's forthcoming book, *Merlin Bay*, and a book by a fellow novelist, *Passionate Kensington* by Rachel Ferguson. The world they portrayed was about to change for ever. The same column, in a stark contrast to these women's novels, notes the publication in the same week of Hitler's *Mein Kampf* in English.[1]

Following her mother's sudden death of a heart attack in May 1939, whatever Richmal might have felt about the prospect of living alone, she had little time to get used to the idea. In early September, Gwen and her family moved in to live with Richmal as war was declared. Her nephew, Tommy, joined the army and did not return home permanently until 1946. Undaunted, in November, Richmal went up to London for lunch with Margaret and Rose Fyleman, a children's author, to celebrate her birthday.[2] In 1940, Jack joined the RAF and was promoted to Flight Lieutenant. He served in Iceland under Commodore Cecil George Wigglesworth, believed to be one of the models for W.E. Johns's Biggles.[3] Jack's family lived with Richmal during his army service.

In common with everyone else, the war had an impact on all aspects of Richmal's life and that of her family and it is reflected in her writing. The William stories during the war reflect both day-to-day experience on the home front and political currents in the build up to and during the war.

J. McVeigh, *Richmal Crompton, Author of Just William*, Literary Lives, https://doi.org/10.1007/978-3-030-96511-2_15

Crompton's novel *Narcissa* (1941) is a powerful classical allegory on the evil of corrupting and malevolent power and two other novels are representative of life on the home front.

* * *

On the advent of war, Richmal first joined the ARP (Air Raid Precautions) as a volunteer and then the Auxiliary Fire Service. She also volunteered in a local canteen. Rather crudely named Communal Feeding Centres, renamed as British Restaurants, were set up during the Blitz in 1940 and any town with a population of over fifty thousand had at least one. By 1944 they were serving an average of six hundred thousand meals a day across the country.[4] Bromley's first communal canteen, called a Civic, opened in April 1941:

> For ten pence people could have a self-service meal of soup (1d), meat and two vegetables (6d), pudding (2d) and a cup of tea (1d). In the first week 970 meals were served, and in the second week this figure went up to 1,300. Another Civic Restaurant was opened in Bromley High Street in June 1941, and in 1942 two new ones were opened.... By early 1944, the High Street restaurant was serving between ten and eleven thousand meals per month while the others were serving 13,000 between them.[5]

Richmal would have met RAF personnel at the canteen in Keston, Bromley, where the emergency control room for Biggin Hill Aerodrome was situated. It was used in 1940 when Biggin Hill came under heavy bombardment.[6] There was a huge community effort on the home front and local people volunteered in the running of these canteens, in the production of food itself, as well as in the ARP and the Fire Service.

During the winter of 1939–1940, the coldest for forty-five years, ration books were issued, and food rationing began in January 1940. It was urgent that the nation began growing more of its own food and production increased during the war on farms, small allotments and in private gardens. It was estimated that by the end of the war ten percent of all food in Britain, including eggs and pork as well as vegetables, came from allotments. Rose gardens were replaced by potatoes, green vegetables, hens and pigs, and the garden of Richmal's home was no exception.[7]

An Anderson air raid shelter was installed in her garden too. It was used by the family during the Blitz[8]:

> These were made of a shell of corrugated steel, six feet high, four and a half feet wide and six and a half feet long. They were buried four feet deep into the

ground, then fifteen inches of soil heaped over the curved roof. There was an opening on the side of one end where you could place a door or cover.[9]

In a story published in 1941, the Brown family head to their shelter after a siren heralds another air raid. William is disgusted that his hammock has been taken down, despite the frequency with which he had fallen on the heads of his family when he tried to use it. He decides that it has been a rotten raid and warns his mother that when he is blown up she will be sorry that she has not given him any more chocolate. William mistakes a screaming bomb for the sound of the twelve-thirty train letting off steam.[10] He thinks he can hear another bomb, but it is only the screams of the Bevertons arriving. They are an unwelcome mother and daughter, whom Mrs Brown has kindly invited to join them in the shelter, much to Mr Brown's annoyance. William's innocence about the impact of the bombs is dry satire at a time when everyday life meant facing the horrors of war.[11]

During the thirties, the threat of another war was never far away, and many local residents signed up to become volunteers in the Auxiliary Fire Service and the ARP. In addition to permanent fire stations, local auxiliary stations were established. From September 1938, their duties included distributing gas masks and training people in the community to use them.[12] If a bomb fell, the wardens nearest the spot would hurry over to assess what help was needed, and then rush back to the control centre to ring through their report before returning to the incident: 'I go into a house, decide who's alive and who's dead, tot up the number of victims and what is necessary in the way of fire services, ambulances, demolition etc.,' wrote one Kent ARP warden.[13]

Her niece Margaret remembers that Richmal was one of many thousands who volunteered. She began her duties the day before war was declared and Gwen's family moved in:

Aunt Richmal had taken an ARP course, passing her exam in 1938.... Auntie was called up for voluntary duty from 6.00am to 2.00pm on September 2nd [1939], the day we moved our possessions to The Glebe. For a while she was on night shift at an ARP post at the boys' County School but managed to change over to daytime work at No.4 Report Centre in Hayes, near to [her home]. Finally, she settled into the Auxiliary Fire Service but much to her disappointment was not allowed to man a fire engine because of her 'dead' leg, as she called it. She had fancied herself in a helmet but had to be content with telephone and tea-making duties.[14]

Richmal left home at five o'clock in the morning to go on duty, driving along unlit country roads in the dark because of the blackout.[15]

At the beginning of the war, Crompton was asked to write a story for the Bromley Civil Defence service's 1939 Christmas newsletter, Arpeggio. She was always noncommittal about the location of William's village, and 1939 was no exception. However, the story is clearly based in Bromley where William is visiting one of his aunts, who is an Air Raid Warden. Left to his own devices, he endeavours to enliven her surroundings:

> He had trimmed his aunt's tin hat with a length of ribbon and a large feather in order to give her a little surprise, but she had been neither grateful nor surprised.... Feeling his popularity at a low ebb, he set off for a walk into the country, meaning to do a little quiet fishing at Keston ponds. But he found the A.F.S at Keston ponds and the A.F.S found William. Neither of them knew exactly how he became inextricably entangled in the hose, but he retired after about a quarter of an hour, soaked to the skin, his vocabulary enriched by some of the choicer phrases of invective of the English language. His aunt received him coldly. During his absence she had discovered that his gas mask carrier (in which he had punched holes for humanitarian purposes) contained his collection of snails, that he was using his gas mask as a sponge bag and his sponge bag as a home for his pet frog. She had further discovered that he had adorned her gas mask with an inked moustache and a false beard.... He'd done all he could to cheer his aunt up and make her Christmas a success and he got no thanks or gratitude.[16]

In the story, William causes further chaos for the local ARP. It was later revised and published as 'William Does His Bit,' although his aunt no longer lives in Bromley.

The threat of bombing was close to Richmal's home, which was a few miles from Biggin Hill where a Royal Air Force base was located. RAF personnel drove up and down the road past her house to and from the airfield. Margaret, Richmal's niece, remembers waving to the planes in the garden as they returned to the airfield.[17] By the end of the war, fifty-two squadrons from twelve countries were based there.[18]

Planes from the base were part of the evacuation of over three hundred thousand Allied troops from Dunkirk between 27th May and 4th June 1940:

> While they were being rescued by the Royal Navy and a fleet of small boats sailed by their owners, RAF fighters - including Hurricanes and Spitfires from Biggin Hill - kept German airplanes away in a long series of battles in the air.[19]

From August 1940, the airfield was targeted by German bombers for ten weeks. On the 18th, five hundred bombs were dropped on Biggin Hill. By the end of the month, it was being bombed twice a day.[20] An attack on 30th

August was the heaviest on any airfield in Britain and resulted in thirty-nine deaths and twenty-five service personnel were injured.[21]

> "If any aerodrome is in the forefront of the battle and right in the frontline it's Biggin," observed a young pilot whose squadron had just been posted there. "The whole place had a desperate air of total war and mortal combat. Broken Spitfires and Hurricanes, hangers in ruins, filled in bomb craters everywhere and so much general bomb damage that one is left in no doubt whatever that this is total war. In spite of all this, the fighters still fly and the station is still fully operational."[22]

In September 1940, the focus of the German bombardment switched from airfields to cities, with London as the main target.[23]

On 6th September, incendiary bombs caused fires in Bromley town centre and the London blitz began the next day[24]:

> Then on Sunday 15th September 1940 came what is regarded as the turning point in the Battle of Britain. This time the bombers were met by British fighter planes which drove them back. Much of the battle was fought in the skies above Bromley. Bombs were dropped as the German planes tried to escape. All over the area houses were damaged and people were killed.[25]

Crompton's contemporary Elizabeth Bowen recalls the devastating impact of the bombing in her wartime novel, *The Heat of the Day* (1949):

> The autumn of 1940 [in London] was to appear, by two autumns later, apocryphal, more far away than peace.... More bombs would fall, but not on the same city.... Everywhere hung the heaviness of the even worse you could not be told and could not desire to hear.[26]

One Bromley resident comments to her daughter in September 1940: 'It is easier to tell you what isn't bombed than what is.... The Aunties seem to get quite a lot of air raids still, but not so bad as it was.'[27] Aunties were under threat across the town and surrounding area.

In 1940, William too was under threat in central London. Many readers of weekly children's magazines and comics were horrified when their favourite magazines were abandoned during the Second World War due to paper shortages. Owen Dudley Edwards notes that this brought more disruption into children's lives:

> Many of them were already cruelly strained by personal evacuation, parental enlistment, nocturnal darkness and so on, and now the closest friends in their

imaginations may have gone, perhaps shortly to be followed by some of their closest friends in life. The bombs were already falling: *Happy Mag*, where William's triumphs and disasters had made their monthly appearance since December 1922, vanished … [in] May [1940], George Newnes's premises – which housed its production – receiving a direct hit. William survived, in book form and (from August) in *Modern Woman*.[28]

Bromley's biggest air raid of the war was on 16th April 1941, when seventy-four people were killed, two hundred injured and over fifteen hundred were made homeless. Three hundred and sixty-five fires were reported.[29] A few days later, twenty-one personnel from the Auxiliary Fire Service from Beckenham were killed during a bombing of a fire station in Bromley-by-Bow, London.[30] Further high explosive and incendiary bombing in 1943 and early 1944 caused extensive fires across Bromley and the surrounding area.[31]

Shortly after the D-Day landings in 1944, a new German 'secret weapon' hit Britain, the V-1 flying bomb or doodlebug. In June, a fire station and council depot in Bromley was hit by the first V-1 in the area.[32] Margaret remembers the falling of bombs on her first night home with her mother Gwen, after leaving Richmal's home, where her uncle Jack and his family would soon be moving:

> We stayed up all night, fully dressed. A flickering flame from the engine showed up in the dark sky, then the engine cut out and seconds later came a huge explosion. This was something new…. If the engine was still making a noise as it passed over the house, we were safe, at any rate from that one … It was the silence between the cut-out and the crash that was so unnerving.[33]

These bombs were followed by a second 'secret weapon' in September 1944, the V-2, new rockets fired from Holland. They were incredibly loud, unpredictable and devastating: 'A single V-2 could cause a crater as large as 50 feet wide and 10 feet deep.'[34] The most serious local incident caused by V2 bombs was in November 1944, when a public house used by RAF personnel from Biggin Hill was destroyed.[35] Twenty-one people were killed and almost one hundred were injured less than a few miles from Richmal. Then, on 1 April 1945, just before five o'clock:

> Thirty-four-year-old Ivy Millichamp was in the kitchen of her bungalow in Orpington in Kent while her husband Eric, a shift worker, slept in the front room. When a V-2 landed in a nearby garden Mrs Millichamp was killed instantly by the blast, the last civilian in Britain to die as a result of enemy action.[36]

Orpington is also close to Richmal's home. Despite the Anderson Shelter, her home was hardly a safe location for her, or her family. Nevertheless, she remained there and was volunteering in the community when fires rampaged across the area following bombing raids.

* * *

Richmal's writing life ebbed and flowed in wartime. She was in regular touch with the publisher of her adult novels, Macmillan, where the future Prime Minister Harold Macmillan was in charge. At the end of 1939, she received a gift of books from him:

> I can't tell you how pleased I am to have them. I had read reviews of them and had them on my library list but should not have got them for some time. They are just the sort of book that one wants to keep and read again, and they will help to enliven the very monotonous hours of my A.R.P. vigils![37]

In May 1940, Macmillan was appointed Parliamentary Secretary to the Ministry of Supply in Winston Churchill's coalition government. Richmal wrote to congratulate him.[38]

Crompton's agents offered Macmillan a new collection of short stories, *The New House and other stories*, in the summer of 1942.[39] The collection was not published. Two stories written from the narrator's point of view stand out. 'The New House' is set in 1939. Julie is afraid of the new home where she has moved with her husband Humphrey and son Dickie. A sense of foreboding overwhelms her, and she is terrified of being left alone. The war is closing in on the family. In 'A Diary,' the narrator reflects on her long marriage to a man she has never loved and who fails to understand her: 'I do not blame him for this,' she comments, 'because I am unlike other people and other people have always called me peculiar.'[40] Her life changes when Wamble comes back: 'Wamble is rather like an elephant, but with a long, sharp beak instead of a trunk and strong webbed feet like an ostrich. He is about four feet high and can appear and disappear at will.'[41] Her relationship with the imaginary Wamble takes her into a dark place from which she can never return.

In August 1944, Crompton's latest novel, *The Roundabout* was also rejected by Macmillan.[42] She wrote to Daniel Macmillan in January 1945 explaining that:

> [It] was written in very difficult circumstances, as I had my brother (invalided out of the R.A.F) and his family living with me while they looked for a house, and I had all the cooking and house-keeping to do, as well as my part time war work at an N.F.S. [National Fire Service] station and a canteen, so that it

was written mostly in odd half hours, with my eye on the clock and my mind in the kitchen, which may account for its diffuseness.

This one [*Westover*] may not be much better, as I wrote it against time during the two months that my brother's family evacuated because of the flying bombs and I had the place to myself.

Life is a little easier now, as my brother has found a house and the N.F.S. station where I did part time duty has closed down.

I suppose that eventually the world will return to normal, but it seems difficult to believe![43]

A reader for Macmillan adds that although she 'is one of the best women novelists writing for women…. in this attempt to write a sort of Forsyte Saga about women in the Victorian era, she has overdone it.'[44] Further research might confirm if this manuscript formed the basis of *Family Roundabout* (1948), an enjoyable family saga that is tightly structured. Assuming that it is based on the earlier submission, we can imagine Richmal returning to revise her manuscript after the war when at least some semblance of normality would have returned to her day-to-day routine, although, of course, the impact of the war continued into the fifties and beyond. It is not surprising that in the heat of conflict on the home front she struggled to maintain a clear view of the pre-war world the novel portrays. She was right to think that *Westover* is not one of her best, but it is extraordinary to think that it was written in 1944 during bombing raids and that she was living alone at the time.

* * *

William stories in the thirties take a wry look at impending war and the comedy in them is sharp in some and less successful in others. Some reflect the political and social climate in Britain in the thirties and in the build up to the declaration of war in 1939 amongst conventional middle-class communities. Macmillan withdrew two stories from *William and the Detective* (1935) in the mid-nineteen eighties on the basis that they would cause offence and they would continue to do so.[45] First published in 1934, 'William and the Nasties,' features the Nasties, based on the Nazis, who harass a Jewish shopkeeper. The story alludes to the persecution of the Jewish community by Nazis. The other, 'William and the League of Perfect Love,' features Jumble fighting and killing rats.

The evacuation of children at the beginning of the war was the largest mass movement of people in British history, followed by further evacuations in 1940 and during the Blitz. In September 1939, one and a half million school children, teachers, mothers with small children and disabled people and their carers were evacuated, although this was less than expected.[46] Many middle-class homes 'received over a million evacuee school children, infants and mothers, the bulk of them drawn from the poorest and most congested parts of the major cities and towns.'[47] In 1940 in Bromley, following the invasion of Belgium and Holland, hundreds of refugees were billeted with local people or moved into empty houses.[48] And then, by September 1944, almost nine thousand people were evacuated from Bromley.[49]

In May 1940, William knocks on the door of an elderly woman, telling her that he has been sent by Chamberlain to find out if she has any vacant rooms for 'vacuees. She replies sadly that she does not need a vacuum and can manage adequately with her old-fashioned broom.[50] The Outlaws have fun when they dress up with flowerpots on their heads, which are their stand-ins for gas masks and, with other local boys, they decide to have a go at 'detramination,' as opposed to decontamination, which involves taking their clothes off and being hosed down.[51]

Owen Dudley Edwards suggests that in the William stories Crompton is the best observer of Home Counties England during the war:

> Crompton succeeded, not by pretending to be on the child's side - she is an adult, writing from an adult perspective and making adult's points which a child feels adult by sharing - but by fairly clear indications that in child-adult war she would not pretend adults were necessarily moral superiors to children.[52]

The comic images of William lighten the mood for a moment, but with a wry satirical edge, when the dangers of war were ever present in the years these stories were published.

* * *

Turning to Compton's novels, classical allusions work to powerful effect in her novel *Narcissa* (1941), which is a disturbing tragedy featuring another of Crompton's mother figures. This is an allegorical tale about the nature of power and evil written amidst the horrors of the Second World War. Crompton's themes can be dark and foreboding, and satire, comedy and bildungsroman are discarded for tragedy and horror. In these stories, Crompton's commitment to allegory, significant in many of the William stories, are key features of her writing. At times, the very walls, and rooms we live in are imbued with an evil spirit. We can see this theme in earlier writing from the nineteen twenties in a collection of short stories, *Mist and other stories* (1928), and her novel *The House* (1926). They are like gothic horror stories in the tradition of *Jane Eyre* (1847) by Charlotte Bronte and *The Fall of the House of Usher* (1839) by Edgar Allen Poe.[53]

Several of the stories in *Mist* are based on a haunted or evil house and garden that become characters in the story. She wrote one allegorical novel on this theme, *The House* (1926), in which Crompton reimagines the glories of gothic horror for her own ends. The history of the people who have lived in a house, to which new owners have moved, has penetrated its walls to such an extent that it has become a place of malevolence and unhappiness. Donald is attending Cambridge University and, when he visits the house bought by his parents for the first time, he becomes conscious of something within it emanating 'from the chinks of the floor and the walls, filling the air with a hostile influence.'[54] He feels the evil, malignant, and destructive will of the house, and is overcome by a black inferno of horror: 'Rank evil emanated from every brick.'[55] The house has an evil spirit that attacks Donald with its horrible inaudible sounds that 'dragged him like little clutching arms downwards, downwards.'[56] His anxiety about the supernatural forces emanating from the house increases as he becomes worried about the health of his family. Thwarted in love, the malevolent forces in the house lead his sister to attempt suicide after she hears the whole house full of voices, whispering to her softly and laughing.[57] His mother hears them too and feels like she is in hell. Eventually, she is broken by her fear and dies. The death of Donald's father follows as the house lures him too into thoughts of fear and self-loathing. Both his spirit and his flesh are broken. A local hermit describes to Donald the evil thoughts that imbue the house. He tells him:

> And evil thoughts are the strongest things in the world. They're stronger than evil deeds or evil words.... An evil thought does not die—it goes to swell the power of evil in the world—it enters other men's hearts ... it goes about tempting—tempting.[58]

The evil demonic spirit embedded in the house becomes a metaphor for the undercurrents inherent in family life, and in our inheritance from our past, and that of others like us. Its power lies in confronting us with inner voices that represent our greatest fears and failures. As George Orwell knew, our greatest torment can come from within ourselves.[59] Donald resists the spirit's temptations, but others more culpable or vulnerable are overwhelmed. Crompton's representation of evil is most successful in a later novel published during the early years of the Second World War.

In *Narcissa*, Crompton returns to the power of evil, but here it resides in a person, not a place, who embodies all that is corrupting humanity at a time of conflict. The novel charts the rise and fall of a tyrannical egotistical woman who is the epitome of narcissistic malevolence and the misuse of power. It can be read as powerful propaganda, embodying the extent to which malign forces had dominated social and political life since 1939.[60] In her memoir about life on the home front in England during 1940, *Where Stands A Winged Sentry* (1941), Margaret Kennedy writes mournfully that:

> There was a time in the summer of 1940 when it almost seemed as if sheer badness was a dominating principle.... A sense of deadly peril weighed upon us, but far worse was the fog of falsity, of betrayal, spreading all over the world its weary, bitter disgust and doubt.[61]

Crompton shares this sense of badness and peril in this novel.

At the beginning of *Narcissa*, Stella is a dazzling, beautiful young woman, who charms most of the people she meets, but she is a monster. Is she also a murderer? She marries and has two sons. Stella is incapable of love and only one son manages to escape her obsessive clutches. We follow Stella over forty years of a life that encapsulates every aspect of the deadliest sins.

Doreen's husband, Hugh, had previously been engaged to Stella. He is fatally injured whilst crossing the channel to rescue young soldiers trapped on the beaches of Dunkirk in late May to early June 1940. Doreen believes that, 'He had died in doing that which of all things he had most longed to do. The world he knew and in which he was at home was crumbling.'[62] At the end of the novel, many years since they last met and after Hugh's death, Doreen decides to go in search of Stella. These scenes are set in 1941, the year the novel was published. When she sees Stella, Doreen is confronted with an image of an evil, dangerous clown, a hideous caricature of her younger self. Stella's true nature is on show at last and Doreen runs from her 'feeling as if in the grip of a nightmare.'[63] Some might be cajoled into believing Stella's narcissistic lies, but people like Doreen, who can see her for who she really is, never will. Published in the midst of war, this allegory encapsulates the utter destruction, both mental and physical, wrought by power unchecked and an obsession to rule.[64]

In *Mrs Frensham Describes a Circle* (1942), Crompton writes about the experience of families on the home front. Mrs Frensham is living on Sidbury Common, three miles from Pollard Hill Aerodrome, so the area is bombed frequently.[65] Sidbury Common is three miles from Medleigh, a pleasant country town.[66] Scenes in the novel depict families hiding in shelters or under the stairs during raids, coping with incendiary bombs, collecting shrapnel in their gardens and learning to live alongside allied soldiers. Many of the bombs falling in the area are part of raids moving on to London.[67]

We also meet Miss Fraser, who volunteers to take telephone calls in the AFS station following bombing raids:

> It was a small room, lit always by artificial light (as the window was blocked by sandbags), containing two desks and a small table on which were the telephone, log-book and message pad. A shelf ran round the wall holding files and records, as well as a heterogeneous assortment of odds and ends - tins of paint, coffee, brass polish, shoe polish, balls of string, lengths of rope, electric torches, a bag of apples, and a Stenor hose-repairing outfit. A large map of the district hung on the wall with red dots for the hydrants, and here and there various coloured pins that marked "Road closed", "Road partially obstructed", "Main out of order". By the door stood the officers' rubber boots, tin hats and respirators ready for use in emergency.[68]

Miss Fraser makes a note in her log when an Air Raid Warning Red is received, sounding six short blasts on the hooter. She then sits tense:

> It might all start in a second at full pitch, out of the blue, as it were.... Salvos of gunfire, bursting of bombs, fires everywhere, the walls falling in ... and she would sit here with the telephone, giving and receiving messages, calm and unmoved until the end.... She put the Fire Call pad directly in front of her. Every second was important for a fire call, of course.[69]

The AFS station is indeed hit in an air raid and Miss Fraser is killed, one of eighty local people killed in one night, 'many of them at their posts of duty.'[70] The novel is a rallying cry for tolerance and an appreciation of the huge contributions and sacrifices made by ordinary people.

It reflects on the discrimination Jews experienced in England. One of the families featured in the novel is Jewish. Mr Stoneberry came to England after the First World War and changed his name from Steinberg. His character is described as unselfish and kind.[71] However, other descriptions of him and another man in the novel reinforce some unacceptable and discriminatory stereotypes about Jewish people that were regrettably common in this period.[72]

Mr Stoneberry's son Simon, who has been educated at Harrow and Oxford, falls in love with Ellen, a young woman who is his neighbour. He watches as lorries full of soldiers with tin hats and rifles pass through the village, and he reflects on the tragedy of war for all young men:

> He thought of Voltaire's prayer, 'Grant that the shades of difference between the atoms called man may no longer be the signals for hate or persecution' - a prayer that was still unanswered after two hundred years.[73]

Viki, a friend of Simon's, saw her mother battered to death in the Berlin pogrom—in November 1938—and has been told 'indirectly but with sickening detail' of her father's death in a concentration camp.[74] She is haunted by what she has seen. Yet, despite her suffering, she tells Simon vehemently, 'I don't want to forget – ever.'[75] Simon 'thought of all those men and women he had known ... butchered, tortured, driven to madness and suicide.... The world would be the poorer for the loss of them.'[76] Viki finds Ellen smug and self-satisfied in her suburban idyll which is 'intolerant of everything outside itself.'[77] She cannot live in the village where she is surrounded by people who have no understanding of such suffering and her own experience as a Jew. She tells Simon:

> "They've been bombed, I know.... They've been hurt physically and driven from their homes, but they've only played at suffering. They don't know what it is to breathe fear with every breath you draw, to feel the very air around you sick with cruelty ... to lie awake at night in the sweat of terror lest you've said anything that could be twisted against you, to see the people you love just – vanish and never to know what's happened to them, to wonder every morning whether it will – get you before night. They've never known that."
> "Please God they never will," said Simon.[78]

Simon experiences discrimination in the village. He knows that the attitude of some of his local friends changes once they know he is Jewish. Ellen challenges her mother's discrimination about what the war means to 'them.'[79] Simon talks to Ellen about his heritage. They plan to marry. In the early years of the war, when information about the Holocaust and the horror of the persecution and murder of Jews was emerging in Britain, this novel is an attempt, albeit unsuccessful, to face up to their experience in Europe and on the home front.[80]

In the rather melodramatic *Weatherly Parade* (1944), Jo, a young English woman, marries Karl, a German, in the late nineteen thirties. In scenes set in Germany in 1937, Karl is caught up fighting against Nazi oppression and Jo's parents are terrified that she is in danger:

> After the Nazi seizure of power, letters from Karl and Jo had become more and more infrequent till finally a Dutchman had brought a letter from her to Jim [Jo's father], which he had smuggled out of Germany, telling him that Karl had been put into a concentration camp because of his anti-Nazi activities, that Jo herself was constantly watched and had been questioned several times by the Gestapo, that all her letters were opened and that it was no longer safe for her to write to him or receive letters from him. She was expecting a baby in five months' time.[81]

Her father helps Jo escape to England. Karl is tortured and killed. By 1940, Jo is driving an ambulance during the blitz and working with refugees. She knows that the allies are:

> fighting something so monstrously evil that no one who hasn't lived with it can know how evil it is. If we're to conquer it, we can't afford to fritter our strength away on emotions ... can't afford to hate. You hate something that you can – partially, at any rate – understand. This is beyond understanding, beyond hatred. We can only fight it blindly.[82]

Karl has fought, like Hugh, against violent conflict and the misuse of power. This is emotional anti-war propaganda after long years of conflict.[83] Crompton is at her strongest when drawing larger than life, allegorical or exceptional characters and circumstances, as well as those experiencing strong emotions, even in the most conventional surroundings, and these wartime novels capture this quality.

* * *

Family Roundabout ends as the Second World War approaches. Inside this biographer's copy of Crompton's *Family Roundabout* (1948), is an invoice for three shillings and six pence from the Universal Book Club addressed to the reader who bought it in 1949. Their home was close to Hanworth Air Park that manufactured airplanes during World War Two. In 1942, a seventeen-year-old cadet, who lived in the same road as the first owner of this book, was killed and six others were injured in a tragic accident when a pilot of a Spitfire overshot the boundary at Hanworth.[84] The Second World War anticipated at the end of Crompton's novel, although not by Mrs Willoughby the matriarch in the novel, must have touched the lives of many of the people known to this reader:

> "On the whole," said Mrs Willoughby after a short pause, "quite a fair proportion of our families [are] happy and well settled."
> "Yes," said Mrs Fowler, "but if war comes" ...
> "No one would be safe anywhere if it came, but it won't come," said Mrs Willoughby ... "The whole thing's bluff. He wouldn't dare to fight the British Empire—a common little German upstart like that!"[85]

Did the novel offer this reader comforting memories of a past era amidst the debris of war, or serve as a shocking reminder of a pre-war complacency that could not imagine the horrors to come?

Notes

1. Anon, "Forthcoming Books," *Birmingham Post* 21 March 1939, 4.
2. Disher, M., 152.
3. Edwards, 193.
4. Gardiner, 153–154.
5. Reeves, 65.
6. I am grateful to Nicholas Bennett for this information.
7. Gardiner, 138–139, 143 and Cadogan, 24.
8. Disher, M., 152.
9. Friel, 3.
10. "William the Salvage Collector," 149.
11. Ibid., 155.
12. Reeves, 4.
13. Gardiner, 332.
14. Disher, M., 151.
15. Ashbee, R., vii.
16. Reeves, "William's Unlucky Day," 30–31.
17. Disher, M., 73.
18. Reeves, 52.
19. Ibid., 49.
20. Ibid., 51.
21. Gardiner, 274.
22. Ibid.
23. Ibid., 282.
24. Reeves, 39.
25. Ibid., 40.
26. Bowen, 92.
27. Reeves, 55.
28. Edwards, 39 and 51.
29. Reeves, 46.
30. *Bromley at War* (2005), published by the London Borough of Bromley.
31. Reeves, 72.
32. *Bromley at War* (2005). Also see, *Bromley on the Frontline* (1983) by Blake Lewis.
33. Disher, M., 153.
34. Gardiner, 560.
35. Reeves, 94.
36. Gardiner, 564.

37. British Library Add MS 89,262/2/17. Letter to Harold Macmillan, 8th November 1939.
38. British Library Add MS 89,262/2/18. Letter to Harold Macmillan, 29th May 1940.
39. British Library Add MS 89,262/2/19. Letter to Daniel Macmillan, 18th August 1942.
40. UoR RC/1/1/2/1/8.
41. Ibid.
42. British Library Add MS 89,262/2/20. Letter to Daniel Macmillan, 17th August 1944.
43. British Library Add MS 89,262/2/20. Letter to Daniel Macmillan, 16th January 1945.
44. British Library Add MS 89,262/2/20. Letter to Daniel Macmillan, 17th August 1944.
45. McKibbin notes that the 'casual anti-semitism of the interwar years was to be found at all levels of English life' (56).
46. Gardiner, 18.
47. Stevenson, 140.
48. Reeves, 25.
49. Ibid., 92.
50. Edwards, 62 and "William and the Evacuees," 11. Edwards argues that Crompton is openly criticising Chamberlain in this story and his inability to make himself understood and that in Crompton's war stories there is covert propaganda. William 'is what Britain is fighting *for*; he is also Britain fighting' (175).
51. "William and the A.R.P.," 13. The Outlaws often get words wrong and decide in one story that someone is a misanthropologist. Henry says that part of this word is right. See "William Gets a Scoop" in *William and the Space Animal*.
52. Edwards, 8 2 and 176. For a summary of Edward's discussion of William stories, see John Lester's article in *JWSM* 28, 28–31.
53. In Poe's story about the last of the Usher family, the first-person narrator visits the forbidding mansion owned by his friend Roderick Usher. Roderick fears that the terrible influence of the house has moulded the destiny of his family for centuries and it seems riven with evil intent.
54. *The House*, 100.
55. Ibid., 113.
56. Ibid., 176.
57. Ibid., 270.
58. Ibid., 308.

59. In *1984* (1949), George Orwell's protagonist Winston Smith is confronted with his greater fear in Room 101.

60. See Maroula Joannou's focus on feminist anti-fascist narratives of the nineteen thirties in her chapter "Anti-fascist Writings," '*Ladies Please Don't Smash These Windows': Women's Writing, Feminist Consciousness and Social Change 1918–38* (1995).

61. Kennedy, 4.

62. *Narcissa*, 296.

63. Ibid., 301.

64. Stella is one of the most controlling mothers in Crompton's fiction. In "The Mother" (1929), published a decade before the start of the Second World War, Crompton writes about the all-consuming and dangerous control of a jealous mother. Mrs Carswell loves her son, 'but it's an utterly selfish love, and an utterly selfish love is one of the most terrible things in the world' (58). Similar stories feature in one of her short story collections, *Sugar and Spice* (1929), in particular "The Woman Who Was Greedy." This is a story about a nasty woman whose husband and son are killed as a result of her maniacal control of their lives. It is a story that Crompton returns to again to powerful effect in *Narcissa*. Also, see "The Last Rung" and "Leila Faraday" in the same collection.

65. *Mrs Frensham*, 45.

66. Ibid., 47.

67. Ibid., 114.

68. Ibid., 154.

69. Ibid., 161.

70. Ibid., 277.

71. Ibid., 76.

72. Whyte, 152. Whyte comments that 'Crompton was no more anti-Semitic than most of her contemporaries.'.

73. *Mrs Frensham Describes a Circle*, 207.

74. Ibid., 195.

75. Ibid., 196.

76. Ibid., 197.

77. Ibid., 203.

78. Ibid., 197.

79. Ibid., 124 and 209.

80. Ellen refers to pamphlets about Polish concentration camps, 124.

81. *Weatherly Parade*, 214.

82. Ibid., 234.

83. Also, see other studies of British fiction during the Second World War: Jenny Hartley *Millions like us: British Women's Fiction of the Second World War* (1997), Mary Cadogan and Patricia Craig *Women and Children First: The Fiction of Two World Wars* (1978).
84. AIR CRASHES AT HANWORTH AERODROME - Habitats & Heritage (https://habitatsandheritage.org.uk).
85. *Family Roundabout*, 271.

References

Ashbee, Richmal. 1995. "Foreword." In *William at War*, by Richmal Crompton, vii–xi. Basingstoke, Hampshire: Macmillan Children's Books.

Bowen, Elizabeth. 1983. First published 1949. *The Heat of the Day*. Harmondsworth, Middlesex: Penguin.

Cadogan, Mary. 2001. *Richmal Crompton and Her Bromley Connections.* Folkestone, Kent: Lilburne Press.

Crompton, Richmal. 1925. *Anne Morrison*. London: Jarrolds.

———. 1949. *Family Roundabout*. London: Hutchinson Universal Book Club.

———. 2015. First published 1942. *Mrs Frensham Describes a Circle*. Peebles: Greyladies.

———. 1941. *Narcissa*. London: Macmillan.

———. 1926. *The House*. London: Hodder & Stoughton.

———. 1929. "The Mother." In *Ladies First*, by Richmal Crompton, 37–58. London: Hutchinson & Co.

———. 1944. *Weatherly Parade*. London: Macmillan.

———. 1987. First published 1939. "William and A.R.P." In *William and the Air Raid Precautions*, by Richmal Crompton, 1–41. Basingstoke, Hampshire: Pan Macmillan Children's Books.

———. 1996. "William and the Evacuees." In *William and the Evacuees*, by Richmal Crompton, 1–33. Basingstoke, Hampshire: Macmillan.

———. 1988. First published 1941. "William the Salvage Collector." In *William Does His Bit*, by Richmal Crompton, 1–19. Basingstoke, Hampshire: Macmillan Children's Books.

Disher, Margaret. 1990. *Growing Up with Just William By His Sister*. London: The Outlaws Publishing Company.

Edwards, Owen Dudley. 2007. *British Children's Fiction in the Second World War*. Edinburgh: Edinburgh University Press.

Friel, Joanna, Gill Purbrick, Kevin Jennings, Ian Janet Skinner, and Susan Wiffin. 2017. *Chislehurst's Second World War 1939–1945*. Chislehurst: Old Chapel Books.

Gardiner, Juliet. 2005. *Wartime Britain 1939–1945*. London: Headline Book Publishing.

Kennedy, Margaret. 2021. First published 1941. *Where Stands A Winged Sentry.* Bath: Handheld Press.

McKibbin, Ross. 2000. First published 1998. *Classes and Cultures England 1918–1951.* Oxford: Oxford University Press.

Reeves, Graham. 1990. *Undaunted: The Story of Bromley in the Second World War.* Bromley: Bromley Leisure Services.

Stevenson, John. 1984. *British Society 1914–45.* London: Lane.

Whyte, William. 2011. "Just William? Richmal Crompton and Conservative Fiction." In *Classes, Cultures, and Politics: Essays on British History for Ross McKibbin,* by Clare Griffiths James Nott and William Whyte Eds., 139–154. Oxford: Oxford University Press.

16

William, Flawed Hero

Some of the essential requirements for rulers of men and women, boys and girls, in or out of periods of war, are encapsulated in William's heroic qualities. He has the confidence to act and an impulse to freedom that we value, but often lack ourselves. He is brave in the face of adversity and his logic is not hidebound by convention. Crompton's hero has one foot in a day-to-day fictional world full of caricatures of both adults and children that bears some resemblance to real life, but is not realistic, and another in a parallel existence in which his alter ego reigns supreme. In William's mind's eye, his adventures take on mythical proportions as he sees himself 'as an impressive and heroic figure,' who can rise above his ordinary boyhood existence[1]: 'To William life was one long glorious Romance.'[2] He mistakenly believes that other heroes have a much better time of it:

> He went downstairs feeling gloomy and disillusioned. All the people one read about in books–Odysseus and Tarzan and the rest of them—could do anything they liked and nothing ever happened to them.[3]

There are times when William is faced with a sense of failure, but only for a moment or two. William reviews the unsuccessful events of one particular day and dismisses them: 'William's spirit could not harbour a sense of failure for long.' It belonged to:

> the world of fantasy, dreamlike, unreal. With relief, he turned to the world of reality.

© The Author(s), under exclusive license to Springer Nature Switzerland AG 2022
J. McVeigh, *Richmal Crompton, Author of Just William*, Literary Lives, https://doi.org/10.1007/978-3-030-96511-2_16

Thunders of applause arose from the crowd as his car turned in at the gates of Buckingham Palace.[4]

This, of course, is one of the qualities that make him a hero. A hero who is confident and whose approach to life has just that touch of arrogance and egotism that keeps failure at bay, who faces people bravely and with bravado.

William is 'a born leader' and the Outlaws accept him as their hero. 'In spite of his occasional exasperation, Ginger had infinite trust in William's capacity for attracting adventure,' a view shared by all members of the Outlaws.[5] 'With William they would stand or fall as they'd always done.... After all, it was generally more exciting falling with William than standing alone.'[6]

There are a few occasions when the Outlaws are brave enough to question some of William's ideas. William decides to write a play about rebels in history. He is a 'jolly quick play writer' and a good one, or so he believes.[7] He decides that it would make history 'more int'restin'' if they became rebels instead. Henry, as usual, provides some useful background information that inspires William:

"How do rebels start?" said Ginger.
"Well, there's got to be a leader," said Henry.
"I'll be him," said William.
"An' this leader's got to rouse followers by makin' speeches."
"I can do that all right," said William confidently. "I'm jolly good at makin'' speeches.[8]

William 'loved an audience,' and considered himself jolly good at anything he wanted to do.[9]

* * *

Each Outlaw has his own distinctive characteristics: Douglas is invariably gloomy; Henry is interested in history; and Ginger is William's loyal side kick. Ken Waller suggests that:

Henry is the eldest, best informed and probably most intelligent of the Outlaws, hence his occasional abortive attempts to wrest leadership of the Outlaws from William. But he manifestly lacks William's charisma and imaginative leadership. Douglas is on one occasion said to be the tallest but is relatively slow witted, with the least natural inclination to court danger and with the largest measure of conscientious scruples over the more lawless of their exploits. Without William, Douglas would achieve little (except an uneventful life). Ginger, William's life-long friend … though thin and wiry can match William in wrestling and tree-climbing. His is a willing, natural lieutenant, but no more [and has a more down to earth approach to life].[10]

In a story from 1966, the Outlaws' personalities are captured in one scene where they have decided to brighten up some boring letters with historical references:

Henry, whose energies were chiefly taken up in supervising the spelling of the other three, tried to confine his historical references within certain roughly defined limits…. William's references spanned the whole field of history with wild abandon…. Douglas confined himself to the only historical film he had seen … Ginger, who had recently read a book called *Scenes from English History*, gave a brief account of his experiences in the Crusades.[11]

Henry corrects William when he gets his facts wrong and takes life more seriously than his friends. He remains in William's shadow.[12] Douglas is the Eeyore of the Outlaws. He often has misgivings about their plans:

"I've never known you do anythin' without havin' a sort of feeling that something's going to go wrong with it."
"Yes, an' it gen'rally does," said Douglas."[13]

The boys are excited by William's idea of a circus in their barn until Douglas dampens their enthusiasm by wondering how they will acquire any animals: 'To Douglas's credit be it said that having uttered his exhortation to caution he was always content to follow the other Outlaws on their paths of lawlessness and hazard.'[14] He preferred a quiet life, but was no coward, a characteristic shared by William and the other Outlaws.

* * *

In an intertextual allusion to Homer, in one story, Ginger and William miss the point by suggesting that they could escape from, rather than into, a house using a wooden horse. Ginger asks William how they can find a wooden horse big enough for them both and who is going to push it. His friend finds these objections unhelpful.[15]

William becomes Crompton's classical hero. Fans Ben and Margaret Sherriff suggest that William:

like some Greek god, introduces chaos which results, ultimately, in a new and improved order, but, like a force of nature, he remains unchanged, unrepentant, unfazed, briefly disgruntled maybe, but essentially full of boundless self-confidence in his own worth ... William remains a creative catalyst, a bringer of change, an irritant to the hidebound, almost like some impish classical messenger sent by Zeus to stir us up.[16]

His 'Pegasean imagination soared aloft on daring wings' and he is always on the side of the righteous.[17] In classical myth, Pegasus is a winged horse tamed by Athena herself, a feat Crompton tried to achieve in William's case. The image of her as Athena seems apt.[18] William is her mischievous and playful self and her inner (most) voice advocating the values she believes are important.

There is an underlying tension between William's logic and strategies, and the powers of Fate, which pursues him throughout his adventures like a guiding spirit, often undermining his plans and preventing him from doing what he wants.[19] In the first book, *Just William* (1922), we hear the narrator's voice:

> I have said that William did not know where he was going.
>   *But Fate Knew.*[20]

In this instance, William literally does not know where he is going as he careers down a road on his brother's new bicycle. Like the girl in the Hans Christian Andersen fairy tale *The Red Shoes*, he has chosen to be in the situation he is in, yet powers outside his control are determining what should happen to him, whilst, as usual, he has not considered the consequences of his actions. William does not know how to stop and get off the bicycle, as 'his feet pedalled mechanically along.... William wondered if people would be sorry if he dropped down dead,' which, as we know, is the fate of the girl in her red shoes who cannot stop dancing.[21]

It is Fate that has the upper hand and often takes control when William is trying to master a situation. Whether this is the fault of William or Fate is not always clear:

> William was an entirely well-meaning boy. That fact must be realised in any attempt to estimate his character, but Fate had a way of putting him into strange situations, and the world in general had a way of misunderstanding him. At least, so it always seemed to William.[22]

On one extremely rare occasion, William is speechless and 'The Medusa's classic expression of horror was as nothing to William's at that moment.... But the Fates were closing round him.'[23] As if determined by the Gods, William our hero, like Odysseus, is under the wings of both Fate and Athena herself.

English author Adam Nicolson suggests why Homer still matters and finds in *The Odyssey*, which charts Odysseus's adventures on his way home from the Trojan wars:

> someone speaking about fate and the human condition in ways that other people only seem to approach obliquely.... I felt Homer was a guidebook to life. Here was a form of consciousness that understood fallibility and self-indulgence and vanity, and despite that knowledge didn't surrender hope of nobility and integrity and doing the right thing.[24]

In *The Odyssey*, we are given the hope that there is a chance 'to stand out against fate.'[25] Of course, Odysseus survives his entry into the city hidden inside a wooden horse. Unfortunately, Nicolson adds that 'Socrates was impressed by Homer's decision ... that no hero should ever eat iced cakes,' so William is clearly not quite the same kind of hero as Odysseus.[26] Nevertheless, he too can be self-indulgent and vain, whilst also, at least when faced with pomposity, doing the right thing.

Odysseus and William do share some surprisingly similar characteristics. Odysseus can 'niftily find [his] way around the obstacles life throws in [his] path,' he is a 'slippery trickster' and an ingenious man.[27] William is a trickster too. In Nicolson's understanding of Odysseus's virtue, we can see aspects of William: 'Homer shapes Odysseus to be the universal man' and Crompton has similarly shaped William.[28] Nicholson believes that Homer offers 'a form of reassurance that in the end there is some kind of understanding in the world' and 'the *Odyssey* [is] a version of what we are and what we might yet be.'[29] Similarly, William offers reassurance and hope. We aspire to have his confidence and his belief that everything will work out alright in the end.

Spanish philosopher Fernando Savater declares that 'No one ... explains us to each other so profoundly' as William Brown. He 'is the hope itself that we will never lack the gumption to get out of a tight place'[30]:

> [He] is brave, and even rash on occasion ... William is impetuous, but he loves the calculated ins and outs of strategy; he seeks the joy of discovery and the challenge of risk rather than booty.... he is imaginative but logically so; he is romantic insofar as this disease is still compatible with irony, pragmatism, and

a taste for cream buns.... he is Ulysses [the Roman name for Odysseus], he of the winged and subtle word, he who invents a thousand stories and ... the best advocate of his own cause.[31]

Savater believes that William adopts the hero's point of view throughout Crompton's stories: he has 'the state of mind that makes a hero immortal.... William never hesitates over anything essential; that is his magic.'[32] He has the confidence to carry on despite any setback. We follow him hoping that some of his resilience might rub off on us too.

* * *

Crompton agrees with the Outlaws that William has 'a love of adventure for its own sake, a fearlessness and courage that is the stuff of which heroes are made. And he lives, of course, in a dream world in which he *is* a hero.'[33] He is the sort of boy who is 'an enemy of civilisation and all its meaning-less conventions.'[34] Despite their caution about William's loose hold on facts and the tendency for most of his plans to go wrong, the Outlaws look up to him as their hero. His optimism, refusal to accept failure, his ability to root out pomposity and greed and his endless imagination brought respite to his readers during the long years of the Second World War and subsequently when further fame and fortune followed Crompton from the autumn 1945. William became a hero to tens of thousands, especially children, as his adventures brought laughter to post-war Britain on the radio. After the war, Crompton touched the lives of families across Britain, whilst she managed to keep the upheaval in her own family away from public scrutiny.

Notes

1. "William and White Satin," 169.
2. "William's Mammoth Circus," 119.
3. "William and the Chinese God," 65.
4. "William Brown Hero," 87.
5. "Kidnappers," 96.
6. "The Outlaws Deliver the Goods," 142.
7. "William the Bold," 36.
8. Ibid., 43.
9. "William and the Early Romans," 18. Crompton did not keep accurate records about some of the details in the stories, and the Outlaw's surnames is one example. Ginger Merridew is also known as Flowerdew.

See "The Mystery of Oaklands," *William* (1929). Crompton told one fan that Douglas's surname was Frinton and Henry's was Bates, but these surnames do not appear in the stories. In a letter by Richmal dated 6th January 1966, she gives Henry's and Douglas's surnames to a fan—see the *JWSM 11*, February 2001, 25–27. Also, see Ken Waller for his discussion on Ginger's first and surname in "What was Ginger's Name?", *JWSM 12*, August 2001, 26–28. He suggests that Ginger's first name was Horatio, another classical hero. Michael Grosvenor Myer also identifies Ginger's surname as Merridew and Flowerdew in *Notes and Queries*, December 1993, 505.

10. Waller, 22.
11. "William and the Masked Ranger," 15.
12. "William the Money Maker," 98 and "Their Good Resolution," 170.
13. "Violet Elizabeth Wins," 24.
14. "William and the White Elephants," 113.
15. "William Does Bob-a-Job," 148.
16. Sherriff and Sherriff, *JWSM* 35, 19.
17. "William the Reformer," 59.
18. See Chapter 18 for a discussion of Crompton's sense that she could not control William.
19. Fate appears in many stories, including "William the MoneyMaker," "William and Photography," "The Fête," "William All The Time," "Kidnappers."
20. "William the Intruder", 51.
21. Ibid.
22. "Just William's Luck," 147.
23. "The Outlaws," 151–152.
24. Nicolson, 6.
25. Ibid., 60.
26. Ibid., 27.
27. Ibid., 60.
28. Ibid., 242.
29. Ibid., 12 and 61.
30. Savater (2010, 28).
31. Ibid., 31–33. Crompton also believes that William is a Romantic figure. A new hero features in a book he has been reading: 'William was not a romancist for nothing. He had ceased to be William. Dick the Dauntless swaggered down the path to the gate with a dark scowl on his face ("William's Secret Society" 128). Savater also comments on the 'versatility of [William's] verbal talent' that is 'literally inexhaustible … No

less admirable is his gift for carrying on a conversation whose meaning and context he knows absolutely nothing about.'
32. Ibid., 37 and Savater (1982, 66).
33. RC/1/1/2/3. *Trade News* 18 August 1956, 28.
34. Ibid.

References

Crompton, Richmal. 1927. "William and the Chinese God." In *William - In Trouble*, by Richmal Crompton, 61–79. London: George Newnes Ltd.
———. 1927. "William's Mammoth Circus." In *Wiliam - In Trouble*, by Richmal Crompton, 106–134. London: George Newnes Ltd.
———. 1927. "William and the Early Romans." In *William - In Trouble*, by Richmal Crompton, 13–38. London: George Newnes Ltd.
———. 1948. First Published 1928. "William the Money Maker." In *William - The Good*, by Richmal Crompton, 97–119. London: George Newnes Ltd.
———. 1949. First published 1932. "Their Good Resolution." In *William - The Pirate*, by Richmal Crompton, 170–187. London: George Newnes Ltd.
———. 1951. First published 1929. "The Outlaws Deliver the Goods." In *William*, by Richmal Crompton, 138–163. London: George Newnes Ltd.
———. 1953. First published 1924. "Kidnappers." In *William - The Fourth*, by Richmal Crompton, 89–107. London: George Newnes Ltd.
———. 1953. First published 1924. "William Makes a Night Of It." In *William - The Fourth*, by Richmal Crompton, 210–226. London: George Newnes Ltd.
———. 1961. First published 1922. "Just William's Luck." In *William Again*, by Richmal Crompton, 147–164. London: George Newnes Ltd.
———. 1961. First published 1923. "William the Reformer." In *William Again*, by Richmal Crompton, 58–73. London: George Newnes Ltd.
———. 1961. First published 1923. "William's Secret Society." In *William Again*, by Richmal Crompton, 108–131. London: George Newnes Ltd.
———. 1984. First published 1927. "William and the White Elephants." In *William - The Outlaw*, by Richmal Crompton, 100–127. Basingstoke, Hampshire: Macmillan Children's Books.
———. 1984. First published 1927. "William - The Outlaw." In *William - The Outlaw*, by Richmal Crompton, 1–17. Basingstoke, Hampshire: Macmillan Children's Books.
———. 1985. First published 1933. "A Rescue Party." In *William - The Rebel*, by Richmal Crompton, 26–50. Basingstoke, Hampshire: Macmillan Children's Books.
———. 1990. First published 1922. "The Outlaws." In *Just - William*, by Richmal Crompton, 150–167. Basingstoke, Hampshire: Macmillan Children's Books.

————. 1990. First published 1922. "William and White Satin." In *Just - William*, by Richmal Crompton, 168–185. Basingstoke, Hampshire: Macmillan Children's Books.

————. 1990. First published 1950. "Violet Elizabeth Wins." In *William - The Bold*, by Richmal Crompton, 1–35. Basingstoke, Hampshire: Macmillan Children's Books.

————. 1990. First published 1950. "William - The Bold." In *William - The Bold*, by Richmal Crompton, 36–66. Basingstoke, Hampshire: Macmillan Children's Books.

————. 1990. First published 1922. "William the Intruder." In *Just - William*, by Richmal Crompton, 33–56. Basingstoke, Hampshire: Macmillan Children's Books.

————. 1991. First published 1958. "William Does Bob-a-Job." In *William's Television Show*, by Richmal Crompton, 136–156. Basingstoke, Hampshire: Macmillan Children's Books.

————. 1993. First published 1966. "William and the Masked Ranger." In *William and the Masked Ranger*, by Richmal Crompton, 1–26. Basingstoke, Hampshire: Pan Macmillan Children's Books.

————. 1993. First published 1968. "William Brown, Hero." In *William the Superman*, by Richmal Crompton, 69–87. Basingstoke, Hampshire: Macmillan Children's Books.

————. 1993. First published 1968. "William's Adventure Society." In *William the Superman*, by Richmal Crompton, 88–112. Basingstoke, Hampshire: Macmillan Children's Books.

Nicolson, Adam. 2015. *The Mighty Dead: Why Homer Matters*. London: William Collins.

Savater, Fernando. 1982. "The Outlaws' Triumph." In *Childhood Regained: The Art of the Storyteller*, by Fernando Savater, 53–67. New York: Columbia University Press.

————. Summer 2010. "The Outlaws' Triumph." *The Just William Society Magazine 26* 28–37.

Sherriff, Ben and Margaret. Winter 2014. "Sixteen of the Best: Richmal's Richmal." *The Just William Society Magazine 35* 18–23.

Waller, Ken. April 2002. "William—His Personality in Childhood and Later Life." *The Just William Society Magazine 13* 20–26.

Part V

(1946–1969)

17

William Becomes a Postwar Hero on TV and Radio

The years shortly after the war brought Crompton further professional success and celebrity status when William became a star of radio and stage plays. During this period, Crompton continued to work in collaboration with Thomas Henry, the illustrator of the William stories, whom she met for the first time in the fifties. She also collaborated with other writers on the successful BBC radio plays from 1945. William stage plays written by Alick Hayes, who worked on many of the BBC William radio productions, were more successful than those by Ireland Wood in the thirties, reflecting the success of William on and off the page. Another new venture in this period, Jimmy stories about a boy aged seven, introduced a new Crompton character.

As Crompton's public fame continued to grow, in her own life complex family circumstances were hidden from prying eyes. Despite changes in the lives of women during the war, when they worked on the home front as never before in jobs previously dominated by men, life at home in the forties and fifties remained traditional, at least on the surface, supported by a strong long-standing community and family values and conventions. Women's lives could suffer if uncomfortable subjects were discussed in public, they sought public attention, or the moral codes expected of love and marriage were broken.

* * *

The Brown's middle-class family life was in tune with similar families who enjoyed radio and television at home, both of which became hugely influential forms of mass home entertainment.[1] In October 1923, 'William Goes

© The Author(s), under exclusive license to Springer Nature
Switzerland AG 2022
J. McVeigh, *Richmal Crompton, Author of Just William*, Literary Lives,
https://doi.org/10.1007/978-3-030-96511-2_17

to the Pictures,' the opening story of the first William book, *Just William* (1922), was transmitted on BBC radio as a children's programme.[2] Then, after a gap of over twenty years, a season of William plays was broadcast on the BBC from October 1945; the series ran for seven years until the autumn of 1952.

Following the broadcast of the first programme on the BBC Light Programme, in October 1945, for listeners of all ages, the BBC believed that the series would catch on and it was indeed hugely popular. They decided to move the broadcast from 6.30 pm to 8.45 pm, immediately after *The Carroll Levis Show*, 'a happy go lucky care-free entertainment.' They were confident that the audience from this show would be carried over to the William series, which was clearly being targeted at adults given the later scheduling. The Overseas Service was also interested in promoting the series at this early stage in its existence.[3]

By the autumn series in 1946, the BBC planned the timing of the programmes so that they were more convenient for children, as well as adults.[4] They had received over two hundred complaints from children about the timing of the repeat daytime programme on Sundays which clashed with their attendance at Sunday school.[5] The aim now became for the programmes to reach both children and adult listeners.[6] Crompton wrote many of the plays for the early radio series in collaboration with BBC writers, including Alick Hayes and Rex Diamond. In 1947, after the first two radio series in 1945 and 1946, Diamond realised the potential for the stories to reach audiences of all ages:

> … Alick Hayes had put his finger on the one weak spot of radio entertainment, that is the gap between young listeners and older ones. *Just William* was the ideal link which brought little Johnny Green, Mr Green and Grandfather Green to the loudspeaker simultaneously…. So, in October 1945, was born the nearest approach to perfect family listening that twenty-three years of radio [had] offered.[7]

William certainly had a national impact and by April 1946 the series had an audience of nine million.[8] David Schutte has identified that Richmal Crompton wrote fifty-five of the ninety-nine radio plays broadcast in five series from October 1945 to December 1952.[9] The 1948 and 1952 series were written exclusively by Crompton.[10] Schutte suggests that in the later series her voice is much clearer and 'the scripts come closer to the style that we know and love as the William of the books.'[11]

In 1946, an article in *The Daily Mail* criticised the William radio series for encouraging bad behaviour in boys. Four boys in Wolverhampton caught breaking and entering and stealing oranges and eggs were allegedly influenced by William's antics in the series. Crompton defends her hero, claiming that William's pranks are innocent and inspired by the best motives.[12] William's retrograde behaviour was treated less seriously in the early twenty-first century. A twelve-year-old boy was hauled into court for assaulting a man with a sausage, a cocktail sausage no less, much to the court's dismay at the futility of the charge. The judge compared the boy's experience with an episode in William Brown's life, commenting that even William 'would have struggled to terrorise someone with a bite-sized snack.'[13]

As all fans of William will know, Richmal Crompton works magic with words. In November 1948, she gave a talk about this very subject on BBC *Woman's Hour*. She argues that each word has 'a life and personality and character of its own, quite apart from its meaning – some friendly, some unfriendly, some gloomy, some cheerful, some beautiful, some ugly.' In her view, some words convey their meaning by their sound, such as 'cosy': 'You can't say the word without being drawn into an atmosphere of closed curtains, heaped up fire, the right book, the right person and the sound of the rain on the window outside.' She likes the woman who said of the dictionary, 'It's such an interesting book, but I wish the stories weren't so short.'[14]

Since the nineteen nineties, the BBC audiobook series based on the original stories, adapted and narrated by Martin Jarvis, have brought a new generation of children and adults into the fold of Crompton fans. In a live recording by Jarvis in May 2019, a member of the audience put it perfectly.[16] Richmal Crompton does not talk down to children, she commented, which was why she enjoyed the William stories so much as a child. Martin Jarvis captures this quality in Crompton's original writing. The stories are ideal for reading aloud, as Martin Jarvis has proved. He gives us a distinctive William who sounds ageless. The care Jarvis takes with each word and phrase, the detailed attention to the tone of even the snappiest retort emphasises the nuance in each story. His performance also reminds us that it is often other adult characters in the stories who we laugh *at*, whilst we laugh *with* William. His attention to Crompton's language and his precision timing to heighten the comedy are critical to our enjoyment.

* * *

In addition to radio and stage plays, Crompton achieved success in films and on television after the Second World War. The first film, *Just William*, in 1939 was followed at the end of the forties by *Just William's Luck* (1947), and *William Goes to Town* (1948), which was later released in 1953 as *William at the Circus*. Val Guest, who went on to have a successful career as a film

Fig. 17.1 Aunt Richmal and Richmal Disher in Denmark late nineteen forties[15]

director, wrote and directed the films from the forties. *Just William: The Book of the Film* (1939) includes the six stories on which the first film is based.[17] *Just William's Luck*, by Crompton and published in 1948, is based on the later film. It is the only William novel and features his adventures over one day. Many years later, Crompton's great, great-nephew, Jonathan Massey, starred in a new re-creation of *Just William's Luck*, which he adapted and co-produced in collaboration with the Shedload Theatre company. The play was performed at the Edinburgh Festival Fringe and other venues in the UK and Europe in 2017–2018. Crompton's creative and performing spirit lives on.

The next book, *William the Bold*, was not published until 1950. Crompton was less prolific after the war, publishing a William book on average every two years, rather than annually. Only eleven novels appeared, roughly a quarter of her total. By the late forties, many of Crompton's best William stories are behind her and fewer individual stories were published in *Home Notes* in 1949–1954, when the publication of William stories in magazines ended. *William and the Space Animal* (1956), the thirtieth book, and the books that followed are based on new stories published for the first time.[18] Nevertheless, from 1945, Crompton was still writing at a steady pace, and she continued to do so until she died. The later William stories lack the satirical edge and exuberant narrative of the pre-war stories, whilst her novels return to the themes of her earlier novels, but with a more mature, reflective, less passionate tone.

In 1946, the first stage play, *Just William* by Alick Hayes, was performed in Birmingham and later that year at the Granville Theatre, Fulham and at the Wimbledon Theatre in January 1947.[19] Fan Robert Kirkpatrick notes that Alick Hayes's play was not based on any of Crompton's stories.[20] Simon Procter, another fan, has discovered that in 1947 the play was performed in local theatres across England and Wales. A live broadcast of a performance from Granville Theatre was shown on BBC television in December 1947.[21] It was revived briefly in 1950 in a production at Christmas in the New Theatre, Bromley, starring Arthur Lowe, who later became famous for his role as Captain Mainwaring in the popular BBC television series *Dad's Army*. Further performances were held in a handful of local theatres in 1962.[22] This first play was followed by *More Just William*, also by Alick Hayes, which had its London premiere at the London Palladium in December 1947.[23]

* * *

William appeared on television with Violet Elizabeth on 25 August 1946 in a programme about London Zoo, but it was another ten years before a regular series appeared.[24] The first TV series, *Over to William*, adapted from original Richmal Crompton stories, was a live broadcast by ITV in 1956.[25] In May 1962, the first BBC television series began with six weekly episodes, followed by a second series in 1963.[26] Two ITV London Weekend Television series were broadcast in 1977, ending in January 1978. The ITV series was well received with both Bonnie Langford as Violet Elizabeth and Diana Dors as Mrs Bott receiving 'special praise.'[27] For fans Jane Furnival and Andy Tribble this series 'has become a classic.'[28] Further BBC series appeared in 1994–1995 and 2010.

In 1975, a BBC reader's report on draft television scripts for a William series highlights that it is the creativity in Crompton's writing, not the plots that allowed the stories to live on into the seventies:

> The William books owe their success to the unvarying formula they used for thirty or so years; an adaptation for children of the farce techniques and a portion of the verbal ones of Wodehouse. They rely on confusions in the boys' minds about the nuances of adult behaviour, indeed of reality itself, and on a convention whereby this muddle always sorts itself out neatly to a desirable conclusion. The plots need a vast amount of coincidence to work at all and it is for this reason that Ms. Crompton was wise to leave them in a vaguely twenties neverneverland, despite gestures towards updating in some of the later stories.... I suspect that this overtly unrealistic treatment and the distancing it involves are the reasons for the amazing popularity of these slightly repetitious adventures of a scruffy child of the rural middleclass; these and the verbal skill with which William's speech is represented.[29]

As this reader identifies, William has one foot in the real world, and another in a world filled with his adventures. His success lies in the quality of Crompton's writing and storytelling. Many William fans enjoy the P. G. Wodehouse Bertie Wooster stories, which have been popular on television too. As Martin Jarvis has identified:

> Crompton's near-contemporary, P.G. Wodehouse, published *My Man Jeeves* in 1919 and William was to encounter several blithe young men (usually besotted by Ethel) who bore a jaunty resemblance to Bertie Wooster. William, though, like Jeeves, had the infinitely superior brain.[30]

The history of William on screen and radio is a story of collaboration between Crompton and other writers, directors and producers who have influenced versions of William on radio, television and film. These and other gate-keepers, including journalists, and especially Martin Jarvis, have helped to make William a classic that is popular with adults and children alike.

* * *

Thomas Henry Fisher, known professionally as Thomas Henry, who created the illustrations for most of the published William stories, was Crompton's most influential collaborator. He was commissioned from the second story published in *The Home Magazine*, 'The Outlaws,' in March 1919.[31] His

William illustrations encapsulate the period in which the stories were first published. Henry illustrated the stories until his death and they were, and have continued to be, a hallmark of the William stories.

Crompton met Henry at the Nottingham Book Festival in 1958, but otherwise they kept in touch by letter.[32] Paul Ashbee remembers that after his death in 1962, she became 'very sensitive about William's anatomy in the hands of the new illustrator, Henry Ford … Thomas Henry had been, via letters, a firm friend for a long time' and she remembered the meeting at Nottingham with affection.[33] From 1947 until his death, Thomas Henry drew a weekly 'William' cartoon strip for *Woman's Own*: 'This usually consisted of three panels, and relied heavily on 'sight-gags' rather than any dialogue.'[34] Kirkpatrick notes that the narrative ideas for the strips were originally created by Crompton, but she decided to withdraw, and Henry subsequently both wrote and designed them.[35] Illustrations by both Henry and his successor, Henry Ford, appear in *William and the Witch* (1964). Henry Ford 'illustrated the final four William books. He also continued the William picture strip in *Woman's Own* for seven years.'[36]

Norman Wright has suggested that for the 'William collector the illustrations are almost as important as the text'[37]:

> It took a couple of dozen stories before the artist finally perfected his interpretation of the character with his saggy socks and resolute chin, but by 1924 both textually and artistically William had become the archetypal anti-authority character that is now instantly recognised by countless enthusiasts the world over.[38]

William's fans, who may or may not collect the books, both agree and disagree with this perspective on the importance of the illustrations. For some what matters most is Crompton's writing, for others the illustrations are integral to their enjoyment.[39]

* * *

Crompton introduced a new character in this period. Jimmy stories, about a boy of seven, were published from 1947 until 1951 in *The Star*, a London evening newspaper.[40] They were illustrated by Thomas Henry. She wrote eighty-seven stories and sixty-two of them were published in two books, *Jimmy* (1949), and *Jimmy Again* (1951), which surprisingly featured another illustrator, Lunt Roberts. The original illustrations were restored by Macmillan when the books were republished in the late nineties.[41] David Schutte and Paula Wild have uncovered the twenty-five previously uncollected stories.[42]

The Jimmy plots echo themes in the William books. The boys are often shadowed by a girl of five called Araminta Palmer, who wants to be part of their adventures and has 'a despotic nature.'[43] Jimmy is in awe of his older brother, Roger, 'an ordinary boy of eleven, but in Jimmy's eyes he was a super boy of unparalleled strength and skill and courage.'[44] Roger is in a gang with two friends, Bill and Charles, called the Three Musketeers who meet in Roger's toolshed. He has a scruffy, 'nondescript mongrel' dog called Sandy.[45] Archie Mould is Roger's bitterest enemy and Jimmy's enemy is George Tallow. Mr. and Mrs. Jellybag are the owners of the local grand house, The Grange. Jimmy often gets into William-like scraps, supported by his friend, Bobby. They eat all the raisins, catch a thief by mistake, make resolutions on New Year's Day, and help a little girl escape from boarding school.[46]

* * *

As the frantic pace of Crompton's writing life continued, her family's life was fraught and demanded her attention too. In both her professional and personal life, she kept her private affairs away from most people outside the family. She was a past master at keeping herself to herself and her public and private lives separate. In her life she seems to epitomise the self-control, self-sufficiency and reticence that Alison Light sees in the lives of middle-class women after the First World War.[47] Like Mrs. Fowler, she kept her rebel self within.[48] Richmal's disability no doubt influenced the world's view of her, and she 'put on a front' and kept her personal feelings about its impact on her life to herself. In 1969, Richmal was remembered by Winifred Finlay, a children's author, as someone 'who fought bravely against her physical handicap.' She also describes her as 'a brilliant conversationalist, wonderfully vital and very clever.'[49] There were also wider pressures within her sister's family that meant it was important to keep their private lives away from prying eyes as much as possible.

One local resident in Chislehurst remembers Richmal coming to his house for meetings of the residents' association, and they met at other local events. She was careful to conceal her disability and did not talk about it. Illness and disability were not considered appropriate subjects for discussion in social gatherings of the time. Richmal did not have the status of a celebrity in the area, which would have been considered poor taste. In those days it would have been considered 'bad form' to get into the papers and self-advertisement, even for recognised professionals, such as accountants, was frowned upon. In his view, social structures and the nature of the professions were rigid, and writers would have received little professional recognition within the middle-class circles of Chislehurst. Also, there was hostility towards women who were ambitious. Richmal's self-deprecation mirrored society's expectations of someone in her position. He can see her character types in William reflected in the lives of the middle classes living in the area in the nineteen fifties; they are especially accurate about pre-war society. She commented to him on one occasion that Ethel's character was 'a bit dated' in the context of post-war social changes.[50]

When she moved from Bromley to Chislehurst in the early nineteen fifties, Richmal was supporting those close to her with life changing events. In 1954, when she bought her final home, her niece Richmal moved from Bristol to Kent with her new husband Paul and their infant son, Edward. Their stay in Bristol had not been easy for the couple and had affected her Aunt Richmal and mother Gwen too.

In November 1953, Richmal had no doubts about the purchase of a house she had seen in Chislehurst. She decided to buy it immediately. It just felt like her home.[51] It abutted Chislehurst Common and National Trust land was directly opposite. The centre of Chislehurst was some distance away. She would have had no option but to drive into the village or take a taxi. The property is secluded, with a garden at the back, a gate and a short driveway. A wooded area to the front kept it hidden from the road. It was often passed by walkers on their way through the woods. One of her readers remembers passing the house as a young girl on her family's regular walks when Richmal was living there. She wondered what this famous author was like but, in common with most people of the period, did not expect to find out about her private life, as we would expect to now.[52] This is a slightly more isolated location than her previous home, an imposing, large house on a relatively busy road that celebrates the success of Richmal Crompton. Gwen, Richmal and other members of the family were frequent visitors but, with fewer bedrooms, one of which became Richmal's study, the house could not accommodate as many guests. Richmal moved to Chislehurst in February 1954. In her early sixties, a desire to have a home without any stairs that was smaller and easier to manage would have influenced her decision to move.

Towards the end of 1953, her niece Richmal was facing a significant turning point in her life. In December, she gave birth to her first child, a month after Aunt Richmal found her new home. Richmal and her fiancé Paul, whom she met through a shared interest in archaeology in 1949 when Richmal was a history student at Westfield College in London, had moved to Bristol where Paul was training to be a teacher. He had high hopes of developing his career in archaeology, but this was proving elusive. Subsequently he went on to become a leading British archaeologist. The couple were married in September 1953 whilst they were living in Bristol. The wedding itself took place in Bromley and it is likely that Richmal's mother and aunt would have attended. Richmal and Paul's son Edward was born in December 1953. In the summer of 1954, Paul secured a teaching post and the family moved from Bristol to Kent. He taught history at a school in South-East London until the nineteen sixties. In 1969, he moved permanently to Norfolk with Richmal and their children, having already taken up an academic post at the University of East Anglia. Over the previous fifteen years, Auntie Richmal continued to be close to her niece and her family and saw them frequently.

Throughout their childhood, Richmal and Paul's children, Edward and Kate, believed that their parents were married in 1952. This was a fiction repeated as they were growing up and one in which Richmal's mother Gwen and her Aunt Richmal colluded. The couple celebrated their fiftieth wedding anniversary in 2002, a year earlier than their actual anniversary. Their children discovered the truth many years later, but never discussed it with their parents, or anyone else in the family. Richmal, their great aunt, died when they were still children, and would not have discussed it with them when they were so young.

At the end of September 1953, Gwen writes to her daughter in Bristol to tell her that she has started to tell the neighbours in Bromley about her marriage, so, she comments, 'it should get round now.'[53] Her aunt Richmal, she goes on, had tea with another neighbour who asked her when Richmal and Paul are to be married. Richmal confirms that they are married, and the neighbour asks if they are planning to have a baby: 'R. said "I hope so."'[54] Both sisters were working hard to construct a story about Richmal and Paul's marriage and Edward's forthcoming birth that the family maintained when Richmal and Paul moved back to Kent in the summer of 1954. By the time they returned from Bristol, Richmal had moved to a new area where her neighbours did not know her family.

Nineteen fifties Britain continued to embrace many of the conventions of the pre-war era and, despite changes in the lives of women between the wars in the twenties and thirties and during the recent one, pregnancy before marriage would still have been something to hide, if at all possible. Throughout the couple's stay in Bristol and for the rest of their lives, Richmal was circumspect, tactful, supportive and loving. Aunt Richmal was not rigid or hidebound by convention in her outlook. In both her personal life and her writing, she is interested in the different decisions people make about their lives and how these decisions influence their futures, often despite society's expectations and conventions. As she no doubts learnt at school and university, rules are made to be broken, as many of her characters, especially William, know. In other writing, characters try to come to terms with what has happened to them and both fate and convention often, but not always, determine that they have little choice.

Richmal's support for her family was practical as well as emotional. She gave financial support to her sister and brother in the nineteen fifties and went on to pay for school fees, holidays and other costs for her nephews and nieces, as well as their children. She gave money to Jack, Gwen, and her niece Richmal.

Both Jack and Richmal contributed a few ideas for her writing. Her other nephews and nieces, as well as great nephews and nieces, were the source of some stories too. She would share her writing with her niece Richmal's children, asking for their ideas and what they thought about some of her vocabulary and plots. The whole family was involved in aspects of her writing life. As her family knew, Crompton was a keen observer of people and she was always looking for new ideas. Her niece Margaret remembers that some of the incidents in the William stories:

> really did happen and scattered through the early books I can find the plots which relate to family or neighbourhood incidents that would have sparked off the ideas. Yet the real attraction of the stories lies in the way they are written – the humour is largely in the writing. Richmal had a superb sense of the ridiculous and her everyday conversation was littered with amusing observations of absurd people and situations. She always watched people, especially in public places like trains and restaurants, and noticed detail that we would never have spotted.[55]

Richmal made scribbled notes about things she overheard in the family and whilst listening to other people. Scraps of paper were found in her old home and together make up an intriguing archive of her thoughts as a writer. She wrote these down, as well as ideas for her stories, on the back of fan letters, bills, royalty statements from her agent and minutes of meetings. Having a treasured notebook to hand to chart her writing journey was never her style.

As she grew older in the fifties and sixties there is an edge to her voice when she talks about her fiction in interviews for the BBC and newspaper journalists, and her final novel is a sombre yet hopeful reflection, not on William, but on what has been important to her in her life of writing. William never grows up, whilst his narrator casts her wry eye over the lives of adults who may grow older but fail to accept the responsibilities expected of them. William encapsulated Crompton's optimism and remained her most significant hero, but his creator lost some of her sparkle as the years passed.

Notes

1. Stevenson, 408–410.
2. See Brian Doyle, "Just William on Radio."
3. BBC Written Archive C167 R19/602, 2 November 1945.
4. BBC Written Archive C167 R19/602, 18 June 1946.
5. BBC Written Archive, Report on Programme correspondence April–June 1946.
6. BBC Written Archive C167 R19/602, 5 December 1946.
7. Diamond, 24. His article initially appeared in *The World Radio and Television Annual* 1947, after there had been two series on the radio in 1945 and 1946 (24).
8. BBC Written Archive P157/1, *Evening News*, 29 April 1946.
9. Schutte, "Publisher's Notes," *William the Terrible*, 12. David Schutte has published the radio plays written by Crompton in six volumes: *William the Terrible* (2008), *William the Lionheart* (2008), *William the Peacemaker* (2009), *William the Avenger* (2009), *William the Smuggler* (2010), and *William's Secret Society* (2010). Many of these plays are not based on stories from the William books (12).
10. See Schutte, *William the Smuggler*, 214–215.
11. Schutte, "Publisher's Notes," 12.
12. BBC Written Archive P157/1, 31 January 1946.
13. UoR RC/1/9/2. *The Times*, 23 August 2007, 5.
14. BBC Written Archive Woman's Hour—The Magic of Words—1 November 1948 Light Programme.
15. UoR RC/3/6/093.
16. I overheard this conversation in an interval during the recording.
17. The stories were "The Outlaws and Cousin Percy," "William to the Rescue," "The Outlaws and the Triplets," "William and the Wonderful Present," "The Outlaws and the Fifth," "William Enters Politics."
18. Schutte, *William the Immortal*, 74, 80 and 84. Although, there is just one story previously published in *Home Notes* in *William and the Space Animal* (1956), "A Helping Hand for Ethel" (74).
19. Kirkpatrick, *JWSM* 28, 10. Kirkpatrick notes that there are no records to date of amateur or professional performances of *William's Half Holiday* by Ireland Wood and *William and the Artist's Model* (1956) by Crompton, based on "Violet Elizabeth Wins."
20. Ibid., 11.
21. Ibid.

22. I am grateful to fan Simon Procter for information on performances of the plays.
23. Kirkpatrick *JWSM* 28, 11. Simon Procter advised me that the play was performed in a few provincial theatres just prior to the London premiere under the title *Just William the Second*.
24. *Radio Times*, 25 August 1946, 25. Issue 1195 (bbc.co.uk), featuring actors from the radio plays.
25. Brian Doyle notes that this as a forgotten series and he describes it in "The Mysterious Case of the 'Missing' William Television Series."
26. Doyle, "William's Television Show," 22.
27. Doyle, *JWSM 6*, 25.
28. Furnival and Tribble, 20.
29. BBC Written Archive T48/184/1, 24 January 1975.
30. Jarvis, 54.
31. Kirkpatrick 2021, 17. See Kirkpatrick's article on Henry's career in *JWSM* 43.
32. Ashbee, 7.
33. Ibid.
34. Wright, 35.
35. Kirkpatrick (2021, 19).
36. Wright, 37.
37. Ibid., 28.
38. Ibid.
39. Hopefully, future research will consider the extent to which the William stories are a collaboration between Crompton and Henry.
40. David Schutte also writes about the publication of the Jimmy stories in "Jimmy's Secret Past" in *JWSM 4*, June 1997, 8–10. He notes here that the stories were originally illustrated by Thomas Henry.
41. Kirkpatrick (2021, 20).
42. Schutte and Wild, *Jimmy Returns: Jimmy and the Bull*, 2. The twenty-five previously uncollected Jimmy stories are available to members of The Just William Society in five volumes: *Jimmy and the Bull* (2016), *Jimmy and the Jellyfish* (2017), *Jimmy and the Lettuces* (2017), *Jimmy and the Despot* (2018), and *Jimmy's Vampire* (2018). They include Thomas Henry's original illustrations. Also see, Kirkpatrick *JWSM* 43, 20.
43. "Jimmy and the Cake," 14.
44. "Jimmy's Fossil Hunter," 10.
45. "Jimmy Upsets the House," 18.
46. See stories in The Just William Society editions on Jimmy.

47. Light describe this as 'a special kind of emotional economy' in middle-class women's lives in the interwar years (212).
48. See *Women, Identity and Private Life in Britain, 1900–50* (1995) by Judy Giles.
49. Soutar, 9.
50. Based on an interview with the author in January 2020.
51. UoR RC/2/1/2/1. Letters to Richmal Ashbee, 30 November 1953 and 5 December 1953.
52. I am grateful to Alysoun Sanders for sharing her memories with me.
53. UoR RC/2/1/2/2. Gwen to her daughter 30 September 1953.
54. Ibid.
55. Disher, M., 24.

References

Ashbee, Paul. 2007. '*Auntie*': *Richmal Crompton As I Knew Her.* The Just William Society.

Crompton, Richmal. 2018a. "Jimmy and the Cake." In *Jimmy and the Jellyfish*, by Richmal Crompton, 12–15. The Just William Society.

———. 2018b. "Jimmy Upsets the House." In *Jimmy's Vampire*, by Richmal Crompton, 16–19, The Just William Society.

———. 2018c. "Jimmy's Fossil Hunter." In *Jimmy's Vampire*, by Richmal Crompton, 8–11. The Just William Society.

Diamond, Rex. Summer 2011. "Just William on the Radio." *The Just William Society Magazine 28* 24–26.

Disher, Margaret. 1990. *Growing Up with Just William By His Sister.* London: The Outlaws Publishing Company.

Doyle, Brian. July 1998a. "The Mysterious Case of the 'Missing' William Television Series." *The Just William Society Magazine 6* 29-30.

———. July 1998b. "William's Television Show." *The Just William Society Magazine 6* 21–27.

———. August 2000. ""Just William" on Radio." *The Just William Society Magazine 10* 13–17.

Furnival, Jane and Andy Tribble. Summer 2011. "William and the Television Monster." *The Just William Society Magazine 28* 16–23.

Jarvis, Martin. 2019. "Just Brilliant." *Daily Mail*, 2 March: 54.

Kirkpatrick, Robert. Summer 2021a. "Thomas Henry." *The Just William Society Magazine 43* 16-21.

———. Summer 2011. "William on the Stage." *The Just William Society Magazine 28* 10–15.

Light, Alison. 1991. *Forever England: Feminity, Literature and Conservatism Between the Wars*. London: Routledge.

Schutte, David. 1993. *William—The Immortal An Illustrated Bibliography*. Stedham, Midhurst: West Sussex: David Schutte.

———. June 1997. "Jimmy's Secret Past." *The Just William Society Magazine 4* 8–10.

———. 2008. "Publisher's Notes." In *William the Terrible*, by David Schutte, 11–13. Petersfield, Hampshire: David Schutte.

Schutte, David and Paula Wild. 2016. "Preface." In *Jimmy Returns*, by Richmal Crompton, 2. The Just William Society.

Soutar, Joy. 1969. "When There's Trouble, There's William." *Northampton Chronicle & Echo*, 18 January: 9.

Stevenson, John. 1984. *British Society 1914–45*. London: Lane.

Wright, Norman. May 2005. "The William Books of Richmal Crompton." *Book and Magazine Collector* 26–39.

18

Richmal Crompton in Her Own Words

By 1960, at the age of seventy, the recognition as a serious author that Crompton had worked so hard for, eluded her. Her popularity did not necessarily reflect an appreciation of the breadth and depth of her imagination in William and her other writing by the reviewers, journalists, critics, and other gatekeepers who influenced her reputation. A contemporary review of her last novel, *The Inheritor* (1960), describes it as 'a tale of village life seen through the eyes of the family who used to live at the manor.'[1] This is a narrow unimaginative perspective on the novel. Such stereotyping in the press can only have reinforced her miscast public image as a suburban author of light comic fiction, family sagas and domestic novels about quiet village life and undermined any more considered evaluation of her oeuvre and the quality of her writing in the William stories.

In her sixties and seventies, Crompton received greater attention in the media than ever before, including the BBC, national and local newspapers, and specialist magazines. She took the opportunity to write about her life as an author in some published and unpublished articles. They provide an insight into a lifetime of writing. In a more light-hearted piece, she reflects:

> I have been touched to learn from some parents that the William stories have helped them understand the maddening creatures with whom they have to deal. Honesty, however, compels me to add that others have found William's activities so unedifying that they have forbidden him [in] the house.[2]

© The Author(s), under exclusive license to Springer Nature Switzerland AG 2022
J. McVeigh, *Richmal Crompton, Author of Just William*, Literary Lives, https://doi.org/10.1007/978-3-030-96511-2_18

Her most rewarding moments are when she reads over something she has written 'and finds that it isn't so bad, after all.'[3] In common with other authors, she loves writing and 'wouldn't do anything else for all the tea in China!'.[4]

This Life has explored the little we know about the make-up of Richmal Crompton Lamburn's character. It has focused on her most famous character and the character of her alter ego as a writer and on her writing itself, the vocation that lies at the heart of Richmal Lamburn's life. This chapter explores the idea of character in her life of writing. Her comments about William and her approach to writing give some insight into her perspective on William's character, and the character of her writing.[5] Her character both as an author and a woman is misconceived by journalists in some of the articles published in this period. Crompton writes about writers as characters in her last novel, which reflects several of the themes she cared about throughout her writing life. Richmal Crompton Lamburn, as ever, remains in the shadows. We learn more about Richmal as a person after her death as many people write to her family to share how she made a difference in their lives. It is in their letters that the character of Richmal comes to life, although her innermost room remains out of reach.

* * *

The Inheritor (1960), Crompton's last novel, is a domestic comedy in which each character has his or her specific part to play. We do not come to know them over time, instead we see them performing in scenes and anecdotes when they are faced with significant turning points and their lives may be about to change forever. For some this happens when they finally face up to something about themselves or their circumstances and realise they have the opportunity to change. If they lack self-awareness, Fate takes a hand and offers them a new direction. In this novel, Crompton returns to the themes that have been important to her throughout her life of writing in characters who are writers or teachers, have a disability, or face domestic abuse, amongst others. If we approach the novel as a drama, not a saga, the closing scenes serve as a fitting note of optimism as the curtain falls.

Di and her husband Leonard are both authors. She writes popular sentimental novels that sell well and, according to her husband, are based on 'the good old formula' that she uses in every novel.[6] She publishes about four a year and she works on them for an average of eight hours a day. Her husband writes a novel every three or four years that is acclaimed by the critics and ignored by the public. He works on them for about two hours a day, which enables him to maintain 'the freshness of his creative faculties.'[7] He is much in demand as a speaker for literary societies. It is his wife's income that funds the family's household. Leonard is jealous of his wife's success and takes his revenge by making fun of her work. He is embarrassed to be associated with her, fearing her status as a popular author will mar his highbrow reputation. By the end of the novel, Leonard finds to his surprise that his latest novel is selling well. Having spent years criticising best-sellers, he now finds that he has written one: 'He remembered R.L. Stevenson's, 'There must be something wrong with me or I should not be popular,' and almost shared his attitude.'[8] Meanwhile, Di's latest novel has been turned down and she faces the reality that there is no longer a public for the sort of books she writes. In Crompton's case, by 1960 there was not a public for her novels either, although she did not write sentimental novels and was never considered highbrow. This novel reflects on the status of popular authors and the extent to which you can ever be both popular and a serious writer and what this means for an author's reputation.

Di lives in the same village as her aunt and uncles, Lucy, Nicholas and James. Di's mother Magda lives a whirlwind life of social visits and travel. She occasionally visits her family and her carefree lackadaisical approach to even the simplest domestic arrangement exasperates them. She reflects that selfishness is a gift and she has been fortunate enough to have been born with it. Magda is the most self-aware member of her family. She is a free spirit who travels wherever she wants and does whatever she wants, irrespective of her conventional duties towards her family, who she clearly loves, whilst her siblings seem trapped in the village where they were born and to which they have returned late in life following retirement.

Nicholas's leg was amputated after he was wounded in battle, and he has worn a prothesis for nearly twenty years:

> A secret resentment, bitter and ineradicable, had always prevented his coming to terms with it or even trying to come to terms with it. He still wore it clumsily and ineffectively. There were times when it seemed to take on a malignant personality of its own, gloating over his disability, rousing a futile childish hatred in him.[9]

He reflects on his disability:

Sometimes he saw himself with disconcerting clarity and was amused by the little orgy of self-pity in which he occasionally indulged and which never failed to give him a certain acrid satisfaction....[10]

He could not have explained even to himself why he had never come to terms with his disability. It was partly a stubborn childish pride. If he couldn't have everything, he'd have nothing.[11]

He feels resentful because his siblings ignored his disability, 'yet he knew that he would have felt even more resentful if they had offered sympathy.'[12] He regularly experiences pain, which he fails to discuss with his family, as one suspects neither did Richmal.

The siblings have sold the estate where they grew up and Nicholas, James and Lucy are living in a small house nearby. Nicholas lives somewhat apart from everyone, amidst the village and his family and yet not quite connecting with anyone. His sense of identity lies in his love of his childhood home. James and Magda, on the other hand, decide in old age to leave the village and find their sense of belonging elsewhere, whilst his sister Lucy stays and discovers a new vocation in partnership with a friend. The family fragments, but each member finds a way of life that suits them better. Nicholas returns to his childhood home, which has now become a residential home for older people:

He was back again where he'd started, he thought. In a sort of prison—a prison that he'd carried with him all his life and from which he had never wanted to escape. But, after all, didn't everyone carry their prison about with them? You couldn't escape from yourself.... Perhaps there was no such thing as freedom and, if there were, it would be unendurable.[13]

Another character, Monica, is trapped in a different kind of prison, and is overwhelmed by fear. She is afraid of her husband and has run away to the village with her son Timmy to escape her husband's emotional abuse and violence. Her husband finds her and plans to abduct Timmy. Perversely, as he plots further abuse of his family, he quotes Terence, a Roman dramatist. In doing so he seeks to hide his real intentions in plain sight:

"I like to help people when they're in trouble. *"Homo sum. Nihil humani a me alienum puto."* That, you know, is one of the most frequently misquoted lines in the Latin language. "Humanum," say the ignorant fools."[14]

Critics agree that this quote, from the opening scene of Terence's play *The Self Tormentor*, 'has become Terence's most famous, and yet most misappropriated, line.'[15] Andrew Cain argues that 'Both pagan and Christian writers almost uniformly took this comment to refer to the virtue of humane feeling or compassion ... but in fact [the character] Chremes is referring to a meddlesome curiosity in others' affairs.'[16] In Crompton's reference to Terence, Monica's husband does not care about the concerns of others, he is deliberately duplicitous, controlling and scheming. He is viciously meddling in his wife's life and is scornful of those who think that humanity has compassion.

There is a reference to the voice of our innermost selves in the novel. Di's daughter Janet asks Mrs Crumbles, who works for the family, if it is possible to know if a person is good or bad. Mrs Crumbles advises Janet to listen to her 'little man' inside her. 'Mind you, you've got to treat 'em right,' she tells Janet.

> "They're same as yumans that way. You can't be on with 'em one minute an' off with 'em the next. "All right," they'll say, "'ave your own way. If you'd sooner 'ave me room than me company, I'll 'op it."[17]

Her 'little man' seems to reside in Mrs. Crumble's innermost room. We might also call this voice the instinct that tells us if something is right or wrong. Is it fanciful to think that William has the features of a 'little man' too? Reading can help us to think about how we are feeling and to gain some perspective; it becomes a guide. What would William do in a particular situation? We are unlikely to follow in his footsteps, but his perverse logic might give us food for thought, as does Mrs. Crumbles's advice.

This novel has a sense of closure after a lifetime of writing and it offers another opportunity to understand what Crompton cared about; her writing is based on serious themes, albeit that her genre of choice is often comedy. In this novel, as elsewhere in her fiction, pomposity and selfishness must be exposed, and each of us should listen to our guiding spirit. If we can grow up and open our eyes, whatever our age, we may become more self-aware about our circumstances and how we might change our lives and those of others for the better. It is hard to escape evil and malevolence, and this can rarely be done alone. Accepting who we are, including our shortcomings, is an achievement. Our sense of belonging does not have to be in a place, such as a particular house or room, although it often is. We always carry with us the essence of who we are, and part of life is accepting this, and coming to terms with it. A source of happiness is being true to ourselves. For Crompton, the proper study of mankind should focus on the character of men and women and the relationships between them, and it is a task to which she devoted her writing life.

* * *

Crompton's articles about William encapsulate many of his qualities. William is a flawed, yet usually honourable hero. He is a complex character who, on the one hand, seems ageless when his fans see aspects of his character in themselves and in people they know, whilst on the other, he is a bumptious child with boundless energy and enviable joie de vivre who reminds them of childhood and their favourite reading as a child. Crompton wrote that William is:

> Towsled, unruly, adventurous, he is the enemy of civilisation, and all its (to him) meaningless conventions.... One has a sort of liking for him, qualified by irritation and sometimes despair. But there is nothing vicious about him and his apparent wickedness is generally the result of good intentions that have gone astray. One of his troubles is that his powers of invention are unbalanced by foresight or any reasoned weighing up of consequences....
>
> Despite his cult of toughness he is tender-hearted, generous and affectionate with a strong sense of justice and dogged loyalty to his friends. In fact, once you become William's friend anything may happen to you. Perhaps I should qualify the term 'tender-hearted' for he is, as are most of us, a strange mixture of opposites. He is both tender-hearted and cruel....
>
> Another good point is that he is essentially truthful. Such untruths as he is guilty of arise chiefly from the daydream he is living in at the time. Like all children he is a colossal egoist and his day-dreams centre invariably round his own powers and success and heroic achievements. Such day dreaming is, I think, a normal part of the make-up of all healthy minded children and goes to the making of a sane and balanced adult.... deliberate calculated unkindness he never forgets or forgives.
>
> Lastly, beneath his brusque exterior he is deeply sensitive but with a pride that makes him at all costs conceal his hurts. You may hurt him desperately by a careless word, but you'll never know you've done so....
>
> William, as the William we know, says goodbye on the day he washes his face without being told to and vanishes forever on the day he smears back his hair with hair oil, leaving in his place a boring and self-conscious youth who spends his money on gramophone records instead of lollipops and is painfully anxious to do and say the right thing.... [though] even then something of William will linger on to peep out at unexpected moments and disconcert himself and others.[18]

William's ambition to live up to his daydreams, although he rarely succeeds in doing so, is also part of many people's make up, whatever their age, the difference being that many adults keep their dreams to themselves for fear of failure and derision.

If we are prepared to accept Crompton's approach, why might daydreaming make us sane and balanced into adulthood? In part, it is an aspect of our imagination that encourages us to be positive and have hope; to conjure up our dreams, even if we never actually follow them. It might be the hope that kills you, but it also helps us to get through the rigours of day-to-day life, or even the most extraordinary and difficult circumstances. Of course, hope can be a bitter companion and can fail us in the end. Nevertheless, it engenders a spirit that can keep us going. It is this spirit of optimism that we see in Euphemia, Matty and Millicent Dorrington. Stella's family loses hope under her malevolent influence. One of the important elements of William's daydreams is that they seem achievable, at least to him. So, if he has the confidence to try, maybe we can too. Less demonstrative characters in Crompton's work, like Millicent Dorrington, David Wilding, Bridget, and Mrs Fowler, have William's sense of what it means to be truthful, fair, and have a strong sense of justice. They too have daydreams, as do many of Crompton's other characters, which for some means love, possibly marriage, and family, whilst others follow different dreams, often with the help of someone else's guiding hand, like Euphemia, Beatrice and Matty. William is creative in his approach to problem solving and time in his company gives the reader a moment to think about the art of the possible. He also reminds us that it is not always possible to know what the unintended consequences of any action might be and that perhaps all we can do is to take a risk and wonder 'what is the worst that could happen?'

* * *

Crompton wanted to be recognised as a serious novelist, but William had other ideas. In an interview, she told Gerry Allison, 'I hoped to become a novelist.... I have written a large number of novels, though they have always been overshadowed in the reading public's mind by the William books.'[19] She wrote in one article:

[F]or many years I looked on William as 'my character'. He was my puppet. I pulled the strings. But gradually the tables have been turned. I am his puppet. He pulls the strings. For he is resolute, indomitable and inclined to be tyrannical. Like all characters who have been over-indulged by their authors, he insists on having his own way. He refuses to co-operate in some plots. He makes fantastic demands on others. He pushes his way unceremoniously into situations in which he has really very little concern.[20]

'With the ruthlessness and tenacity of purpose that have always characterised him, he took and held the field,' she said.[21] Crompton is celebrating William here; he is loved by his fans and has become part of British cultural history. She is showing awareness that William had a hold on her reputation, but also perhaps that the influence of other gatekeepers, including those who had reimagined William during her lifetime on the stage, radio and television, had meant that she no longer had complete control over her original creation.

She commented in an article for *The Writer* in 1952, and in others published into the sixties, that she wrote William stories as pot-boilers whilst she tried to establish herself as a writer. Crompton comments that at the beginning of her career, she 'wrote the William stories—rather carelessly and hurriedly,' which needs some explanation given the quality of her language, style, and tone.[22] As she knew, several other so-called pot-boilers had become classics of literature, read by both children and adults. Crompton cites as examples Conan Doyle's Sherlock Holmes stories, Robert Louis Stevenson's *Treasure Island* (1883), and Hans Christian Andersen's fairy tales.[23] She noted that Stevenson was so ashamed of writing what he described as a story for children that he used a pseudonym when it was first published, fearing that his reputation would be harmed.[24] Implicit in Crompton's stories about popular writers, including in *The Inheritor*, and her statements that she wrote the William stories hurriedly, lies questions about whether popular fiction can be understood as serious literature discussed at literary societies (and in universities) and about the status of dual audience fiction. In Crompton's case, she was serious about writing as an author, it was integral to her life, and in these stories, she wrote complex, sophisticated narrative for both adults and children that became a classic of English literature.

In 1956, in an article with the title, 'Just Frankenstein,' Crompton tells journalist Kenneth Allsop: 'Frankly I resent William taking over my work.... The William books have always been just pot-boilers to me.' Allsop describes visiting Crompton at home as an:

> arsenic-and-old-lace moment. Chintzy chairs. A red December rose on satin-wood table. Bright coal fire.... And a smiling, grey-haired woman in tweed suit, blue cardigan and pearls who told him: "I have created a Frankenstein monster. I could wring the horror's neck at times."[26]

Fig. 18.1   Gwen, Richmal and Aunt Richmal[25]

By the time she reached her seventies, the idea of William as a monster became a feature of her interviews and her tone can feel somewhat jaded. In 1965, one journalist notes that,

> … no-one is more astonished at his survival than his creator, who admits, wryly, that she herself has lost her identity to "the boy," that William has become a monster while she exists as a frail, suburban Dr Frankenstein…. in spite of something that resembles a love-hate relationship with her creation, she had become, she murmurs, his property.[27]

In the case of Mary Shelley's monster, it has been created a monster because of the monstrous ambitions of his creator Dr. Frankenstein. This drives Frankenstein in turn to become monstrous too as his obsessive ambition drives out all consideration for his family and the consequences of his actions.[28] After a lifetime of drawing intertextual connections in her writing, Crompton creates one of her most evocative analogies. In Mary Shelley's novel, *Frankenstein* (1818), published one hundred years before Crompton's writing life began, Frankenstein has created a creature which is neither god nor man, in the world and yet not of it, like William. The creature's existence takes over the life of his master and similarly Crompton is William's mistress and she pulls the strings until, like Frankenstein's monster, her creation gets out of hand. Of course, it is important to remember that William is a trickster, rather than a monstrous demon, although some of his aunts might disagree. There is a distinct touch of irony in Crompton's analogy here. Monstrosity in William's case is an endearing quality.

In 1966, Crompton comments that there was a period when she wrote and published a William book and a novel each year. She found it a relief sometimes to get away from him and work on something more serious. She gave up writing novels in 1960 because, she says, 'There is not much call nowadays for quiet stories about families and village life—rather a vanished world.'[29] One wonders if she has lost faith in both William and her novels, or is this just a light-hearted quip about how her novels were described by her contemporaries? When someone who has worked on at least one William collection and a novel every year for seventeen years, and will publish over ninety books in their lifetime, comments that some of her writing is not serious and that the rest is quiet and out of touch, we should ask ourselves, does she mean it?

She was extraordinarily prolific in the nineteen twenties and thirties, but this can mask the range and depth of much of her writing. Of the twelve novels she published from 1925 to 1930: three could be described as a family saga, the Wildings trilogy; one is a darker morality tale of evil, *The House* (1926); four follow young girls and women as they grow up, *Anne Morrison* (1925), *Millicent Dorrington* (1927), *Four Graces* (1929), *Naomi Godstone* (1930); one follows young people when they visit the same place for a holiday and watches them as they grow up, *Blue Flames* (1930); two are village sagas, *Leadon Hill* (1927) and *Abbots' End* (1929); and one is a story of social change on a new housing estate that reflects the period in which it was written, *Roofs Off* (1928). The Crompton of the twenties and early thirties or the author of her novels published during the Second World War would not have made a similar comment. One almost wonders if she is mirroring back to the journalist what he wants to hear.

In the same article, the journalist Michael Moynihan recreates a familiar contemporary portrayal of Crompton and her home:

Beechworth is tucked away among trees down a muddy lane ... The drawing-room is cosy in an old-fashioned way, firelight warming the trolley's silver teapot, plates of thin, crustless sandwiches and the remains of Miss Crompton's 76th birthday cake.

Miss Crompton herself is neat and alert and smiling, with white hair and eyes she would most likely describe in one of her more sympathetic female characters as 'twinkling.'.... She talks about [William] with a mixture of tolerant amusement, bewilderment and outright resentment—rather as, one supposes, Conan Doyle might have tried to put Sherlock Holmes in his place....

Miss Crompton is active despite her lameness ... As she talks, it is difficult to imagine the enfant terrible hunched dutifully beside her.[30]

Of course, this is meant to be affectionate but, typecast as an older aunt-like figure with a disability, Crompton was easily pigeon-holed. A society obsessed by age, robust physical health, and physical appearance, then and now, is prone to stereotyping older and disabled people and fails to see the tousled rebel within. One can certainly imagine a vibrant, deviously innocent and inadvertently wise William sitting resplendently on her shoulder or by her side. I doubt that he would ever be dutiful, but William is a well-meaning boy who has good intentions, unlike many of the adults around him. To some extent this article asks one of the questions at the heart of this Life: how could she have created William? Other similar interviews in this period failed to see beyond her outward appearance and touched on the same question.

In November 1968, two months before she died, Crompton suggests that 'I always say that [William] is the outlet of all my criminal tendencies, so I've led quite a blameless life.'[31] She is baffled, or so she claims, by William's success:

> "I confess it is all a mystery," she says. "All I can suggest is that William must have some characteristic that is common to all human beings. Love of adventure? Inventiveness? Burning curiosity? Courage? The stuff of heroes."[32]

She denies any maternal feelings and refutes any suggestion that William was the son she never had, a popular assumption that people made for years.[33] Crompton came to resent some of his success she admits in another interview published a month later: "'If I had known that William was going to steal the limelight I would have taken a pseudonym for the novels.'"[34]

In an appearance on BBC *Woman's Hour* in July 1968, she is asked whether she would have liked to write something else apart from the William stories. She replies, polite but with restraint, that,

> I did write about thirty novels, but I think that William overshadowed them so much that the people who liked William didn't like a book by me not about William, and the people who disliked William then they dislike any book by me. So, I think that my novels did not get quite a fair chance.[35]

After a writing career spanning fifty years, she could have responded more robustly. Crompton confirms in the interview that she began to write the

William stories entirely for adults about children and that now 'I occasionally find myself writing down a bit [to children], but I try not to.'[36] If she receives any complaints about his influence, she points out that, 'Original sin existed long before I put pen to paper.'[37] She acknowledges that people used to be terribly surprised that she was a woman: 'Richmal sounds so much like Richard.'[38] Again, their surprise was perhaps rooted in the same question that underlies her interviews in this period: how could a rather prim and law abiding single woman have created William? The voice of the vibrant, hopeful and incredibly ambitious young writer in her twenties and thirties has not been lost altogether, but it would not be surprising if she had not felt a little downhearted towards the end of her life.

* * *

After *The Inheritor*, Crompton carried on writing William stories until her death. In 1970, the last collection, *William the Lawless*, was published posthumously.

In September 1960, a decade before the demise of William, Richmal was admitted to hospital with a heart attack and she was ill again in 1961 when she fell and broke her leg whilst staying with her brother in Sandhurst, Kent. She was admitted to Tunbridge Wells Hospital and then went home with the support of a live-in carer.[39] In 1968, she broke a leg again, her 'good' left leg, and spent another lengthy stay in hospital.[40]

There is no available evidence to confirm this, but one possibility is that Richmal experienced the consequences of post-polio syndrome, also known as PPS. As Gareth Williams notes:

A sizeable proportion of polio survivors eventually suffer worsening or reawakening of muscle weakness. This can begin decades after the original attack, and in some cases can be more disabling....
    The cardinal features of PPS are the new onset of muscular weakness, pain and fatigue, together with physical and mental tiredness affecting the whole body. Muscles other than those originally paralysed are often involved, sometimes with deep, burning pain and tenderness over tendons and other 'trigger points.'[41]

Post-Polio Syndrome was not identified until the end of the twentieth century. As Barry North suggests:

It is now accepted that people who have had polio, even those who are described as having made a full recovery from the disease, may experience new and hard-to-explain physical symptoms some thirty to fifty years after the original onset of the disease.[42]

We do not know if this condition affected Richmal and it would not have been diagnosed during her lifetime Nevertheless, she dealt with the ongoing consequences of polio throughout her adult life.

Jack writes just after Christmas that year telling her that he was in 'a rather bad way.' He had fallen in his garden and managed to crawl back to his house where he lay until the following morning before being admitted to hospital.[43] Life was catching up with both of them. Richmal died on 11th January 1969 in Farnborough Hospital. She had last met up with Gwen and Paul and Richmal Ashbee and their children, Kate and Edward, at their home a few days before.

In a letter dated 1st January 1969, shortly before Richmal died, Joan Braunholtz, the ex-pupil from Bromley High School who became a life-long friend, was worried about her, especially as a national newspaper had published her address in an article and mentioned that she lived alone: 'I know you are not afraid of anything, but all the same, I thought it was not very good.'[44] One is inclined to agree. A couple of months before, we can hear something of these women's friendship in one of Joan's letters. She tells Richmal:

What you said about William made me think that he is a sort of Prodigal Son, I mean, he is the primitive, natural, spontaneous adventurous part of ourselves which we all have to repress in order to fit into conventional society – But he is capable of rebirth, and like the Prodigal Son, I think one can imagine William in later life rising to heights to which Violet Elizabeth, like the elder brother, never could! I think all these characters in fiction, which seem to keep their appeal forever ... respond to something deep in ourselves, especially if it's something we normally have to repress.[45]

Joan and Richmal's joy in literature and wide-ranging interests enriched their friendship as well as their own lives. In one of their last letters, Joan shares her reading with Richmal and looks forward to seeing her again in the Spring.[46] Sadly, they did not meet again. Joan wrote to Richmal's niece a few days after she died:

I had known her for over fifty years, and for about the last twenty years had spent a day with her about four times in the year and looked on her as my most valued friend. She was unique, one always had that marvellous sense of being instantly understood, her sympathy covered an immensely wide field and was very deep.[47]

Fig. 18.2 Richmal Crompton Lamburn in Rome 1952[48]

Joan reminds us of Richmal's courage, her astuteness, intellectual life, and her ability to build lasting friendships.

Richmal Ashbee received letters of condolence from people who came from almost every aspect of her aunt's life and from across the world. A fellow pupil from St Elphin's had always kept in touch and regarded Richmal as a great friend. She enjoyed meeting her every year. Another ex-pupil had last heard from her at Christmas. A fellow student from Royal Holloway still met her from time to time, telling her niece that, 'No appraisal of her work as a writer is likely to do justice to her gallantry, her generosity ... serene wisdom, sense of humour, human understanding, which made all contact with her such a joy.' Two friends from her membership of the London Lyceum Club wrote fondly and another friend: 'loved her, probably more than I loved my own mother. Can I say more? Just two or three weeks before her Birthday we had her with us for a day and took her to the theatre. She was a sheer delight to be with.' One pen friend who had known her since he was an evacuee in the Second World War had been corresponding with her for almost thirty years and had received a letter from her only four weeks before. A fan who had read William stories all her life speaks for many others when he tells Richmal's niece that: 'Whenever we are worried or unhappy a chapter of William always banished gloom, and his sayings are known by heart in our house.'[49] This fan and her close friends wrote to Richmal over countless years, but sadly her letters to them are lost, or at least remain hidden. Richmal was clearly a loyal and caring friend. She made lasting friendships in every corner of her life.

In 1965, Dan O'Neill comments on William that:

> He has captured the loyalty of children since 1922 and perhaps the real reason
> is that the stories have never been written for children. To reread William is
> to discover satirical (and often snobbish) observations on life that escape the
> 10-year-old engrossed with his first reading.[50]

On Richmal's death four years later, there were many accolades for William in the press that reflected this loyalty. To Bob Wynn he is a rare hero who had never let him down:

> He has remained the eternal rebel, always preaching sedition (and occasionally
> going out on the streets for the cause), the friend of all outlaws, the exponent of
> equal shares for all, especially of gobstoppers.... After all, we were not terribly
> alike.... I suppose it was the rebel in him that appealed.... He did at times
> have an almost classless appeal, and this I think helped towards his universal
> popularity.[51]

He feels that all boys, whatever their class, 'have some problems in common' and many of them are exemplified in William's life.[52]

Crompton's fans know that William is not a life-like boy, yet he is a touch-stone with whom they identify both as children and adults. One obituary reflects that: 'Perhaps her creation serves a moral purpose.... Just when we are about to tick off some scruffy schoolboy for bumping into us, we are rebuked by an image of ourselves as Richmal Crompton's William.'[53] Her fans know that her writing has elements of myth and allegory and that their quality lies in part in their ability to unearth a truth that says something about our own lives.

* * *

William is not a real boy; he lives in a world that does not exist, although it is based on the life of some of his early twentieth century middle-class readers. We see the world from his point of view, as he makes fun of its foibles and pomposity. It is Crompton as narrator whose tone and wry voice highlight the comedy of any situation. As far as William is concerned, he is a serious boy. He never grows up, whilst in some of Crompton's novels, we follow young characters, whose world we see from their point of view too as they do grow up and become adults. Her satire reflects on the absurdities of the adult world, which a child reader may miss, and the literary merit in her writing lies in the language, style and tone in stories that speak to both adults and children.

William remains much loved by his fans on his centenary, although the stories are less likely to appeal to new readers given their roots in the early to mid-twentieth century. Adventures today are set far beyond the boundaries of home with heroes who battle evil in more fantastical worlds. On the other hand, if we focus on Crompton's storytelling, adults can be pompous and greedy whatever outer space or other-worldly dimension they come from. His spirit lives on as fans from the UK and abroad continue to read his stories throughout their lives and other readers recognise him as a cultural icon. The mischievous boy is a familiar character in fiction and William-like characters have been reimagined in new literature since Crompton's death and the work of these authors has been popular. As a writer, Crompton remains influential amongst her more recent peers.

Notes

1. *Birmingham Post*, 22 November 1960, 12.
2. "Puppet Pulls the Strings," 41. Also, see *JWSM* 28, 27.
3. Ibid.
4. Ibid.
5. Crompton admitted that she did not keep accurate records about the plots and characters in the William stories and some fans write to her to

correct her mistakes (*The Writer*, 5 and Allison 94). She was keen not to identify William's village, claiming that it was entirely imaginary and might be located in Kent, Surrey or Sussex (Allison, 95).

6. *The Inheritor*, 53.
7. Ibid., 54.
8. Ibid., 190.
9. Ibid., 8.
10. Ibid.
11. Ibid., 42.
12. Ibid., 62.
13. Ibid., 223.
14. Ibid., 151.
15. Starkes, 152.
16. Cain, 387–388.
17. *The Inheritor*, 164.
18. UoR RC/1/1/2/3. Typed and handwritten notes for articles on William. It is undated but mentions that William had been the same age for more than thirty years, so it was probably written in the early nineteen fifties.
19. Allison, 92.
20. "Puppet Pulls the Strings," 41. Also, see Chapter 1.
21. Ibid.
22. UoR RC/1/1/2/3. *The Writer* October 1952, 5.
23. "Puppet Pulls the Strings," 41.
24. Ibid.
25. Held in family papers.
26. Allsop, 4.
27. O'Neill, 5.
28. Shelley, 169.
29. Moynihan, 27.
30. Ibid.
31. Harmsworth,16–17.
32. Ibid, 17.
33. Bruce, 9.
34. Francis, 4.
35. https://www.youtube.com/watch?v=TmEcUabNmYQ.
36. Ibid.
37. Ibid.
38. Ibid.
39. Ashbee, 14.
40. Ibid., 15.

41. Williams, 34–35.
42. North, 388.
43. UoR RC/2/1/1/1. Letter from Jack 27 December 1968.
44. UoR RC/2/1/1/1. Letter from Joan Braunholtz 1 January 1969.
45. UoR RC/2/1/1/1. Letter from Joan Braunholtz 18 November 1968.
46. Ibid.
47. UoR RC/2/9/3. Joan Braunholtz to Richmal Ashbee 13 January 1969.
48. UoR RC/3/6/091.
49. UoR RC/2/9/3. January 1969. Letters to Richmal Ashbee, Crompton's niece, from Doris Kaye, Dorothy Cleary, Margaret Morphew, Marjorie Bronghall, Stas Toegel, Bryan Blades, Clive Arden, Grace Carlton, Anne Fisher.
50. O'Neill, 5.
51. Wynn, 2.
52. Ibid.
53. Brace, 9.

References

Allison, Gerry. 1961. "Forever William." *The Collector's Digest Annual* 91–95.

Allsop, Kenneth. 1956. "Just Frankenstein." *Daily Mail*, 6 December: 4.

Ashbee, Paul. 2007. *'Auntie': Richmal Crompton As I Knew Her*. The Just William Society.

Brace, Keith. 1969. "'William' author: Unfinished book." *Birmingham Post*, 13 January: 9.

Bruce, Stella. 1969. "The Woman Who Created William." *The Star Sheffield*, 13 January: 6.

Cain, Andrew. 2013. "Terence in Late Antiquity." In *A Companion to Terence*, by Antony Augoustakis and Ariana Traill, 380–396. Chichester, West Sussex: John Wiley & Sons.

Crompton, Richmal. 1957. "Puppet Pulls the Strings." *Books and Bookmen*, December: 41.

———. 1960. *The Inheritor*. London: Hutchinson.

—. 1952. "On Writing for Children." *The Writer*, October: 4–5.

Disher, Margaret. 1990. *Growing Up with Just William By His Sister*. London: The Outlaws Publishing Company.

Francis, Sue. 1968. "Just William creator still busy at 78." *Yorkshire Evening Post*, 6 December: 4.

Harmsworth, Madeleine. 1968. "William and the Old Lady of Beechworth." *Daily Mirror*, 20 November: 16–17.

Moynihan, Michael. 1966. "Uncivilised yuman bein'." *Sunday Times*, 18 December: 27.

North, Barry. 2012. "The British Polio Fellowship: its contribution to the development of inclusivity for disabled people." *Dynamis 32 (2)* 361-390.

O'Neill, Dan. 1965. "William Enters the Pop Age." *The Guardian*, 20 April: 5.

Shelley, Mary. 2006. First published 1818. *Frankenstein*. London: Bloomsbury Publishing.

Starkes, John H. 2013. "Opera in bello, in otio, in negotio: Terence and Rome in the 160s BCE." In *A Companion to Terence*, by Antony Augoustakis and Ariana Traill, 132–155. Chichester, West Sussex: John Wiley & Sons.

Williams, Gareth. 2013. *Paralysed with Fear: The Story of Polio* . Basingstoke , Hampshire: Palgrave Macmillan.

Wynn, Bob. 1969. "William's Eternal Appeal." *Morning Star*, 18 January: 2.

Part VI

Fans at Home and Abroad

19

William, At Home and Abroad

During Crompton's lifetime, the William stories were translated into many languages, and they were popular in Spain in particular. The history of the publication of her stories in Spain illustrates how the William stories captured the imagination of international fans, most of whom first discovered the stories in childhood. They felt a connection between themselves and William despite the distance created by geography, culture, politics, and language. William offered a window through which Spanish readers could see their own lives from a different perspective.[1] They and UK fans recognise his influence and continue to turn to him. As the Outlaws know, twenty minutes in William's company helps make sense of the world, although other adults would fail to understand why.

Margaret and Ben Sherriff have identified that more than thirty of the William books were translated into Spanish from 1935, which coincided with the Spanish Civil War [of] 1936–39, and these titles were reprinted in the late 1970s after Franco's death in 1975.[2] William is a rebel and an outlaw, which translates into Spanish as 'proscrito':

which means both "outlaw" in the bandit sense and "political exile"—of which there were many following the Spanish Civil War. Indeed, when the "Outlaws" first appear in the first William books, the Spanish translator had to append a fairly lengthy footnote, explaining that the word "outlaw" in English has very different connotations from its Spanish equivalent, and conjures up positive images of Robin Hood and his merry men, stealing from the rich to give to the poor and so on.[3]

© The Author(s), under exclusive license to Springer Nature Switzerland AG 2022
J. McVeigh, *Richmal Crompton, Author of Just William*, Literary Lives, https://doi.org/10.1007/978-3-030-96511-2_19

The Sherriffs argue that William's life would have felt 'intoxicating and liberating to anyone growing up in the grey, repressive society' of post-Civil War Spain under Franco.[4] William 'recalls that quintessentially Spanish figure, Don Quixote,' although unlike 'poor Don Quixote … William, usually against all the odds, emerges on top. Rebellion and freedom of thought and action are consistently rewarded,' the Sherriffs write.[5] Like William, Don Quixote has his own misconceived romantic version of himself existing on the boundary between life and fantasy:

> For his imagination was so crowded with those battles, enchantments, surprising adventures, amorous thoughts, and other whimsies which he had read of in romances, that his strong fancy changed everything he saw into what he desired to see; and thus he could not conceive that the dust was only raised by two large flocks of sheep.… He was so positive that they were two armies.[6]

William would be equally positive.

Ian Craig has studied the censorship of Crompton's stories during the Franco era, which began in 1936.[7] Many Spaniards suffered in these years. As the Sherriffs observe:

> The 1940s were known as 'the hungry forties,' a period when many Spaniards came close to starvation, and into the 1950s, Spain remained in many ways a cheerless place rife with repression and censorship, in which people were forced into polarised positions—either of right or left.[8]

From 1942, the William books were censored both for their large readership, which according to the censors meant that they might be 'ideologically influential and possibly pernicious,' and for the particular brand of irony and humour that Crompton masters in these stories that highlighted its foreignness.[9] It appeared that 'such nonconformity had become unacceptable.'[10] The publication of the William books was revived in the late nineteen fifties when 'the additional xenophobia applied to children's literature in the early 1940s was relaxed.'[11] At this time, 'the series enjoyed its most prosperous period in Spain.'[12] The stories were again popular in the nineteen sixties, although further censorship followed in 1968 when irony was again rejected as a permissible feature of children's literature.[13] Marisa Fernández López notes that the elements of children's literature that were traditionally banned in Spain until the nineteen seventies were references to sex or religion.[14] And by the nineteen eighties, after the end of the Franco era, the popularity of the stories in Spain was in decline.[15]

As a young reader, philosopher Fernando Savater was astonished 'how easily one slipped into the circumstances of William's life, which after all were entirely different from those of a Spanish boy of my generation':

> The lush green world of a small English town, more like a village than a city, with its cottages, its vicar and his wife, its confusion of pennies, guineas, and half crowns, its greenhouses, its absurd charity teas, all the constant references to a foreign history and culture... each and every one of these things should have placed us at a vast distance from William's adventures... [However, he] was, without doubt, just like one of us.... William was myself, but completely successful, me at my very best, at the tip-top of my energy and good fortune... William was not a more or less unattainable ideal, but the joyous fulfilment of my best possibilities.[16]

Savater believes that the connection between young Spanish readers in the nineteen fifties 'to those British outlaws was a yearning to be free, to escape from stifling rituals, to live life to the full without fear or blame or the vigilance of others.'[17] The Sherriffs suggest that most seductive of all 'would, perhaps, have been the sheer joy and energy of William, intoxicating and liberating to anyone growing up in a grey, repressive society.'[18]

In 1976, Spaniard Juan Campos wrote to Crompton's niece Richmal Ashbee to explain that the stories have 'helped me understand that it was not totally absurd to consider the world of adults as absurd as it seemed to be.'[19] Campos writes astutely on Crompton's connection to his hero:

> It was her secret and innermost self that found expression in the stories and ... allowed her not only to remain law-abiding but, more importantly, beautifully sane. Behind her non-threatening image lay a very sharp observer of much of what is absurd, stupid and inane what underlies..of the child inside even the most uptight and authoritarian of adults.... All adults, even those of us who were quite unlike William as children, have something of this ugly, brave, imaginative and generous boy inside our soul. Or so one would hope.[20]

Much of the humour 'relies on William's dialectical resources and the willingness of the author to take the side of the child in his conflicts with adults.'[21] Campos suggests that William is not a portrait of a real child, but 'the archetype of the hero, never to be humbled even in defeat.'[22]

In Spain, some readers of the William stories, 'feel a personal connection with William Brown, cherish the stories' slapstick and farcical moments, and recognise the wider implications of his challenges to authority.'[23] Savater speaks to many fans when he writes: William 'is the hope itself that we will never lack the gumption to get out of a tight place.'[24]

* * *

In the UK, Crompton's fans are legion. Biography is a process of collaboration between people of the past and present. I have spoken to many fans and others about William and this biography could not have been written without their support. Many fans feel like Miranda Pender that 'he is the only rational person in a pointless and totalitarian world.'[25] Others remember that William did everything they would love to have done but did not dare to do. Stories from a few of their number speak for many.

Miranda thinks that she was probably around ten when she had a closer look at her William books:

> I might not have understood every single word in them, but it wasn't difficult to guess their meaning by the context. I think that one of the things I did appreciate was the feeling that for the very first time, I was reading books that did not give the impression they had been written specifically for children. Richmal Crompton introduced me, without my realising it, to literary constructs such as irony, hyperbole, bathos and alliteration. The sophistication of her language is one reason why I still enjoy reading William books.'[26]

She was introduced to William by her mother Pat whose parents had inscribed in her copy of *William and the Evacuees*, 'to Pat the Permanent.' In 1940, after an unhappy evacuation to Northamptonshire, thirteen-year-old Pat begged to be allowed to return to her family in London, so she became known as Pat the Permanent and spent most of 1940 ready to shelter from air-raids in the cellar. Miranda has reread the stories over and over again. She describes what she calls the cameo episodes within each story. 'Crompton exposes the hypocrisy of the adult world, but she never preaches,' she said. In her view, the stories appeal equally to men and women, boys and girls. After 1950, the stories 'become a parody of themselves and are farcical,' whilst in the earlier stories the 'pace is masterful.' Miranda enjoys their oral quality and 'little touches' that make the language so beautiful.[27]

William offers Tony some light relief. He occasionally reads one story at the end of the day and has kept returning to them over the years since his childhood. William does not belong to the real world, and yet Tony can still identify with him. Most of all Tony values William's optimism and the positive tone of the stories that make fun of the ridiculous and are ridiculous. It is not so much that William's exploits relate in any way to Tony's life, but that he shares Crompton's values. He is often in awe of the humour she can capture within a single sentence.[28]

Tim started to read the stories in 1995 when he was eleven and went on to build his William collection in his twenties. He now re-reads William stories himself and entertains his six-year-old son with the Martin Jarvis stories in the *Meet Just William* series for younger children. When they read the original William stories together, they each find different elements of the stories important. As a child reader himself, Tim remembers them as 'a peephole through which I could look at the adult world.' Tim has also read *Horrid Henry* and more recent *Dennis the Menace* stories with his son, which Tim describes as versions of the William stories 'without heart.' As we all know, William cares about others and even helps them on occasions, although the results of his efforts are invariably unhelpful.[29]

Finally, Jim remembers his mother taking him to the library for the first time, where she left him to explore the children's section on his own:

> I perused the books lining the walls and approached a free-standing bookshelf in the centre of the room, picked out a book, and thought... this book is in the wrong section... it is obviously an adult book as it has no pictures! I flicked through it, found an illustrated page, slowly read the caption (with the help of the illustration), and found it amusing. Intrigued, I turned to another page, and slowly read a line or two. I suddenly realised that I didn't need the illustrations... the words seemed to make sense all by themselves... and I felt compelled to continue... I could read! ... and of course, the book was a *Just William* book. I made my way back to the foyer where my mother was waiting and showed her my first library book. I realised she was impressed with my choice, and proud, I think, of her son. This is one of my clearest memories of my mother. She died when I was very young.[30]

Interestingly, this library is now the Glasgow Women's Library. These few fans reflect what many others know too, namely that Crompton wrote for both children and adults, observing everyday life with an optimistic and wry sense of humour, captured in withering and powerful narrative that stays with us after we have finished reading.

Some of Crompton's readers have gone on to become writers themselves and they acknowledge their debt to her. Javier Marías, a Spanish author of international renown, passionately read the William stories as a child. 'They were a great success in Spain,' he has said, 'I loved them.'[31] In fact, he believes, 'it is in large measure due to this almost invisible English lady, whom many of her fellow-countrymen took to be a man, that I have devoted my life to literature.'[32] Other writers share his passion.

Notes

1. The material on William in Spain is taken from "The Spanish Translations of Richmal Crompton's Just William Stories" in *Transnational Perspectives on Artists' Lives* (2020), edited by Marleen Rensen and Christopher Wiley. This collection of essays demonstrates the significance of transnationality for studying and writing the lives of artists. Whilst painters, musicians and writers have long been cast as symbols of their associated nations, recent research is increasingly drawing attention to those aspects of their lives and works that resist or challenge the national framework.
2. Sherriff and Sherriff 2009, 18. I am grateful to Margaret Sherriff, also known as the translator Margaret Jull Costa, for her support with this aspect of my research on Crompton.
3. Ibid., 24.
4. Ibid., 26.
5. Ibid., 25.
6. Cervantes, Part 1, 112.
7. Craig, 81.
8. Sherriff and Sherriff 2009, 18.
9. Craig, 81.
10. Ibid., 82.
11. Ibid., 95.
12. Ibid.
13. Ibid., 101.
14. Fernández López, 43.
15. Craig, 104.
16. Savater 2010, 29–31.
17. Savater 2009, 28.
18. Sherriff and Sherrif 2009, 26.
19. UoR RC/1/7/2/6 Letter from Campos 14 March 1976.
20. Campos 2007, 29–30.
21. Ibid., 30.
22. Ibid.
23. McVeigh, 101. I am grateful to Marleen Rensen and Christopher Wiley for their permission to use material from my chapter in their edited collection here.
24. Savater 1982, 55.

25. Pender 2008, 6. Also, see "The Story that Makes You Cry with Laughter" Arrowsmith, Derek, Miranda Pender, Elisabeth Middleton, Alan Ring. *JWSM 35* Winter 2014, 24–30.
26. Ibid., 6.
27. Based on a conversation in 2021.
28. Based on a conversation in 2020.
29. Based on a conversation in 2021.
30. Based on a note prepared by Jim, following our conversation in 2021.
31. Marías, *The Guardian*, 5.
32. Marías, *JWSM* 24, 29. Also see, Michael La Pointe, "Ave Marías: An Interview with Javier Marías" *The Paris Review* 12 October 2018.

References

Campos, Juan. Winter 2007. "The Way of William." *The Just William Society Magazine 21* 29–38.

Cervantes Saavedra, Miguel de. 1993. First published 1605. *Don Quixote*. Ware, Hertfordshire: Wordsworth Classics.

Craig, Ian. 2001. *Children's Classics under Franco*. Oxford: Lang.

Fernández López, Marisa. 2006. "Translation Studies in Contemporary Children's Literature: A Comparison of Intercultural Ideological Factors." In *Translation of Children's Literature: A Reader*, by Gillian Lathey Ed., 41–53. Clevedon: Multilingual.

Marías, Javier. Summer 2009. "A Longstanding Debt." *The Just William Society Magazine 24* 29–30.

———. 2018. "The books that made me." *The Guardian*, 13 October: 5.

McVeigh, Jane. 2020. "The Spanish Translations of Richmal Crompton's Just William Stories." In *Transnational Perspectives on Artists' Lives*, by Marleen Rensen and Christopher Wiley Eds., 93–105. Cham, Switzerland: Palgrave Macmillan.

Pender, Miranda. Summer 2008. "What William Means to Me." *The Just William Society Magazine 22* 5–7.

Savater, Fernando. Summer 2009. "The Outlawed Lady." *The Just William Society Magazine 24* 27–29.

Savater, Fernando. Summer 2010. "The Outlaws' Triumph." *The Just William Society Magazine 26* 28–37.

Savater, Fernando. 1982. "The Outlaws' Triumph." In *Childhood Regained: The Art of the Storyteller*, by Fernando Savater Ed., 53–67. New York: Columbia University Press.

Sherriff, Ben and Margaret. Summer 2009. "William and Franco's Spain." *The Just William Society Magazine 24* 17–26.

20

Writers' Homage to Crompton and William

Over the last fifty years, William has lived on with the support of his fans. Not surprisingly, a number of them are authors because, as we know, 'books have a way of influencing each other,' as Virginia Woolf professed.[1] Also, as she and Crompton both knew: 'Fiction will be much the better for standing cheek by jowl with poetry and philosophy.'[2] Crompton's William stories and novels reflect her extensive knowledge of literature, including poetry and classical literature and philosophy. She in turn has influenced more recent fiction.[3] Writers feature as characters in the William stories and his own unique understanding of the books he has read are priceless, as Great-Aunt Jane knew.[4]

Anne Fine, Children's Laureate 2001–2003, is unequivocal that the William collections are 'the best children's books ever written.'[5] 'I have loved William all my life,' she writes. He became 'my own imaginary brother, my closest secret friend.'[6] She believes that there cannot be a children's writer in this country who has not been influenced by Crompton. 'She turned me into a writer,' Fine says.[7] She shares with Crompton a belief that children should be challenged, not patronised and that it is important not to write down to them: 'When you are writing for children, you should never overestimate their knowledge or underestimate their intelligence.... With children, you're often writing about things they've not yet experienced or don't know; adults, on the other hand, are on the journey with you,' she says.[8] A journey of a lifetime for William's adult fans. Fine writes books for young and older children or adults, coming-of-age stories about growing up, as well as stories popular

© The Author(s), under exclusive license to Springer Nature Switzerland AG 2022
J. McVeigh, *Richmal Crompton, Author of Just William*, Literary Lives,
https://doi.org/10.1007/978-3-030-96511-2_20

with children <u>and</u> adults, such as *Goggle Eyes* (1989), identified by Peter Hunt as one of her novels in which the narrative voice erodes the boundaries between children's and adult literature.[9] *Madame Doubtfire* (1987) is another story enjoyed by young and older adults, and that pillories and questions grown-up pretensions. Her books reflect on both the good and ill in all of us, whatever our age.

William has been important to novelist Deborah Moggach too. He was her first love and became her phantom friend in childhood.[10] She felt that Crompton's writing treated her as a grown-up.[11] She learnt a great deal from her about language and how to draw a character who can be contradictory, humane and someone we care about. Moggach believes that Crompton's humour lies in what her characters are trying to do and what we can see is actually happening to them, which in William's case is usually wildly different from his intentions.[12] Her favourite stories are from the nineteen thirties. Moggach 'knew he was simply me, but much more fun. He was also the first person to emerge from a book and accompany me; the first to make me realise that fiction is immortal.' William's bemusement with the adult world is something at odd moments she still feels herself.[13] As a girl, she did not like girlish things, preferring outdoor adventures, although William's were always more daring. He supplied adventures and a more fertile imagination.[14]

Moggach senses William's special qualities. He has been a staunch companion for many years.[15] In *The Carer* (2019), published in the centenary year of the first William story, James read William as a child. When he is older, he remembers meeting a young woman on a train; they start talking:

> "When I was six," James said, "the girl next door built a pub in her bedroom, out of a blanket and chairs, and called it The Rosy Arms." He realised, with surprise, that he'd never told anyone this.
> "That is so *sweet*," she said. "What did she serve?"
> "Liquorice water. Like William Brown."
> She hadn't read the William books so he told her about them. This led on to a disagreement about blancmange – him for, her against. Basically, they nattered.[16]

'Rice-Mould,' the first William story published in *Home Magazine* in February 1919 is about a little girl's love of blancmange.[17] William natters too, which is an underestimated ability and one that not everyone can master. One of William's qualities is that he can natter with everyone, no matter how august they might be. For Moggach the William books are the funniest books of all time.[18] 'Richmal Crompton was a peerless writer who understood that the basis for comedy is the disconnect between how we see ourselves and how others see us,' she said.[19]

At the end of her novel *God in Ruins* (2015), Kate Atkinson acknowledges her debt to Crompton in the portrayal of Augustus. William Brown 'remains for me one of the greatest fictional characters ever created. Richmal Crompton, I salute you,' she writes.[20] At the end of the First World War, Izzie is twenty-four and two young men to whom she was engaged are killed in the fighting. She especially loved Augustus. A few years later Izzie turns to fiction and finds that it is a means of both resurrection and preservation.[21] Her fictional character Augustus is eleven years old and is 'a scuffed, badly behaved schoolboy, his cap glued permanently to the back of his head and a cowlick of hair in his eyes and a catapult hanging out of his pocket.'[22] Izzie's nephew Teddy, who she talks to at length when he is eleven years old and who is her model for Augustus, feels that he will be plagued by her creation for the rest of his life.[23] During his service in the RAF during the Second World War, Teddy thinks that Augustus, 'his grown-up double, as he imagined him,' would have been a spiv and war profiteer, but we do not believe him.[24] Teddy and Augustus are both heroes.

As a boy, Augustus's eavesdropping is rudely interrupted when Cook knocks him on the head with a spoon:

> "That boy *lurks*," he had heard her complaining to their housemaid, Mavis. "He's a regular little spy."
>
> Augustus felt rather gratified by this compliment. Naturally, he *was* going to be a spy when he grew up. As well as a pilot, a train driver, an explorer and "a collector of things."[25]

Like Augustus, William lurks amidst his family and community and eavesdrops on us all too. Augustus's mother tells him that he has given her a headache. He challenges her logic on the basis that he cannot have given her a headache because he does not have one to give her in the first place. His mother's headache 'was not improved by this barrage of reason.'[26] Mrs Brown would have understood.

Sue Townsend, another author who wrote for both children and adults, was introduced to the William stories during a period of childhood illness and they taught her to read:

> William's world may not be familiar to [new readers], but William certainly will be. He is that scruffy boy with the screwed up face and with his own logic, who pedantically questions every rule and sets out to break most of them.[27]

She believes that 'the true genius of his author, Richmal Crompton, is in her richly comic dialogue. In particular William's poor diction, grammar and mordant observations, which still make me laugh.'[28] Julia Donaldson loved the William stories, which she read avidly as a child. He was her childhood hero.[29] Finally, Louise Rennison came to William as an adult, unlike many of his fans. She believes that the William stories 'are really all about standing up for what is right. Never bowing to things which just are not acceptable. These books show you how to display Just William-ness in the face of intolerable circumstances.'[30] It is this quality of Just William-ness that makes William a hero.

In a collection of essays on books that inspired over forty writers, the William stories are high on their list. Antonia Fraser notes that this is 'just after *Treasure Island*, with only *Alice's Adventures in Wonderland*, *Jane Eyre* and *Winnie-the-Pooh* ahead.'[31] Carol Ann Duffy continues to read the stories as an adult and a copy of *William Again* lies waiting on her bedside table.[32] She too believes that 'Crompton is an author who does not patronize the young reader, and her sophisticated vocabulary gave me the habit of consulting the dictionary,' she writes.[33]

Betty Greenway also considers other authors who have turned to Crompton in their own fiction, reimagining William and William-ness in new characters who pay homage to her hero. She illustrates that William has been an influence on:

> many who recall "devouring" or "consuming" the William books. Dylan Thomas was given the third in the series when he was ten, and he went on to "voraciously" collect all he could get his hands on…. His short stories show a marked similarity to these books…. Roddy Doyle, author of *The Commitments*, *Paddy Clarke Ha Ha Ha*, and several books for children, spent a summer with the letter V for "vigour" written in coal dust on his and his gang's stomachs, a word that caught his fancy in the William books…. Miles Kington, humorist and popular English journalist … [calls] them "some of the funniest books ever to be written."[34]

Dylan Thomas learnt from Crompton how to appeal to readers of all ages.[35] Short stories about his childhood by Thomas in *Portrait of the Artist as a Young Dog* (1940) and *Quite Early One Morning* (1954), 'have as protagonists a young boy watching with bewilderment the strange world of adults while engaging in his own hijinks.'[36] Greenway argues that Crompton and Thomas use complex narrative strategies and the adult narrator knows more than the character of the child. As readers we can reflect on what the child thinks has happened and what really has.

The child's experiences in the stories are primary:

> but those experiences are recollected by a more experienced mind that sees
> things not differently but simply more widely. This dual point of view is carried
> over into the characterization of adults as well. Adults often come in for ridicule
> in the stories of both authors, making their works subversive in the way that
> Lurie suggests the best literature for children is.... The stories ... appeal to
> our own doubleness, our past and present selves.... [They] depend on a gentle
> self-mockery. And they also depend upon a close, if sometimes ironic, narrator-
> narratee relationship.[37]

It is this close relationship that puts Crompton firmly in control of the
William stories, especially in the twenties and thirties.[38]

In *Good Omens* (1990) by Terry Pratchett, who was a William fan, and
Neil Gaiman, the lead character Adam is supported by his gang of three
friends, Pepper, Wensleydale and Brian, known as the Them. Pepper is a girl
and is an equal member of the gang; Joan and Violet would be jealous. The
Them have views the Outlaws would no doubt share, such as:

> They had once – at Adam's instigation – tried a health food diet for a whole
> afternoon. Their verdict was that you could live very well on healthy food
> provided you had a big cooked lunch beforehand.[39]

Adam's leadership of the gang is as sacrosanct as William's:

> There was a lazy shifting of position on the milk crate throne. Adam was going
> to speak.
> The Them fell silent. Adam was always worth listening to. Deep in their
> hearts, the Them knew that they weren't a gang of four. They were a gang of
> three, which belonged to Adam. But if you wanted excitement, and interest,
> and crowded days, then every Them would prize a lowly position in Adam's
> gang above leadership of any other gang anywhere.[40]

When a new character, the aptly named Anathema, first meets Adam, she
describes him as a resplendent hero and he bears comparison with William,
although without the curls:

> What Anathema saw was, she said later, something like a prepubescent Greek
> god. Or maybe a Biblical illustration, one which showed muscular angels
> doing some righteous smiting. It was a face that didn't belong in the twen-
> tieth century. It was thatched with golden curls which glowed. Michelangelo
> should have sculpted it.

He probably would not have included the battered sneakers, frayed jeans, or grubby T-shirt, though.[41]

In an inevitable line in the novel, Anathema tells Adam that she has been told that 'you were the worst of the lot of Them.... Adam nodded.'[42] William would no doubt have done the same; delighted that he was considered the best at being worst and oblivious to the irony of the wordplay. Towards the end of *Good Omens*, Adam comments severely, 'I don't see what's so triffic about creating people as people and then gettin' upset'cos they act like people.'[43] Clearly, he is a boy after William's own heart and as sagely wise.

Australian children's author Morris Gleitzman was inspired by Crompton when he read the stories as a child. William is a complex character with his own perverse view of the world. Gleitzman writes:

I think one of the reasons I started writing my own imaginary adventures [was] because I so admired how Richmal did it and her character William Brown.... So many [other] stories had a narrow view of the world and the characters were either bad, bad, bad or good, good, good. I realised very young that I was a mixture of the two and it turns out most people are.[44]

Crompton becomes a talisman for Felix, the lead character in Gleitzman's powerful books for children about a young Jewish boy's experience of the Holocaust and Nazi oppression in the Second World War. Felix's parents, who are murdered in a concentration camp, read William's stories to him. The stories represent everything that has been happy and good in his life before the war. During violent and terrifying experiences, he prays to Richmal Crompton and asks her to help him:

After I wipe my eyes, she helps me think about things. About how she's with me every day, in my thoughts and in my imagination, even though she's not actually physically there.[45]

As well as recalling his happy childhood, whether Crompton represents for Felix a guide, and hope or love and possibly both, these emotions are embodied in Felix's precious memories of his parents and the sacrifices they made to protect him, and in his friend six-year-old Zelda and other characters who love him in return. In the end, it is Felix who matters most of all. A Jewish boy who is good at telling stories that help carry his friends through some of their harshest experiences becomes a man who continues to contribute to others as a doctor and a storyteller. Felix's stories are a poignant and important reminder that stories about the experience of Jews during the Holocaust must continue to be told and never be forgotten.

There are glimpses of William-like characters in J K Rowling's *Harry Potter* series. Hermione has shades of Violet Elizabeth when she is at her most unctuous and Ron has ginger hair and is a loyal and dogged sidekick. Harry has William's bravery in pursuit of adventure. His enemy is fantastical evil that threatens the world, whilst William's enemies are human characters who represent pomposity, narcissism, vanity, gluttony, and greed, amongst other human frailties, which threaten the world too. Much of Crompton's writing suggests that the greatest evil is that which we bring upon ourselves and others in our day-to-day lives.

These authors, who write for children or adults, and sometimes both, know that the William stories are not the pot-boilers that Crompton herself deceptively claimed. They appreciate that the nuances of tone and perspective that lie in the gift of a narrator are at the heart of Crompton's genius.

* * *

She takes a wry look at the character of writers in the William stories.[46] A few of these characters bear some resemblance to Crompton herself, although this is not to suggest that their experiences represent specific events in her own life. Miss Fairlow is one possible candidate for this accolade. Fans Margaret and Ben Sherriff notice that she is sympathetic to William:

> William is a touchstone by whom we can judge the basic decency of the other characters. Those who find William interesting or worthwhile (not a great number!) are rare beings of wonderful insight.... and those who dismiss him, as simply the savage he appears to be, are themselves many leagues from heaven. Many are called, but few are chosen. Miss Fairlow is one of the chosen. She immediately understands William's creative defiance of custom.[47]

Miss Fairlow is a successful author and publishes a book every year, making a lot of money out of it.[48] Despite this lack of highbrow status, she is graciously invited to join the Society for the Encouragement of Higher Thought, and she counts herself lucky, or perhaps not so lucky, to receive an invitation to attend a meeting of these 'Higher Thinkers.' William and Miss Fairlow contribute to some disruption at one of their meetings. William should no doubt share most of the blame as he is responsible for a menagerie of small creatures that scurry across the floor, much to the horror of the society's Higher Thinkers who jump to higher ground, literally not philosophically.[49]

The creative spirit need only turn to William for advice. His logic is a cure to any episode of writer's block. When another writer wants to know what one of his characters would do in a particular situation, William locks up a hapless victim in a shed and suggests that the writer listens to the man's exclamations: "'Anyway, you know now wot he does in reel life. He breaks the door down an' gets out,'" said William.[50] When William meets an author of space fiction for the younger reader, he becomes the face of one of the characters; namely Tonando, 'The Scourge of Mars,' who is a character of supreme and evil intelligence.[51] William is indeed a scourge on his own planet, as the story implies.

In 'Aunt Arabelle in Charge,' The Outlaws meet Anthony Martin, a character based on Christopher Robin, whose mother writes wonderful stories about him.[52] The boy is self-satisfied and arrogant, and William swiftly brings him down to earth when he catches Anthony indulging in shoddy behaviour. William might be many things, but he is never shoddy. Anthony is thereby persuaded to be interviewed by Ginger's Aunt Arabelle, who is an 'agony aunt' for a women's magazine, and the pompous Christopher Robin is knocked down 'a peg or two.'

* * *

On other occasions, William is influenced by the stories he has read, such as Aime Tschiffel's *Tschiffely's Ride* (1933), in which he records his horse ride across deserts and mountain ranges and through jungles. William picks up Robert's library copy and is lost to all around him:

> It was about a man who travelled ten thousand miles with two ponies from Buenos Aires to New York, beset by danger on every side—crocodiles, electric eels, vampire bats, and fever.... It was an adventure after his own heart. It would need a little adjusting, of course.... Still, William was not the boy to give up a perfectly good plan because of a few initial difficulties. He'd take Jumble instead of the two ponies.[53]

William returns home after a failed attempt to set out on his adventures with his dog Jumble, although 'by now he was almost convinced that he actually had walked around the world.'[54] It is this ability to turn even the most inauspicious events into a success that makes him such a talisman. Jumble is by William's side from the very first William book:

> There was a picture in that year's Academy that attracted a good deal of attention. It was of a boy sitting on an upturned box in a barn, his elbows on his knees, his chin in his hands. He was gazing down at a mongrel dog and in his freckled face was the solemnity and unconscious, eager wistfulness that is the mark of youth. His untidy, unbrushed hair stood up round his face. The

mongrel was looking up, quivering, expectant, trusting, adoring, some reflection of the boy's eager wistfulness showing in the eyes and cocked ears. It was called "Friendship".[55]

As we learn in later stories, William is not quite as innocent as this portrayal suggests. Nevertheless, Jumble's devotion rarely waivers throughout the books.

In another story, William, as ever, decides to act based on whatever experience he has just had. He reads *Robinsoe Crusoe* (1719) by Daniel Defoe and dreams of being shipwrecked on a desert island. Joan joins him as his chief mate. William is pleased that she does not expect a more prominent role. They meet a vagabond who they call Friday. He steals William's clothes. William walks home through the village wearing a borrowed suit that is far too big for him, with a tablecloth bundled up under his arm. As he makes his way down the village street looking more like a vagabond himself with every step, local families come out and laugh at him. The owner of the suit requests that it is returned to him, and William is left with no option but to wear the tablecloth for the remainder of his journey: 'Even William's spirits were crushed by the repeated blows of fate.'[56] The story starts out like a parody of *Robinson Crusoe* but becomes almost a version of 'The Emperor Has No Clothes.' Ethel and Robert collapse into screams of laughter on his return home. Joan telephones that evening and his self-esteem is restored. She thought he looked nice in the tablecloth. Violet Elizabeth would not have been so supportive.

In an example of crossover reading in Crompton's own fiction, when William and Ginger read Agatha Christie-like detective novels, previously read by their older brothers, they decide to become private sleuths. William's literal take on the plots seem to suggest that the police struggle to find any murderer, so William decides that it would be 'more fun bein' the man that comes along an' finds out all about it when the detectives have stopped tryin',' which is his perspective on Christie's Poirot-like character.[57] They remember a story in which a man discovered a dagger by unscrewing the top of the murderer's umbrella and that another murdered his victims with poison at the end of a tie-pin, which the boys thought was jolly clever. Sherlock Holmes by Conan Doyle, with a bloodhound rather than Watson, is alluded to in 'The Great Detective,' the latest play by the village dramatic society in which a detective appears wearing a dressing gown and smoking a pipe. Having seen the play, William, with Jumble at his side, transforms immediately into a detective: 'Jumble wasn't exactly a bloodhound, he was a bloodhound as much as he was any kind of dog. Jumble was all sorts of dog. That was what was so convenient about him.'[58] On another occasion, William has been reading one of his brother's books and decides once again that he is jolly clever and should be Sherlock Holmes. He suggests that Ginger takes on the role of Watson. He is the straight guy to William's lead.[59]

Shakespeare's plays are also subject to Crompton's comic genius. In one story, Joan, his young neighbour and ardent supporter, who they willingly allow to take part in the Outlaws' adventures, offers William some advice based on Shakespeare's *Much Ado About Nothing*. This is during one of his campaigns to support Ethel's love life, and thereby himself. However, his efforts flounder and he sternly suggests to Joan that she reads books with more sense in them: 'This Shake man simply doesn't know what he's talkin' about. It's a good thing for him he *is* dead, gettin' us all into a mess like this!'[60] A school master tries to tell William about a man called Bacon who, it is alleged, might have written Shakespeare's plays. William gets confused and thinks that this might instead have been a man called Ham[let]. William decides that if they call everyone Eggs the teacher's story might be less muddled. He tells the headmaster about their lesson:

> Please, sir, he told us that he thinks that the plays of Shakespeare were really written by a man called Ham and that Shakespeare poisoned this man called Ham and stole the plays and then pretended he'd written them. And then a man called Bacon pushed a woman into a pond because he wanted to marry his mother. And there's a man called Eggs, but I have forgotten what he did except that—[61]

Hamlet and breakfast collide as Shakespeare's genius is brought down to earth and becomes all the greater for it. Crompton pays homage to, rather than makes fun of, a play that is embedded in our cultural memory, as of course is William. Other writers have similarly paid homage to her.

* * *

Alison Light warns biographers to be wary of the different shadowy selves that our subjects create, 'since we all make fictions of ourselves in order to live.'[62] In Richmal's case, our sense of who she was is masked by her professional image. She played many parts both on and off the public stage and she often feels out of reach, watching us from the sidelines. Fiction helps us to understand the world around us and Richmal knew this. Like other women writers in this period, she focused on the private and domestic with one foot in the past and another firmly rooted in the present. One of her most distinctive qualities is an ability to focus on the everyday whilst appreciating that what she can see has wider implications for her family, her community, and her class.[63]

William is aghast at the life led by grown-ups, especially his parents. The 'dullness of people in general was simply beyond him'[64]:

> He had come to the conclusion that morning that there was a certain monotonous sameness about life. One got up, and had one's breakfast, and went to school [or work], and had one's dinner, and went to school [or work], and had one's tea [or dinner], and played [or watched television], and had one's supper, and went to bed.[65]

William is entranced instead by the potential adventure that life offers. In William, we see thoughtfulness and irreverent strategy alongside a literal approach to life, with a hint of guile and obtuseness. He is a figure who both emboldens and makes fun of many of our most human characteristics, some good, some less so.

'William is me,' his fans say wistfully. It is this connection that lies at the heart of William's success with adult readers. We empathise with him; we care about him; his experience resonates with the life of his fans even when their circumstances are different. During her lifetime, as Crompton professed herself, William took on a life of his own. She could no longer control him, and William became a cultural icon, for many represented by Thomas Henry's drawings of William, but encapsulated for most by William's character and the adventures he pursues and by Crompton's storytelling. One of the many remarkable things about him is the extent to which he can create an adventure on his home turf. He does not have to go in search of it in faraway places. Adventure is all around him on the home front, which suggests that we only need to look at the world around us through his eyes to find it for ourselves.

Richmal Lamburn, and her alter ego the writer Richmal Crompton, remain in the wings, whilst William takes centre stage. Much still remains hidden about Richmal's life. It is hoped that the reader can now see something of Richmal Crompton's view of the world, through her biographer's eyes at least. Since her death, William has taken on a life of his own and his fans, other writers, and readers within and outside the UK have recreated a William who lives on.

This Life has tried to look at the world through the eyes of both Crompton and William and found, not surprisingly, that they share common values. A number of her novels are comedies, whilst others have a different tone, but nevertheless they share aspects of William's view of the world.

In *A God in* Ruins, Teddy's mother Sylvie tells him that the purpose of Art "'is to *convey* the truth of a thing, not to *be* the truth itself.'"[66] His aunt Izzie's definition of art is broader:

"Art is anything created by one person and enjoyed by another."

"Even Augustus?" Sylvie said and laughed.

"Even Augustus," Izzie said.[67]

Like Izzie:

Teddy didn't believe art ('Art,' he thought, acknowledging his mother) should be didactic, it should be a source of joy and comfort, of sublimation and of understanding ('Itself,' in fact.) It had been all these things to him once. Nancy [his wife], however, tended towards pedagogy.[68]

William is both Everyman and no-one, a character who did not exist, or at least only in the innermost room of his creator and in his fans and other readers' eyes. William is a 'little man,' an inner voice or monstrous demon depending on the turn of any given plot, peeping out behind Crompton's shoulder, who urges us to have hope, confidence, and faith in ourselves. In her portrayal of him, as well as other characters, Crompton's pedagogy informs her writing, and she knows how to convey the truth of things. And, with apologies to Kate Atkinson, 'when all else is gone, Art remains.' Even William, Euphemia, Millicent, and Matty.[69]

Notes

1. Woolf, 98.
2. Ibid.
3. A few examples here suggest the extent of Crompton's influence on more recent authors for both children and adults in the UK and elsewhere. A more in-depth study will no doubt reveal others.
4. See this reference to Great-Aunt Jane in Chapter 9.
5. In an interview for this biography.
6. Fine, Anne. *William the Bad*.
7. In an interview for this biography.
8. Ibid.
9. Hunt, 14.
10. Interview with author in March 2020.
11. Ibid.
12. Ibid.
13. Moggach 1988, 62.
14. Ibid.
15. Ibid.

16. Moggach, *The Carer*, 179.
17. More, 71. An early mention of liquorice water came in another classic text nearly four hundred years earlier, *Utopia* (1516) by Thomas More: 'Utopians … drink no beer, only wine, cider, perry, or water—sometimes by itself, but often flavoured with honey or liquorice, which are both very plentiful.' I am grateful to Michael Wace for telling me about this source for liquorice water.
18. Moggach, Deborah. "I fell out of bed laughing: writers on their favourite funny books." *The Guardian* 7 January 2017. 'I fell out of bed laughing': writers on their favourite funny book | Fiction | *The Guardian*.
19. Ibid.
20. Atkinson, 545.
21. Ibid., 35.
22. Ibid., 52.
23. Ibid., 53.
24. Ibid., 261.
25. Ibid., 534.
26. Ibid., 50.
27. Townsend, Sue.
28. Ibid.
29. Donaldson, Julia. "Books that Made Me," *The Guardian* 18 June 2021. Julia Donaldson: 'Edward Lear taught me that there can be a lyrical beauty in nonsense' | Books | *The Guardian*.
30. Rennison, Louise.
31. Fraser, xix.
32. Ibid., 251.
33. Ibid., 247.
34. Greenway 2002, 99–100.
35. Greenway 2001, 134.
36. Ibid.
37. Ibid., 137–138.
38. In 1953, a journalist reports that Crompton first realised that William had become a legend when Thomas himself was described in an obituary as a mixture of Peter Pan and Just William (Sue Francis *Yorkshire Evening Post* 6 December 1968).
    Critics have alluded to echoes of William-like characters in a range of other fiction since the nineteen fifties, such as the Peanuts cartoon, which first appeared in 1950, and Kingsley Amis's *Lucky Jim* (1954). See Penelope Gilliatt 'Introducing Peanuts' *The Observer* 31 December 1967,

17 and 'A Puritan Reformed' by John Horder *The Guardian* 5 February 1964, 8.

39. Gaiman and Pratchett, 138.

40. Ibid., 139.

41. Ibid., 147–148.

42. Ibid., 148.

43. Ibid., 367.

44. Gleitzman, Morris. See "Some of my books are serious and some are funny but to me they are not so very different." *The Guardian* 6 January 2015. Morris Gleitzman: Some of my books are serious and some are funny but to me they are not so very different | Children's books | The Guardian.

45. Gleitzman, Morris, *Then* 139. The family of books about Felix are *Once* (2005), *Then* (2008), *Now* (2010), *After* (2012), *Soon* (2015), *Maybe* (2017). Gleitzman explains that he calls these books a family of books because he came to see Felix and his friends as a family, and they can be read in any order. They are a family of books rather than a series. (See 'Dear Reader' appendix to *Maybe*).

46. Also see, for other examples, Jenifer in *The Quartet* (1935), Clare in *Steffan Green* (1940), Arnold Palmer in *Family Roundabout* (1948). Palmer's marriage to Judy is based on complacency and self-obsession and she wearies of his appetite for constant praise as his literary reputation declines, and although he is still a best seller his creative impulse is now exhausted. Like Di's husband in *The Inheritor*, in the case of Palmer's novels:

> They were now feats of virtuosity, written to a formula, repeating over and over again the situations and characters that had first won him success. His tricks of style were becoming accentuated, and his work afforded a happy hunting ground for the parodist. (246)

47. Sherriff 2006, 11.

48. "William the Showman," 162.

49. Ibid., 170.

50. "William's Helping Hand," 219 and 228.

51. "William Among the Chimney Pots," 84.

52. Edwards, 101 and Hunt, 55. See *William the Pirate* (1932).

53. "William the Globe-Trotter," 175–176.

54. Ibid., 192.

55. "Jumble," 248.

56. "William Gets Wrecked," 246.

57. "The Mystery of Oaklands," 18.
58. "The Great Detective," 167.
59. "William on the Trail," 21.
60. "William and the Matchmaker," 151.
61. "William Holds the Stage," 43.
62. Light, 205.
63. The American sociologist C. Wright-Mills published his ground-breaking book, *The Sociological Imagination*, in 1959 in which he argues that the life of an individual and the history of society are intrinsically linked. Is this an imagination that Crompton understood?
64. "A Busy Day," 26.
65. "The Helper," 157.
66. Atkinson, 15.
67. Ibid., 35.
68. Ibid., 97.
69. The full quote in *A God in Ruins* reads: 'And when all else is gone, Art remains. Even Augustus' (528).

References

Atkinson, Kate. 2015. *A God in Ruins*. London: Transworld.
Crompton, Richmal. 1949. *Family Roundabout*. London: Hutchinson Universal Book Club.
———. 1949. First published 1932. "William Holds the Stage." In *William - The Pirate*, by Richmal Crompton, 36–57. London: George Newnes Ltd.
———. 1951. First published 1929. "The Mystery of Oaklands." In *William*, by Richmal Crompton, 13–43. London: George Newnes Ltd.
———. 1953. First published 1924. "William the Showman." In *William - The Fourth*, by Richmal Crompton, 158–174. London: George Newnes Ltd.
———. 1959. First published 1922. "A Busy Day." In *More William*, by Richmal Crompton, 13–32. London: George Newnes Ltd.
———. 1959. First published 1922. "The Helper." In *More William*, by Richmal Crompton, 157–173. London: George Newnes Ltd.
———. 1961. First published 1923. "The Great Detective." In *William Again*, by Richmal Crompton, 165–179. London: George Newnes Ltd.
———. 1961. First published 1923. "William's Helping Hand." In *William Again*, by Richmal Crompton, 212–230. London: George Newnes Ltd.
———. 1961. First published 1923. "William Gets Wrecked." In *William Again*, by Richmal Crompton, 231–251. London: George Newnes.

―――. 1984. First published 1925. "William and the Matchmaker." In *Still - William*, by Richmal Crompton, 127–152. Basingstoke, Hampshire: Macmillan Children's Books.

―――. 1990. First pubished 1922. "Jumble." In *Just - William*, by Richmal Crompton, 228–248. Basingstoke, Hampshire: Macmillan Children's Books.

―――. 1991. First published 1958. "William Among the Chimney Pots." In *William's Television Show*, by Richmal Crompton, 109–135. Basingstoke, Hampshire: Macmillan Children's Books.

―――. 1986. First published 1937. "William the Globe-Trotter." In *William - The Showman*, by Richmal Crompton, 164–192. Basingstoke, Hampshire: Macmillan Children's Books.

―――. 1991. First published 1958. "William on the Trail." In *William's Television Show*, by Richmal Crompton, 1–27. Basingstoke, Hampshire: Macmillan Children's Books.

Edwards, Owen Dudley. 2007. *British Children's Fiction in the Second World War*. Edinburgh: Edinburgh University Press.

Fine, Anne. 2015. *William the Bad Introduction*. Kindle Edition: Macmillan Children's Books.

Fraser, Antonia. 2015. *The Pleasure of Reading*. London: Bloomsbury.

Gaiman, Neil, and Terry Prachett. 2014. First published 1990. *Good Omens*. London: Transworld.

Gleitzman, Morris. 2017. *Maybe*. London: Penguin Random House UK.

―――. 2008. *Then*. London: Penguin.

Greenway, Betty. 2001. "The Influence of Children's Literature—A Case Study: Dylan Thomas and Richmal Crompton." *Children's Literature Association Quarterly 26.3* 133–139.

Greenway, Betty. 2002. "William Forever: Richmal Crompton's Unusual Achievement." *The Lion and the Unicorn 26.1* 98–111.

Hunt, Peter. 2001. *Children's Literature*. Oxford: Blackwell.

Light, Alison. 1991. *Forever England: Femininity, Literature and Conservatism Between the Wars*. London: Routledge.

Moggach, Deborah. 2019. *The Carer*. London: Tinder Press.

―――. 1988. "My Hero." *The Independent*, 8 October: 62.

More, Thomas. 1972. First published 1516. *Utopia*. Harmondsworth, Middlesex: England: Penguin.

Rennison, Louise. 2015. *William Again Foreword*. Kindle edition: Macmillan Children's Books.

Sherriff, Ben and Margaret. Winter 2006. "William Among the Writers." *The Just William Society Magazine 19* 10–15.

Townsend, Sue. 2015. *Just William Introduction.* Kindle Edition: Macmillan Children's Books.

Woolf, Virginia. 2000. First published 1929 and 1938 respectively. "A Room of One's Own." In *A Room of One's Own/Three Guineas,* by Virginia Woolf Ed., 3–103. London: Penguin Classics.

Richmal Crompton References and Selected Bibliography

(* denotes no quotation or discussion in chapters)

Just - William (1922)		
More William (1922)		
William Again (1923)	*The Innermost Room* (1923)	
William - The Fourth (1924)	*The Hidden Light* (1924)	
Still - William (1925)	*Anne Morrison* (1925)	
	The Wildings (1925)	
William - The Conqueror (1926)	*David Wilding* (1926)	*Kathleen and I & of course Veronica* (1926)
	The House (1926)	
William - The Outlaw (1927)	*Millicent Dorrington* (1927)	*A Monstrous Regiment* (1927)
William - In Trouble (1927)	*Leadon Hill* (1927)	*Enter Patricia* (1927)
William - The Good (1928)	*The Thorn Bush* (1928)	*The Middle Things* (1928)
	Roofs Off! (1928)	*Felicity Stands By* (1928)
		Sugar and Spice and other stories (1928)
		Mist and other stories (1928)
William (1929)	*The Four Graces* (1929)	*Ladies First* (1929)
	Abbots' End (1929)	
William - The Bad (1930)	*Blue Flames* (1930)	
William's Happy Days (1930)	*Naomi Godstone* (1930)*	

(continued)

© The Editor(s) (if applicable) and The Author(s), under exclusive license to Springer Nature Switzerland AG 2022
J. McVeigh, *Richmal Crompton, Author of Just William*, Literary Lives, https://doi.org/10.1007/978-3-030-96511-2

(continued)

William's Crowded Hours (1931)	Portrait of a Family (1931)*	The Silver Birch and other stories (1931)*
William - The Pirate (1932)	The Odyssey of Euphemia Tracy (1932)	
	Marriage of Hermione (1932)	
William - The Rebel (1933)	The Holiday (1933)	
William - The Gangster (1934)	Chedsy Place (1934)	
	The Old Man's Birthday (1934)	
William - The Detective (1935)	Quartet (1935)	
Sweet William (1936)*	Caroline (1936)	The First Morning (1936)
William - The Showman (1937)	There Are Four Seasons (1937)	
William - The Dictator (1938)	Journeying Wave (1938)*	
William & the Air Raid Precautions (1939)	Merlin Bay (1939)	
Just William - The Book of the Film (1939)		
William and the Evacuees (1940)	Steffan Green (1940)	
William Does His Bit (1941)	Narcissa (1941)	
William Carries On (1942)*	Mrs Frensham Describes a Circle (1942)	
	Weatherly Parade (1944)	
William and the Brain's Trust (1945)*		
	Westover (1946)	
	The Ridleys (1947)	
Just William's Luck (1948)	Family Roundabout (1948)	
		Jimmy (1949)
William - The Bold (1950)	Frost at Morning (1950)	
		Jimmy Again (1951)
William and the Tramp (1952)	Linden Rise (1952)*	
William and the Moon Rocket (1954)*	The Gypsy's Baby (1954)	
	Four in Exile (1954)	
William and the Space Animal (1956)	Matty and the Dearingroydes (1956)	
	Blind Man's Buff (1957)*	
William's Television Show (1958)		

(continued)

(continued)

	Wiseman's Folly (1959)*
William - The Explorer (1960)*	*The Inheritor* (1960)
William's Treasure Trove (1962)	
William and the Witch (1964)	
William and the Pop Singers (1965)	
William and the Masked Ranger (1966)	
William the Superman (1968)	
William the Lawless (1970)*	

Index

© The Editor(s) (if applicable) and The Author(s), under exclusive
license to Springer Nature Switzerland AG 2022
J. McVeigh, *Richmal Crompton, Author of Just William*, Literary Lives,
https://doi.org/10.1007/978-3-030-96511-2

Ingram Content Group UK Ltd.
Milton Keynes UK
UKHW022002220323
419010UK00003B/18